The Man Behind the Bayeux Tapestry

The Man Behind the Bayeux Tapestry

Odo, William the Conqueror's Half-Brother

TREVOR ROWLEY

Cover images: A scene from the Bayeux Tapestry (by permission of the City of Bayeux); Portrait of Bishop Odo (courtesy of the Baron Gérard Museum, Bayeux).

First published 2013

The History Press
The Mill, Brimscombe Port
Stroud, Gloucestershire, GL5 2QG
www.thehistorypress.co.uk

British Library Cataloguing in Publication Data.
A catalogue record for this book is available from the British Library.

ISBN 978 0 7524 6025 3

Typesetting and origination by The History Press
Printed in Great Britain

• Contents •

Foreword 7
Acknowledgements 8

1 Odo de Conteville 9
2 Duke Robert 'the Magnificent' 24
3 The Boy Bishop and Bayeux 39
4 The Duke Becomes a King 64
5 Bishop Odo and the Bayeux Tapestry 83
6 'A Second King in England' 107
7 Odo the Pontiff – A Step Too Far 134
8 'The Bishop Abandoned the Dignity That He Had in This Land' 150
9 'God Wills It' – Odo's Last Expedition 167

Bibliography 183
Index 188

• Foreword •

Odo of Conteville was a larger than life character, who is best known for his dashing appearance on the Bayeux Tapestry as a mounted cleric waving a baton at the height of the Battle of Hastings. In older text books the bishop is frequently characterised in terms of illegally obtaining land from English monastic houses and of rebelling against the king. Generally he is portrayed as a not so loveable rogue, who typified the worst excesses of the Norman conquerors. In recent decades the work of David Bates and others has done much to redress the balance of opinion about Odo amongst historians, but the popular impression of William the Conqueror's half-brother still remains largely a narrow and negative one.

I have spent most of my life working within extra-mural departments, whose task was to make scholarship generated largely within universities, accessible to the world outside. The aim of this book is just that, to try to make Bishop Odo's extraordinary life-story known to a wider audience. In the past I could have anticipated that my book would find its way into the book boxes of the lifelong-learning classes held in towns and villages throughout the country. Sadly such commendable educational activity now appears somewhat archaic and is indeed itself largely historical in character. It would be preposterous for me to try to enlist Odo as a prescient supporter of the great extra-mural tradition, but it should be remembered that he was far from being a loutish philistine. The bishop recognised the value of education and the arts and amongst his less well-known activities was his generous patronage of both.

Trevor Rowley
Appleton (one of Bishop Odo's estates recorded in Domesday Book), Oxfordshire,
30 November 2012

᛫ Acknowledgements ᛫

Thanks are due to those many people who encouraged me to write this book and have helped with information, ideas, typing, translating, editing and drawing. Notably Richard Allen, Pat Combs, Susannah Dyer, Linda Kent, Francoise Laval, Tony Morris, Richard Rowley, Lindsey Smith, Alison Wilkinson snd my wife Jane Rowley.

Thanks are also due to the following individuals and organisations for their kind permission to reproduce illustrations: English Heritage (colour plates 11, 23 and 25, and figure 42), Francoise Laval (colour plate 10), and Alison Wilkinson (figures 4, 11, 22, 36, 41 and 51).

1

• Odo de Conteville •

> The name of Odo is one which will be found constantly recurring in this history, from the day when his bishop's staff and warrior's mace were so successfully wielded against the defenders of England, till the day when he went forth to wield the same weapons against the misbelievers in the East and found in his road a tomb, far from the heavy pillars and massive arches of his own Bayeux, among the light and gorgeous enrichments with which the conquered Saracen knew how to adorn the palaces and churches of the Norman lords of Palermo.

So wrote the venerable Victorian historian, Edward Augustus Freeman in his magisterial account of the *History of the Norman Conquest* (1874–78, 210).

Odo de Conteville, whose name also appears in the form of Odon, Eudo and Eudes, was born in around 1030 in Normandy. He was the half-brother of William the Conqueror and, as Freeman proclaims, Odo's name reverberates throughout the narrative of Anglo-Norman history in the eleventh century. He became Bishop of Bayeux while still in his teens, a position he was to hold until his death. He helped plan the invasion and participated in the Battle of Hastings and the subsequent Conquest of England. He became Earl of Kent with responsibility for the defence of south-east England; he was regent to King William from time to time on the king's frequent visits to Normandy. Odo gained land legally and illegally after the Conquest and his English estates and wealth were second only to the Conqueror's. He was responsible for the building and consecration of a new cathedral at Bayeux.

He developed a powerful cathedral chapter which nurtured many leading figures among the Anglo-French clergy. He sponsored artists, musicians and poets and is widely believed to have been responsible for the making of the Bayeux Tapestry. In 1082 he raised a private army in England with the intention of acquiring the papacy, for which he was arrested and imprisoned for four years by King William. On his release he almost immediately rebelled against the new king, William Rufus, and as a consequence was permanently banished from England. In 1096 he joined Duke Robert Curthose's contingent leaving Normandy on the First Crusade and died a natural death in Palermo, Sicily, early in 1097. These are the compelling headlines for a life that touched on almost every aspect of the Anglo-Norman story in the eleventh century.

• The Making of Normandy •

The Duchy of Normandy was barely a century old when Odo was born, and its rulers had only called themselves dukes for a few decades. The duchy had been carved out of Neustria, a post-Romano-Gallic territory of fluctuating dimensions lying between and including the Seine and the Loire valleys. Neustria originated in the Merovingian fifth century, but by AD 900 it had been moulded to create a buffer territory of the decaying Western Carolingian Empire. In the mid-ninth century, Charles the Bald, King of the Western Franks had carved Maine and Angers out of Neustria in order to confront the Bretons, who at that time were the most serious threat to the Western Franks. Towards the end of the ninth century it was the Vikings who posed the most danger, and the fertile river estuaries of western France, notably, the Loire, Seine and Somme, provided Viking attackers with ready access to inland regions. Pillage and plunder in the Seine Valley in the late ninth century was followed by permanent Scandinavian settlements and eventually by the acquisition of territory in the tenth. Short-lived Viking enclaves were also established in the estuaries of the Loire and the Rhine, but it was only the *Northmanni* in the Seine Valley who were able to create a more permanent political entity on mainland Europe.

Although the detailed history of Normandy's origins is far from clear, the traditional story is that in 911, Charles the Simple, King of the West Franks ceded an area of the Seine Valley around Rouen to a Viking warlord called Rollo. This territory, which coincided with the old Frankish diocese

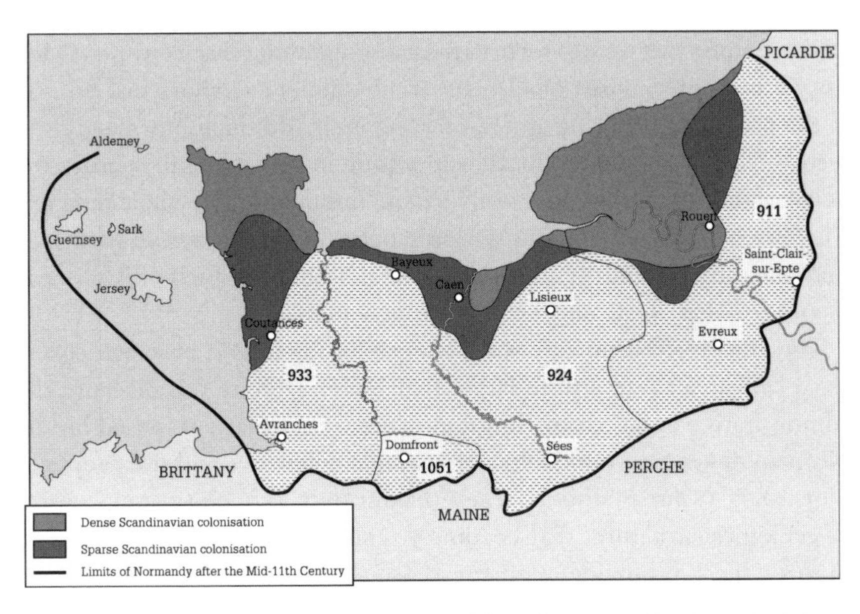

1 Map showing the dates at which land was ceded from the Western Empire to the dukes of Normandy. Ducal authority did not operate fully in the whole of the duchy until the eleventh century. *After the Museum of Normandy, Caen*

of Rouen, was granted to the *Northmanni* in a treaty signed at St-Clair-sur-Epte on the eastern boundary of what was to become Normandy. Reputedly, Rollo converted to Christianity in return for defending the Seine Valley against further Viking attacks. Rollo, known by the title of Count of Rouen, and his son, William Longsword, acquired overlordship of most of the rest of the geographical area that became the Duchy of Normandy during the next thirty years.

It is probable that the Franks did not view Normandy as a permanent creation, and when in 921 an attempt by the Western Franks to bring the Normans to heel failed, a network of semi-independent *seigneuries* was established to act as a buffer, the most notable of which was Bellême, to the south of the duchy. During the later tenth century these territories drifted under Norman influence, although eventually they were to pose serious problems for the Norman dukes (Dunbabin 1985, 66–7). By the early eleventh century the duchy had begun to resemble its neighbours in northern and western France in many ways, but it had still not fully recovered from the physical and cultural damage inflicted by the Vikings and was still in the process of acquiring the military, governmental and artistic features that were to form its most distinguishing characteristics. Odo's story was an integral part of a larger narrative about a territory that was still in the process of repairing and re-creating itself. Although Normandy was recognised as being under ducal overlordship in the late tenth century, the duke's authority did not necessarily extend throughout the whole territory. There were semi-autonomous warlords, operating in the west in particular, until the early eleventh century and it was not until the reign of Richard II (996–1026) that Normandy became a largely unified duchy.

The Duchy of Normandy was a geographically diverse province, covering a land area about a third larger than Wales. Despite this diversity, the administrative organisation and regional system of laws imposed by the Norman dukes gave the duchy considerable coherence and the people of Normandy a sense of distinctiveness (Flatrès 1977, 313). Normandy consists of geological structures that become younger moving from west to east; in this respect, it provides a mirror image of the geology of the southern coastal areas of England. The sandstones, granites and primary schist of the Armorican Massif in the area known as the Cotentin match the geological complexion of south-western England. The Secondary and Tertiary era strata of clays, limestone and chalks which belong to the geological formation of the Paris Basin can be matched in Dorset, Hampshire and Sussex.

Geographically, it has been conventional to divide the duchy into two regions: Upper (Haute) and Lower (Basse) Normandy. Upper Normandy lies to the north-west of the Paris Basin and consists of an elevated Cretaceous chalk plateau lying at an average height of 130m above sea level. The Seine cuts through the chalk, giving characteristically steep cliffs to the north of the river and more gentle undulating escarpments to the south. The valleys of the Seine and its principal Norman tributaries, the Risle and the Epte, have broad alluvial terraces which provided fertile locations for Frankish monasteries such as St Wandrille, Jumièges and St Ouen, founded from the sixth century onwards. Odo essentially belonged to Lower Normandy: he was born there, and while in Normandy spent most of his time there as bishop, only occasionally venturing to Rouen and Upper Normandy on ducal business.

Lower Normandy lies to the south-west of the Seine, sharing some of the geological and geographical characteristics with neighbouring Brittany. In the east it consists of a narrow band of Jurassic limestone, running from Caen through Falaise to Alençon. This is generically known as Caen stone, which is a versatile and attractive building material used for cathedrals, abbeys, castles and parish churches throughout the duchy; Caen limestone was also imported into England after the Norman Conquest. Beyond this, to the west, are older granites and sandstones making up Armorican Normandy and the Cotentin Peninsula. The southern frontier of Normandy lies to the south of a forest belt which follows a quartzite crest of *bocage* upland running from Domfront to Avalois.

The administrative divisions within the Duchy of Normandy incorporated earlier Gallo-Roman and Carolingian elements, particularly in the territorial divisions of the Church. Rouen was the capital and by far the most important town of the province, as its predecessor *Rotomagus* had been of the Romano-Gallic region of the *Veliocasses*. It was also the diocesan centre in late Roman times and from the eighth century the seat of an archbishop. Rouen clerics, keepers of the Gallo-Roman tradition, argued that the dukes of Normandy should extend their dominion to the borders of the ecclesiastical province of Rouen, the former *Lugdunensis secunda*. In the south-east the ducal boundaries extended beyond the diocesan border after they had conquered the lands of the house of Bellême. There are a number of ancient administrative units (*pays*) in the province of Normandy – Bessin, Cotentin, Hiémois, Lieuvin and Avranchin – which can be traced back through the medieval dioceses to Gallo-Roman *civitates* and partly

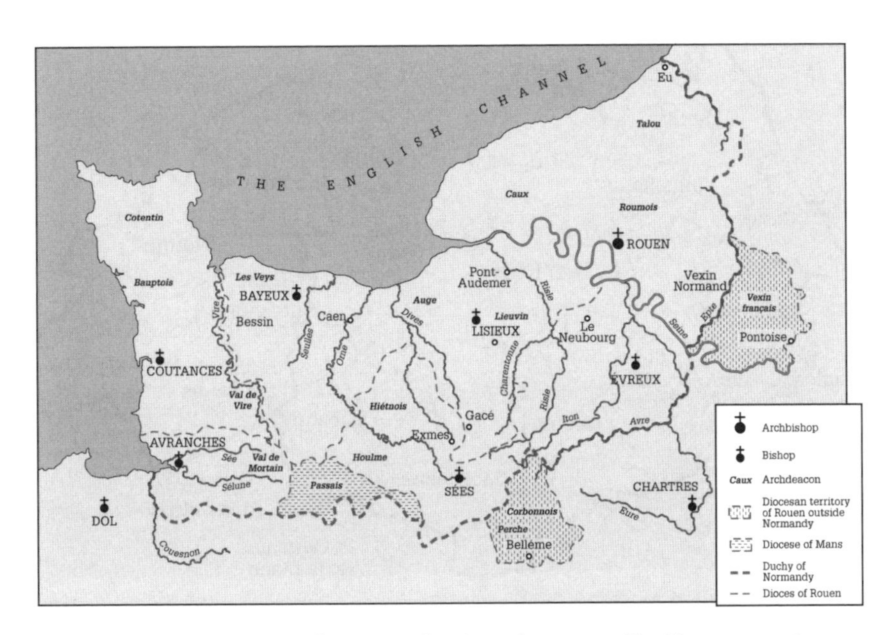

2 The ecclesiastical province of Rouen in the eleventh century. *After Neveux 1995, 16*

survive in the administrative structure of the region today (Flatrès 1977). The area known as the Bessin coincides with the territory of the *Badiocassi*, which lies between the rivers Orne and Vire in the department of Calvados.

• Bayeux and its Diocese •

By the year AD 1000 each of the seven dioceses of Normandy had a bishop for the first time since the Vikings had disrupted the ecclesiastical organisation of the region. Even then, not all the bishops were able to reside within their own diocese, and although several bishops were appointed, they did not live in Bayeux until the early eleventh century. Odo's immediate predecessor, Bishop Hugh (1015–49), was the first post-Viking prelate to reside in Bayeux. Even then, the shifting power of Norman barons meant that a constant watch had to be kept on areas of instability. Odo's appointment at Bayeux was made in order to extend ducal control to the west of the duchy

3 Pre-1789 parishes around Bayeux. The circular configuration of boundaries around Bayeux probably reflect defence obligations dating from the Carolingian era.

by re-establishing the Church and its institutions as powerful aids to and allies of government, as had been the practice in the Carolingian world.

Bayeux had been a Gallo-Roman town, initially called *Augustodurum* and later *Noviomagus Badiocassium* after the local tribe, the *Badiocassi*. It lay on a road running from Rouen to the northern coastline of the Cotentin Peninsula, and was considered the second town of the duchy, until Duke William developed Caen as an alternative to Rouen. Fortified stone towers were recorded at Bayeux in the twelfth century and evidence of a Romano-Gallic theatre, the *praetorium*, public and private bathhouses, and a temple on the site of the cathedral have been uncovered (Neveux 1997). Bayeux was the reputed birthplace of several early Frankish saints, notably St Evroul (517–96), St Evremond (d. c. 720), St Marcouf (b. c. 500) and St Aquilinus (d. 695). During Odo's lifetime, the city was largely contained within the Roman walls, which were in the form of a regular square, following the lines of the original Romano-Gallic *castrum*. The regular grid pattern of roads had largely been broken up, but the rue St Martin which entered at the St Martin gate in the north-east and exited at the St André gate in the north-west was the main through road. It is still the main east–west road of central Bayeux today.

According to tradition, before he became the first duke of Normandy, Rollo is said to have destroyed Bayeux in the 890s and carried off Poppa, daughter of Berenger, the Frankish Count of Bayeux. Despite this, Bayeux was a town which retained its strong links to the early Viking rulers of Normandy – Rollo's son, William Longsword, was born here and Richard I was declared duke in Bayeux as well as in Rouen. During the tenth century Bayeux had a chequered history, often operating outside the control of the duke based in Rouen. For example, in the 940s the city was under the control of an independent, pagan Viking lord, Harold, and it appears that paganism was still common in the Bessin at that late date (Herrick, 92). Duke Richard I built a castle here in the late tenth century in the south-west corner of the walled town in an attempt to assert his authority. Although it was portrayed as an earth and timber motte and bailey on the Bayeux Tapestry, it was almost certainly built of stone.

The diocese of Bayeux was made up of the territories of the *Baiocasses*, centred on Bayeux (*Augustodurum*), and the *Viducasses*, based on *Araegenua* (Vieux-la-Romaine), 5km to the south-west of Caen. The diocesan boundaries were largely defined by rivers and streams or former water channels. To the west, the boundary ran south from the estuary of the River Vire,

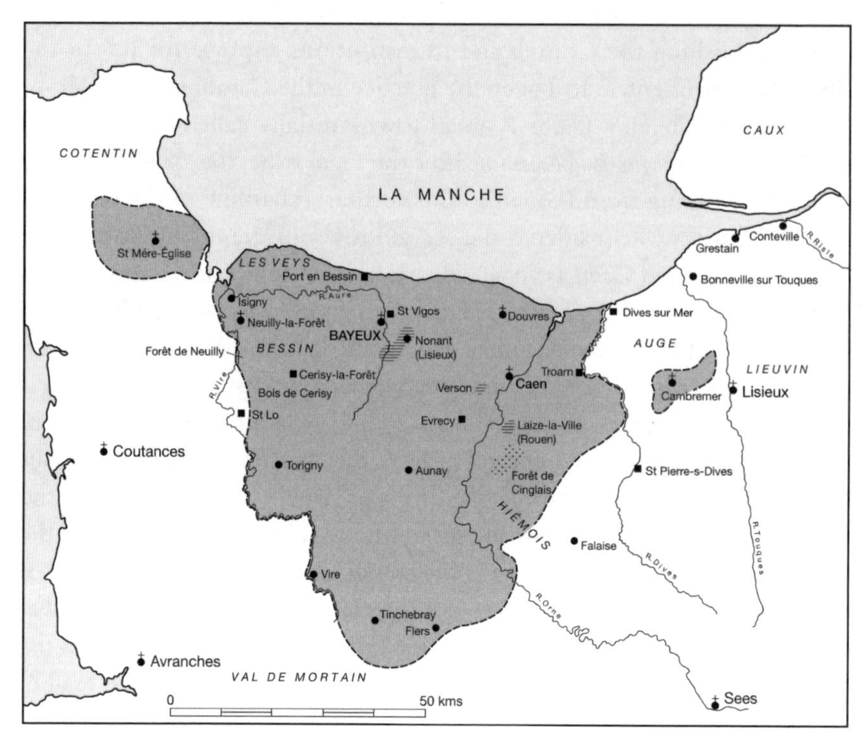

4 The Diocese of Bayeux in the eleventh century. *After Allen*

through Isigny to Vire. It then picked up the Égrenne stream as far as Beauchêne and followed the Halouze stream before cutting north-east to join the Rouvre, a tributary of the River Orne. The border then followed the Laizon to join the River Dives to the north of St-Pierre-sur-Dives, whence it ran northwards following the Dives to its estuary at Dives-sur-Mer. There was a detached portion of the diocese at Cambremer, which lay within the diocese of Lisieux. Several churches dedicated to St Vigor in this separate unit suggest that it was an area converted by Vigor in the sixth century. A second, larger, detached portion of Bayeux diocese, St-Mère-Église, lay in the Coutances diocese to the west of the River Vire in the Cotentin, to the north of Carentan. Conversely, a detached portion of the diocese of Rouen lay within Bayeux diocese at Laize-la-Ville; while Lisieux held a portion at Nonant on the River Aure, where the abbey of Mondaye was built in the twelfth century. Such detached units may have originated as personal possessions of individual bishops that were incorporated under their administration as diocesan boundaries were established.

St-Mère-Église could, however, have also been an outlier of early Christianity during the conversion of the sixth century. There is a spring behind the church at St Mère dedicated to the Celtic saint Mewan or Méon of Brittany. Reputedly, St Méon and his godson St Austell followed St Samson to Brittany in the sixth century (Farmer 1987; Neveux 1995, 13–18).

• Odo's Character •

Odo was an enigma even to near contemporary chroniclers such as Orderic Vitalis, writing a few decades after the bishop's death. Orderic portrayed Odo as eloquent, generous, courtly and ambitious and 'a slave to worldly trivialities'. Orderic repeatedly links the phrase 'the secular' with Odo – eating, drinking, fighting and loving. He was described as a mixture of virtues and vices and later, it was the vices that were emphasised. Added to the cartoon-like depiction of the battling bishop on the Bayeux Tapestry, this created a somewhat roguish and dissolute image, which was pounced on and amplified by later historians. Two episodes in particular have been used to demonstrate Odo's reprehensible character, firstly his treatment of the English and their lands after the Conquest and his role in the rebellion against William Rufus. It was not until the later twentieth century that a more balanced account of the bishop and his deeds was written; when it was pointed out that his behaviour was no better and no worse than many of his contemporaries, including fellow churchmen (Bates 1975). 'He was regarded at Bayeux as a good bishop and his activities in England, while undoubtedly at times oppressive and tyrannical, have sometimes been too severely censured because overmuch attention has been given to the testimony of those that suffered at his hands' (Bates 2004–11). He spent large sums of money on the patronage of churches and monasteries as well as on the education and training of clerks for secular and religious positions.

Much attention has been paid to the apparent incongruity between Odo the bishop and Odo the secular lord. This tension becomes particularly obvious from the Battle of Hastings onwards, when Odo assumes the role of a colonial baron and is often harsh in his dealings with the English. Such apparent conflicts of interest were common during the early medieval period, but those involved had no trouble in operating successfully within both spheres. Characteristically, Odo's own seal shows him as a bishop in clerical dress on one side and as a mounted earl in battledress on the other (colour fig 1). However, he does not seem to have been particularly pious and spent little time on doctrinal studies. 'Odo found the early Cistercian and Savignac literal interpretation of the Rule of St Benedict and emphasis on manual work disturbing' (Bates 1975). Occasionally we find references to his piety, as at St Albans Abbey, where Odo was remembered in the list of benefactors for having returned three hides of land 'for the sake of his soul' (Cownie 1998, 98), but this was a standard clause in such documents.

Orderic was living at a time when there was increased emphasis on the spiritual requirements of the religious life and was generally unsympathetic towards churchmen who meddled in politics (Bates 1975, 2). Hence Orderic's writing combines admiration and censure in his account of Odo's life. Unfortunately it is the censure that has tended to be amplified over the centuries and which often prompts a negative kneejerk reaction to the very mention of Odo's name.

As for his personal life, it is known that he kept a mistress and that they had a son, John, who was born in around 1080. Orderic regretted that, 'Sometimes the spirit triumphed in him [Odo] to good ends, but on other occasions the flesh overcame the spirit with evil consequences. Yielding to the weakness of the flesh he had a son named John', who served Henry I and 'is renowned there for his ready speech and great integrity'. We hear of John from an incident where he brought the news of the death of Henry's nephew William 'Clito', Count of Flanders to him in 1128 (OV, iii, 264). Descendants of Odo continued to play an important governmental role in Normandy and Richard du Hommet, Constable of Normandy under Henry II, was Odo's great-grandson (Power 2002, 76).

In the eleventh century, clergy, even bishops, were known for keeping mistresses. Orderic Vitalis recorded that Robert; Archbishop of Rouen (d. 1037) had a wife called Herleva, whom the bishop claimed he took in his capacity as count. He was also accused of selling church treasures in order to buy women. Orderic observed that 'the practice of celibacy among the clergy was so relaxed that not only priests but even bishops freely shared their beds with concubines and openly boasted of their numerous progeny' (OV, v, 121). Such behaviour became increasingly difficult to defend as the eleventh century progressed and at the Council of Lisieux in 1064 clerical marriages were prohibited in Normandy. Nevertheless, the situation remained unresolved until the Lateran Councils of 1123 and 1139, which ruled definitively against such unions. Part of William's case for the invasion of England was the need to reform the English Church, which was accused of pluralism, concubinage and simony as well as tolerating worldly prelates. William's own Church in Normandy as represented by Odo was vulnerable on this issue and the emissaries that went to persuade Pope Alexander II of the validity of the Norman cause had a difficult time. The pope eventually agreed that the campaign against England could be waged as a Holy War, according to William of Poitiers.

In keeping with the times in which he lived, Odo's brand of Christianity was muscular in nature, with little room for compassion. This was illustrated by an anecdote related by the cleric Lanfranc where Odo had condemned a man, who had killed one of his stags, to wear fetters permanently. The man became exceptionally pious and the sound of his rattling chains became a public symbol of sanctity, until after two years his chains fell off as he prayed prostrate before the altar of the Holy Cross (Cowdrey, 106). Odo along with his fellow Norman bishops is known to have issued anathemas, calling upon God to smite his foes with 'eternal malediction' (Tabuteau 1988, 207). It also appears that Odo preached the virtues of the invasion from his pulpit in Bayeux in order to increase the size of his own contingent in the invading force. At Hastings along with other churchmen he exhorted the Norman troops to destroy their English opponents. According to Odo a leader 'should be gentle as a lamb to good men and to the obedient and humble, but as harsh as a lion to law breakers' (OV, VIII, 151).

• Literary Sources •

The writing of secular history was a relatively new concept in eleventh-century Western Europe. After the Conquest of England several chronicles were written, both in Normandy and in England: some were specifically about King William and the Conquest of England, others were more ambitious historical surveys. It is from these accounts that historians have largely gathered their ideas about and opinions of William, King Harold, Bishop Odo and the other principal players in the Anglo-Norman world of the eleventh century. None of these accounts can be regarded as totally accurate, and none was written with a view to producing objective history.

Perhaps because of his double fall from power there is no contemporary 'Life of Odo', and none of his letters survive. There is a laudatory poem, written by Serlo, one of the Bayeux Cathedral canons, that simply expresses pleasure that Odo has been released from prison. One of the

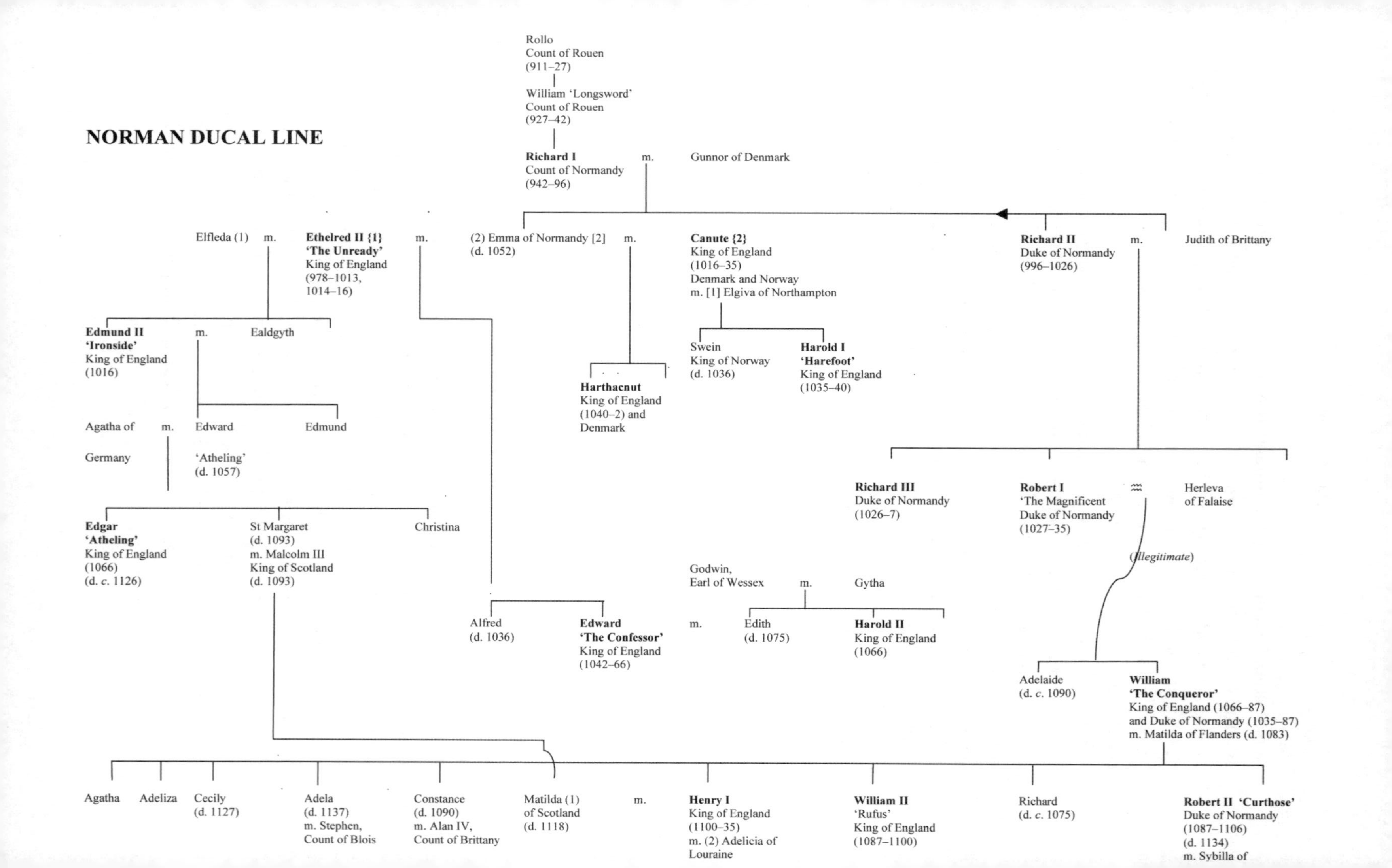
NORMAN DUCAL LINE
Rollo
Count of Rouen
(911–27)
William 'Longsword'
Count of Rouen
(927–42)
Richard I
Count of Normandy
(942–96)
m.
Gunnor of Denmark
Elfleda (1)
m.
Ethelred II {1}
'The Unready'
King of England
(978–1013,
1014–16)
m.
(2) Emma of Normandy [2]
(d. 1052)
m.
Canute {2}
King of England
(1016–35)
Denmark and Norway
m. [1] Elgiva of Northampton
Richard II
Duke of Normandy
(996–1026)
m.
Judith of Brittany
Edmund II
'Ironside'
King of England
(1016)
m.
Ealdgyth
Harthacnut
King of England
(1040–2) and
Denmark
Swein
King of Norway
(d. 1036)
Harold I
'Harefoot'
King of England
(1035–40)
Agatha of
Germany
m.
Edward
'Atheling'
(d. 1057)
Edmund
Richard III
Duke of Normandy
(1026–7)
Robert I
'The Magnificent
Duke of Normandy
(1027–35)
Herleva
of Falaise
(Illegitimate)
Edgar
'Atheling'
King of England
(1066)
(d. c. 1126)
St Margaret
(d. 1093)
m. Malcolm III
King of Scotland
(d. 1093)
Christina
Godwin,
Earl of Wessex
m.
Gytha
Alfred
(d. 1036)
Edward
'The Confessor'
King of England
(1042–66)
m.
Edith
(d. 1075)
Harold II
King of England
(1066)
Adelaide
(d. c. 1090)
William
'The Conqueror'
King of England (1066–87)
and Duke of Normandy (1035–87)
m. Matilda of Flanders (d. 1083)
Agatha
Adeliza
Cecily
(d. 1127)
Adela
(d. 1137)
m. Stephen,
Count of Blois
Constance
(d. 1090)
m. Alan IV,
Count of Brittany
Matilda (1)
of Scotland
(d. 1118)
m.
Henry I
King of England
(1100–35)
m. (2) Adelicia of
Louraine
William II
'Rufus'
King of England
(1087–1100)
Richard
(d. c. 1075)
Robert II 'Curthose'
Duke of Normandy
(1087–1106)
(d. 1134)
m. Sybilla of

earliest surviving sources is the *Gesta Guillelmi II ducis Normannorum et regis Anglorum* (Deeds of Duke William) by William of Poitiers (c. 1020–90), written in the early 1070s (Davis and Chibnall 1998). William was a native of Normandy who studied in Poitiers before returning to become a chaplain to Duke William and then archdeacon in the diocese of Lisieux. After the Conquest he also became a canon of the church of St Martin in Dover. William's account is at times cloyingly sycophantic to his hero, William the Conqueror, but is important for the detail it contains, much of it derived from personal experience. It is possible that William of Poitiers and Odo were associated in some way and there is a suggestion that Odo commissioned him to write the *Gesta*. William depicts Odo as 'uniquely and most steadfastly loyal to the king, from whom he had received great honours and hoped to get still more' (*GG* 166), so it was clearly written before Odo's fall from grace in 1082.

Another early history was the *Gesta Normannorum Ducum* by William of Jumièges (1026–70), written about 1070. William was a monk at the abbey of Jumièges; his account was based on an earlier history of the Normans written by Dudo of St Quentin. Dudo's work, *Historia Normannorum* (1015–30) was revised and eventually updated to 1070 by William of Jumièges, possibly at the command of William the Conqueror (Christiansen 1998). This *Gesta* was later expanded again by the twelfth-century chroniclers Orderic Vitalis and Robert of Torigni (Van Houts 1995). William has little more to add about Odo, but his account of the Battle of Hastings is similar in its details to those depicted on the Bayeux Tapestry. Another account, believed by many to be contemporary with the Battle of Hastings, is the *Carmen de Hastingae Proelio* (Song of the Battle of Hastings) (Barlow 1999). The *Proelio* is attributed to Bishop Guy of Amiens, uncle to Guy of Ponthieu who figures in the early stages of the Bayeux Tapestry, capturing Harold Godwinson on his arrival on French soil in 1064. Odo does not feature at all in the *Proelio*, but it is important in his story because this omission contrasts revealingly with the Tapestry, where Odo plays a leading role. The poem is also thought to be one of very few versions to provide a detailed non-Norman version of events.

Two later accounts are of particular interest: the *Historia Ecclesiastica* (History of the Church) by Orderic Vitalis (Chibnall 1968–80) and the *Roman de Rou* (History of Rollo) by Wace (Burgess 2004). Orderic was born in Shropshire in 1075 to a Norman father and an English mother; when he was ten he was sent to the monastery of St-Evroul-en-Ouche in Normandy, where he spent the rest of his life. His narrative started off as a history of his monastery, but developed into a general history of his age, which he wrote between around 1110 and 1141. Orderic was well informed and a vivid narrator; the range, variety and volume of his account give his history a particular importance. Orderic's perceptive, if often slanted, and his graphic character sketch of Odo has remained with him over the centuries. His attitude to Bishop Odo was ambivalent, torn perhaps between the early praise heaped upon him by William of Poitiers and later accounts of his various calumnies, and which would have been in circulation when Orderic was writing and painted Odo in a very different light. On the one hand, he is described as 'a man of eloquence and statesmanship'; on the other, he was 'frivolous and ambitious'. Orderic seemed on occasion to despair of his subject,'What shall I say of Odo, bishop of Bayeux … ? In this man it seems to me, vices were mingled with virtues, but he was given more to worldly affairs than to spiritual contemplation.'

Wace of Bayeux (c. 1115–c. 1183) was a poet, born in Jersey and brought up in Normandy, who ended his career as a canon of Bayeux Cathedral. His history of the dukes of Normandy started with Rollo and ended with Robert Curthose's defeat at the Battle of Tinchebrai (1106), and appears to have been written between 1160 and the mid-1170s. Wace's history provides details not available elsewhere, in particular, concerning Odo's actions during the Battle of Hastings. Like the other chroniclers, Wace used earlier sources to compose his history, one of which seems to have been the Bayeux Tapestry, which he would have known from his time in the cathedral chapter at Bayeux. Like Orderic Vitalis, Wace paints both sides of Odo's character – as the hero during the Battle of Hastings and as the traitor in 1082.

Of all the contemporary accounts, it is the Bayeux Tapestry which has had by far the biggest impact on the general perception of Odo and of the Norman Conquest as a whole. The Tapestry provides us with a pictorial depiction of the Norman Conquest, often imparting detailed information not available from any other source. It will probably never be absolutely certain who commissioned the Tapestry, but, despite ingenious arguments for a range of other possible sponsors, Bishop Odo remains the clear front-runner in any wager (for recent research into the Tapestry, see Foys et al. 2009; Lewis et al. 2011).

There are also a number of English accounts of the Norman Conquest which contain information about Odo, most notably, the *Anglo-Saxon Chronicle* (Whitelock et al. 1961). The *Chronicle* often covers events tersely, as in its description of Odo as regent, 'the foremost man after the King, and he had an earldom in England'; but on other occasions, such as Odo's revolt in 1088, it provides more details than other accounts. There are several twelfth-century English chronicles, the most relevant of which is that of John of Worcester (d. c. 1140), formerly attributed to the monk Florence of Worcester (Darlington and McGurk 1995 and 1998). John's account provides a partisan English account of the Conquest, particularly, details of Odo and the 1088 revolt.

Other English sources include William of Malmesbury's *Deeds of the Kings of England* (c. 1125–27), which not only includes references to Odo but also provides valuable shrewd observations about the bishop's contemporaries (Mynors et al. 1998; Winterbottom & Thomson 2002). Eadmer, a monk at Christ Church, Canterbury, wrote a *History of Recent Events in England*, which covers the period between around 1066 and 1122 and provides a conventional pen portrait of the bishop and a long account of the Penenden Heath trial (Bosanquet 1964), where Odo was accused of purloining monastic estates, particularly those of Christ Church, Canterbury. Henry of Huntingdon (c. 1088–c. 1154), in his *History of the English People*, again records Odo's role in the 1088 rebellion (Greenway 1996).

There are numerous documents resulting from Odo's work as Bishop of Bayeux, Earl of Kent and regent, but these are 'dry, often difficult to use, and of little intimate significance' (Bates 1975) and have to be carefully sieved to reveal anything of Odo's character. Domesday Book (c. 1086) provides a great wealth of information about Odo as a magnate, as a deliverer of English lands to Normans and as an appropriator of English estates, but a definitive account of Odo's English lands remains to be written.

Surprisingly, there is no modern biography of this extraordinary man, but David Bates has been responsible for the revision of opinions about the bishop. In his doctoral thesis and a series of articles Bates has produced comprehensive accounts of Odo's life, which have established a much more balanced and sympathetic interpretation of the bishop's activities (Bates 1970, Bates 1975 and Bates 2004–11).

2

• Duke Robert 'the Magnificent' •

The story of Odo is inextricably linked to that of his half-brother, William. Without that fraternal relationship he would have probably been a minor lord of Lower Normandy. Odo's dramatic achievements mirror those of his brother and his principal failure was caused by the breaking of the trust that William had placed in him. Between 1050 and 1082 the two brothers worked together; firstly, to build Normandy and the Norman Church, and after 1066 to conquer, pacify and rule England. For the final four years of William's life, Odo was imprisoned and it is unlikely that the two men met during that time.

William the Conqueror was born in 1027/28; his father was Duke Robert I, called 'the Magnificent', allegedly because of his generosity in dispensing treasures when on pilgrimage. William's mother was Herleva, the duke's mistress, who, within a few years of William's birth, married and had two more sons, one of whom was Odo. William became Duke of Normandy in 1035 on the death of his father and Odo's trajectory to the summit of Anglo-Norman society had started.

• Duke Robert I and Herleva •

On the death of his father, Duke Richard II (996–1026), Robert's elder brother, Richard, became duke, while Robert was made Count of Hiémois, a wooded region straddling the dioceses of Bayeux and Séez, as his share of the inheritance. Such divisions of territory echoed the arrangements of the Frankish era, when on the death of a king the empire was divided between all male heirs. Within a year, Duke Richard III died and Robert became duke. There were rumours that Robert had poisoned his elder brother, which resulted in his acquiring an alternative nickname – *le Diable* (the Devil). Subsequently, Robert's time as duke (1027–35) was characterised by the extension of the power and land of a number of baronial families, and he also made clerical enemies by plundering Church property. The Burgundian chronicler Hugh of Flavigny claimed that the duchy was 'debauched with anarchy' under Robert's rule (Bates 1982, 100). Nevertheless, Robert did play an inadvertent role in later Anglo-Norman politics; during his reign he continued to give assistance to the exiled brothers Edward and Alfred, sons of the English king, Ethelred the Unready, and his wife, the Norman Emma. William of Jumièges observed that the English princes were treated by the dukes as members of their own family. The friendship between the Norman ducal family and Edward, who later became King of England, as 'the Confessor', must have contributed to the credibility of Edward having promised William that he would succeed Edward as king. Regardless of the historical veracity of the promise, the strength of this relationship meant that it was feasible to contemporaries that such a commitment could have been made.

Herleva was the daughter of Fulbert, a *pollinctor*, who prepared corpses for burial. According to Orderic Vitalis (1075–c. 1142), her father later became an official of the ducal household (*cubicularii ducis* – duke's chamberlain) (van Houts 1986). We know that Robert occupied Falaise Castle immediately after the death of his father, Duke Richard II, in August 1026, and his liaison with Herleva probably started soon after that. William of Malmesbury observed that Duke Robert kept Herleva as if she was his lawful wife and that he treated her 'with distinguished respect' throughout her life. In addition to her father, her brothers also joined the ducal court. Robert also fathered a daughter called Adelaide, later, Countess of Aumale. Such relationships were common amongst the rulers of Frankish principalities even as late as the eleventh century and concubines were recognised as second-class wives with some rights under customary law – a convention known as 'Danish marriage'. In the 1030s the chronicler Ralph Glaber wrote that the Norman dukes often produced heirs with concubines and compared such procreation with that of the biblical patriarchs of the Israelites. Bates explains that:

> It had been common practice for centuries for young male members of the aristocracy to take on a long-term partner with whom they did not go through a full marriage ceremony of the kind increasingly required by the Church. Such a partner might in due course be supplanted by a wife, or might form a *ménage à trois* with one. The sons of both unions might be considered as potential heirs. (Bates 2003)

Duke Richard III and his brother Duke Robert both embraced this tradition by taking mistresses and producing children outside formal marriage. Robert may have been married briefly to Cnut's sister Margaret, usually known as Estrith, but we know little about this union. It could, however, be linked with the story of Robert sending a large fleet to invade England in 1033, after Cnut refused to recognise the exiled brothers Edward and Alfred (Lawson 1993, 105). William of Jumièges's version of this story claims that the fleet sailed, but was hit by bad weather and shipwrecked off the Breton coast. William of Malmesbury claimed that bad weather prevented the fleet sailing and the boats were left to rot in Rouen and 'much damaged by lapse of time, were still to be seen in Rouen in our own day' (Malmesbury, *Gesta Regum*, 1, 320–1).

Illegitimacy did not carry a social stigma in this context and in the Scandinavian world the child of a concubine was recognised as eligible to inherit. William's birth status was never disguised, although contemporary hagiographers tended to overlook it, and of the Norman chroniclers only the later writers Orderic Vitalis and Wace of Bayeux record a negative, but factually suspect, story about William's illegitimacy. When Roger of Tosny returned from fighting against the Muslims in Spain and heard that William had succeeded as duke, he 'arrogantly refused to serve him, saying that as a bastard William should not rule him and other Normans', and added that 'as a bastard [he] was despised by the native nobility'. Roger died in 1040 in a private war with his neighbours before William was in a position to avenge the insult (OV). It was only in contemporary non-Norman accounts that William was regularly described as *bastardus*. William of Jumièges records a well-known incident that reflected the humble status of the Conqueror's mother rather than his illegitimacy: while Duke William was besieging Alençon in 1050/51, the inhabitants waved hides and skins over the battlements and 'beat pelts and furs in order to insult the duke and despisingly called him a pelterer'. In response to this insult, William cut off the hands and feet of thirty-two of his tormentors. The reprisal was sufficiently horrific to persuade the nearby town of Domfront to surrender without a fight and presumably also sufficient to inhibit anyone else repeating the insult, at least publicly.

• The de Conteville Family •

Some scholars have recently suggested that Herleva's low birth status might have been exaggerated. They point to her brothers being readily assimilated into the ducal court and that sometime after William's birth Herleva being married to Herluin, a petty lord of the Lieuvin (a region to the east of Lisieux), who was probably already an established supporter of Duke Robert. Herluin was a man of modest fortune, but after his marriage he was made *vicomte*, based at Conteville on the southern bank of the Seine estuary. After William became duke, Herluin's estates throughout Normandy increased significantly and he became a member of the 'newly enriched' aristocracy of William's reign (Bates and Gazeau 1990, 22). There were two sons from this union, Odo and Robert, and the date of the marriage is central in determining the vexed question of Odo's birthday. Douglas had very little doubt 'that the marriage took place very soon after the birth of the Conqueror; and that Odo … was born about 1030' (Douglas 1964, 369). On the other hand, Bates argues that it was later in the 1030s, 'a little before he [Duke Robert] set off on his fatal pilgrimage to Jerusalem in January 1035' (Bates 2001, 34). A more recent study of the Norman bishops mediates and places Odo's birth in 1032/33 (Allen 2009, 120). Apart from uncertainty about Odo's birth date, it is unclear which of the brothers was senior. On their father Herluin's death (in 1066) it was Robert that succeeded to his lands, which might indicate that he was the elder, although by this time Odo, as Bishop of Bayeux, was already a wealthy man.

Although Odo was five or six years younger than William, his early education probably ran along corresponding lines to that of the young duke. He may well have had a hard childhood and even removed from the care of his parents (Bates 1975, 5). William of Poitiers implies that Odo was educated in the ducal household and was possibly being groomed for a senior role in government from an early age. Odo and his brother Robert would have enjoyed a similar military training to William's, which served both well as they were later to be involved in military action on

ODO DE CONTEVILLE FAMILY TREE

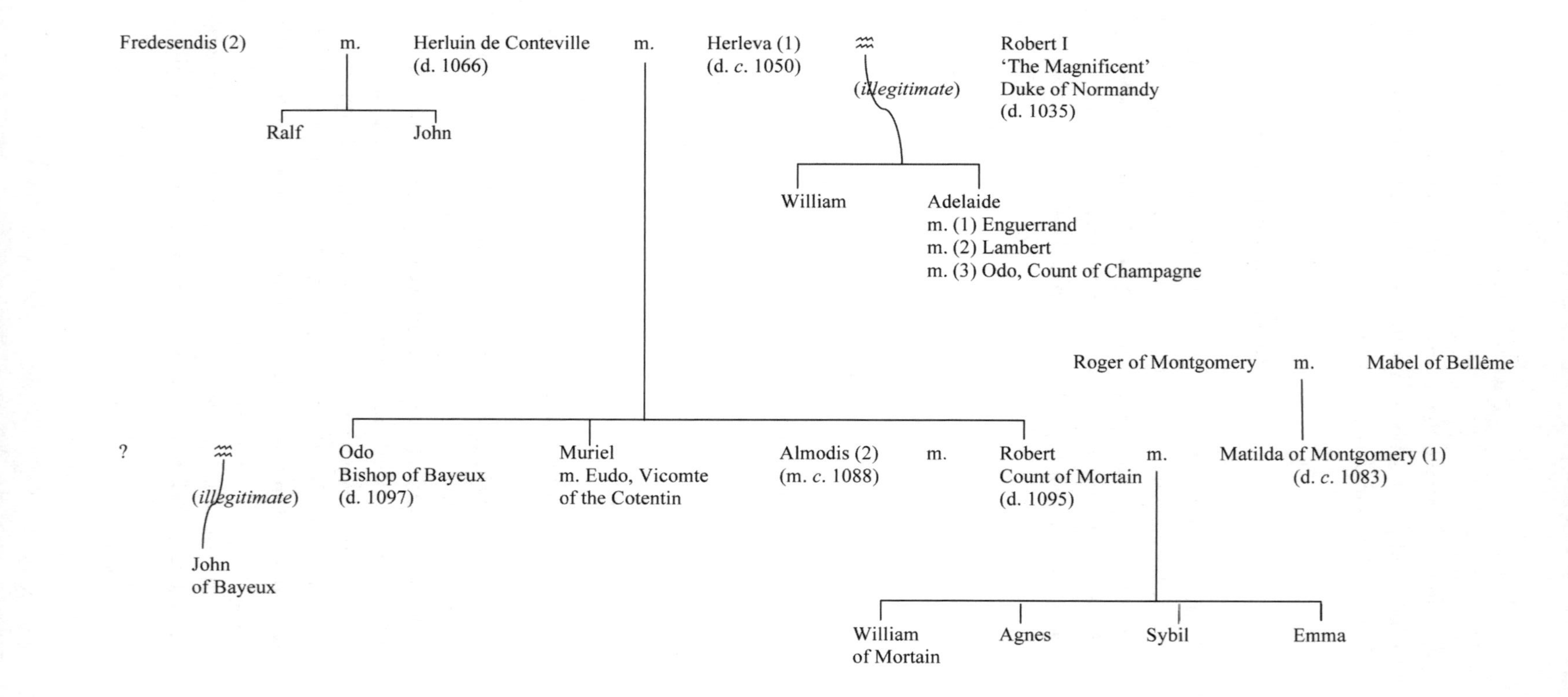

several occasions. Unlike William, however, Odo was literate and it is possible that he did receive some form of clerical education, even to the extent of learning Roman and canon law, which was normal for young French clerics at the time. Sometime before his election to bishop he was ordained a deacon at Fécamp by his second cousin Hugh d'Eu, Bishop of Lisieux. This ceremony may have taken place immediately before Odo's ordination as bishop, but it is also possible that he spent some time at Fécamp between 1046 and 1049. If so, he may well have been taught by the renowned ecclesiastic scholar John of Ravenna, Abbot of Fécamp (Allen, 120–1). John was a long-serving abbot of Fécamp renowned for his spiritual writings, but also associated with the extension of Fécamp's influence into Lower Normandy in the 1050s.

William was lucky in having two half-brothers on his mother's side. Among the Frankish princely class, family rivalry was common, and brothers, in particularly in Normandy, often posed a threat to ducal power. William's own father, Robert, was challenged for the succession by a half-brother, William of Arques. However, amicable relations were more common in ducal families where there was a shared mother. Maternal half-brothers were less likely to make a direct claim for the dukedom and, as happened in William's case, his half-brothers could be relied upon for support and rewarded with powerful positions within the duchy. It was a successful policy and one consequence was that by 1066 'Normandy had established itself as one of the most stable and successful principalities in France' (van Houts 2000, 56).

Odo was deemed to be brighter than his brother Robert, who William of Malmesbury dismissed unkindly as being of a stupid, dull disposition, but admitted that 'he had the courage of his race' and 'no foul crimes are laid to his charge'. We learn more about Robert from an account written by Vital of Savigny, one of Odo's protégés, who became his chaplain. Vital records how he had to intervene to stop Robert beating and abusing his wife, saying that he would have to dissolve the marriage unless the count mended his ways. The picture that Vital paints of Robert suggests a headstrong character given to rages and exaggerated remorse. These rather tepid assessments of Robert's character might have led to his qualities being underestimated, in any case his half-brother William had sufficient confidence in his abilities to delegate important tasks to him both before and after the Conquest of England. Robert appears to have had a shrewd business mind; he established markets with monopolies close to his many castles on his estates in

Normandy and England. He seems to have founded new towns adjacent to his castles at places such as Berkhamsted, Montacute and Pevensey as well as in Mortain itself. Orderic Vitalis noted that Robert was the most important of the Conqueror's followers and he did provide the most ships of all the Norman lords for the Norman invasion fleet (Golding 1991). His loyalty to his family and his generosity to the church may have made him something of a 'grand seigneur' in his later years (Bates 1975, 5).

Odo also had a sister called Muriel, who married a Cotentin lord called Odo au Chapel. This Odo founded an abbey at Lessay (c. 1056) along with his father, and appears as an adviser to William the Conqueror at the council held in early 1066 to consider the response to Harold Godwinson's seizure of the English crown. He might also be one of the men depicted on the Bayeux Tapestry at the feast at Hastings before the battle. It has been suggested that Muriel might have been the Norman woman of that name, who was educated in the school for young noblewomen at Wilton Abbey, before the Conquest and who eventually became a respected poet. While at Wilton, she was curiously advised by the poet/canon of Bayeux, Serlo, 'Far better to remain a virgin in your nunnery than have to take a lover.' (Stephenson 2011, 71–4).

Odo's father, Herluin, went on to marry a second wife, Frescendis, by whom he had two more sons, Ralph and John, about whom little is known. A Ralph de Conteville, who appears in Domesday Book holding lands in Somerset and Devon, is not thought to have been related to Herluin. Odo's father died around 1066 and almost the entirety of his lands went to Robert. Odo received only a small estate; this apparent favouritism may have been because Odo was already in possession of extensive diocesan estates.

• Notre-Dame de Grestain •

Odo's mother, Herleva, died around 1050 and was almost certainly buried at the Abbaye Notre-Dame de Grestain, founded by her husband, Herluin, and their son Robert on the south bank of the Seine estuary in the same year (Gazeau 2007, 24). It seems probable that the abbey was founded as an appropriate burial place for Herleva. In addition to Odo's mother, his father, Herluin, and his brother Robert were also buried here. The abbey was endowed with extensive estates and maritime rights. The pre-Revolutionary parish boundaries show that Grestain was carved out of the two neighbouring parishes of Fatouville and Berville, and given a long stretch of land along the bank of the Seine estuary as it then was, presumably for mooring and fishing purposes. After 1066 Grestain acquired estates in England including a house in London and twenty-nine estates spread over seven counties from Robert's wife, Matilda de Montgomery. Roger de Montgomery gave lands in Sussex at Wilmington, Firle and Beddingham; he also gave the abbey a house in the nearby port of Pevensey to facilitate movement of goods across the Channel (Gardiner 2000). Grestain established Wilmington Priory as a non-conventual cell in the twelfth century, from where the abbey's English lands were administered. Grestain had a bumpy history in the late twelfth century and the Bishop of Lisieux complained to Pope Alexander III that the monks' behaviour was scandalous and that the abbot was a 'dissolute liar'. The abbey was finally dissolved in 1757.

The site occupied the bottom of a slope descending into the Seine estuary. There is evidence of extensive terracing to accommodate the abbey buildings. A spring which fed a pool within the abbey complex was probably the site of an earlier, possibly pre-Christian, sacred site. The only surviving buildings are a heavily built late medieval undercroft, a chapel by the gate

7 Part of the surviving medieval remains of Grestain Abbey, forming the lower part of a later residence.

and part of the perimeter circuit running parallel to the former channel of the Seine. The building materials used include Caen stone, tufa from a local source and flint blocks from the chalk deposits of Upper Normandy. Today, the site is occupied by a few half-timbered cottages, a house built on to the main surviving section of abbey, the former chapel and the perimeter wall. A shady apple orchard covers the earthworks of the former abbey, giving it a quiet, almost mystical atmosphere, appropriate for the semi-legendary status of those who rest permanently here.

• Duke Robert's Pilgrimage and Death •

Duke Robert's short rule is generally judged to have been a troubled one, but by 1034 he appears to have secured and strengthened his ducal authority, which makes his decision to go on pilgrimage to Jerusalem at that point difficult to understand. Despite the inherent dangers of the long journey to visit the Christian sites in Jerusalem and Palestine, pilgrimage to the Holy Land was becoming increasingly popular in western Christendom. Pilgrimage was energetically promoted by the monks of Cluny in Burgundy, who used their far-flung network of contacts and their organisational skills both to urge men to go on pilgrimage and to provide facilities along the way for those that did.

According to Ralph Glaber, around AD 1000 an 'immeasurable multitude' of nobles and common folk took to the pilgrimage road. They were inspired by stories from the Book of Revelation, which foretold the Second Coming of Jesus Christ which would be in Jerusalem at the End of Days (widely interpreted as the Millennium). Although the Second Coming did not materialise, thousands of pilgrims gathered in Jerusalem and interest in the Holy City in the West was greatly enhanced. Attention then turned to 1033, another important date, marking a thousand years after Christ's crucifixion, when there was another major pilgrimage, which anticipated the Second Coming. Glaber tells of how peasants, merchants and nobles began 'to stream towards the Saviour's Tomb in Jerusalem'. The pattern was developing of a large pilgrimage from western Christendom to Jerusalem every thirty-three years or so – there was one in 1064 and at the end of the eleventh century the First Crusade (1095–99) was proclaimed.

At the time of the 1033 pilgrimage Jerusalem had yet to recover fully from the ravages of the Egyptian Fatimid caliph Al-Hakim, who in 1009

8 A portrait of Duke Robert 'the Magnificent' on the right, and his father Duke Richard II on the left. Robert appears to be wearing a Phrygian cap; headwear which was later associated with the French Revolution and liberty, but originated in antiquity and was depicted in Romanesque sculpture at places such as Kilpeck, Herefordshire. *Cartulary of Mont-Saint-Michel, Avranches*

had ordered the destruction of the Church of the Holy Sepulchre and other sacred sites in the city. The site of Christ's tomb had been largely destroyed and only the lower part of the cave structure survived. Al-Hakim had subsequently ordered the tearing down of all the Christian churches and convents in the whole of Palestine as well as the forced conversion to Islam of Christians living in lands under his control. Although later in his reign Al-Hakim turned his destructive attention to his fellow Muslims and became more tolerant of Christians, conditions in the Holy Land remained highly volatile. In the 1020s Bedouin tribes revolted against the Fatimids, seized control of the roads and systematically laid waste the Palestine countryside. Order was not fully restored until 1030 and only then did work begin on the restoration of Christian sacred places associated with the life and death of Jesus Christ (Armstrong 1996, 258–60).

The Normans were enthusiastic pilgrims and an entry for 1017 in Amatus' *Chronicle of Monte Cassino* recounts:

> Forty Normans dressed as pilgrims, on their return from Jerusalem, disembarked at Salerno. These were men of considerable bearing, impressive-looking, men of the greatest experience in warfare. They found the city besieged by the Saracens. Their souls were inflamed with a call to God. They demanded arms and horses ... and threw themselves ferociously upon the enemy. They killed and captured many and put the rest to flight, achieving a miraculous victory with the help of God. They swore that they had done all this only out of love of God and of the Christian faith; they refused any reward and refused to remain in Salerno.

Others were less charitable than Amatus and the Normans' aggressive habits earned them an unsavoury reputation. Eventually, in Italy, Norman pilgrims met with such intense local hostility that John, the abbot of Fécamp, complained to Pope Leo IX that they were being robbed, imprisoned or murdered 'every day' (Sumption 1975, 118). Thus, Norman pilgrims were obliged to travel in large well-armed bands, and it was from such groups that the Conquest of southern Italy had started. Despite these difficult conditions, in 1026 Robert's brother Richard III had financed a pilgrimage to the Holy City. The abbot of St Vanne of Verdun led a group of 700 Normans and pilgrims from other parts of northern France and Angoulême. At Antioch the pilgrims met up with Symeon, a Sicilian Greek monk from Mount Sinai, who was journeying in the other direction to Normandy in order to collect the alms which the duke regularly gave to his monastery. Following what had become the convention for the collection of holy souvenirs, while in Jerusalem, Abbot Richard acquired a fragment of the True Cross, which it is said he concealed in a bag hung around his neck.

The arrival of the news of more peaceful conditions in the Holy Land, brought back by such pilgrims, could have prompted Robert to decide that this was a propitious time to undertake his own pilgrimage. Pilgrimage to the Holy Land by Western rulers was normally linked to penance by men such as the 'terrible count of Anjou', Fulk III, who went to Jerusalem on four occasions after 1002 in order to expiate his crimes. Fulk's journeys were undertaken because of his fear of damnation resulting from all the blood he had shed. By the time of his last visit to Jerusalem when he was an old man, William of Malmesbury claims that Fulk stripped naked and was led by a halter around his neck to the Holy Sepulchre while a servant scourged his back as he called on Christ to accept his penance (Riley-Smith 1997, 28). Count Thierry of Trier, who had killed his archbishop in 1059, was to make the journey for similar reasons. After Robert's death it was alleged that he wanted to purge himself from the guilt of the death of his brother Richard III, who had died unexpectedly in 1026. Such sudden and unexplained deaths were not uncommon at the time and regularly led to accusations of foul play. In this case, some chroniclers claimed that Richard had been poisoned by his brother, although there is no other evidence to support the accusation. The real motives behind Robert's pilgrimage were probably more simple; as D.C. Douglas comments, 'It is not wholly inexplicable that the call to Jerusalem should have been answered by a young man who seems always to have combined within himself a violent lack of scruple with a strain of romantic rashness' (Douglas 1964, 36).

Prior to departing for Jerusalem, Duke Robert convened a special meeting of his Norman magnates in order to tell them of his planned pilgrimage. Apparently, the lords, led by Archbishop Robert of Rouen, unsuccessfully tried to dissuade him. Then, following Frankish tradition and recognising the possibility that he may never return, the duke persuaded the lords to acknowledge his illegitimate son, 7-year-old William, as his successor. According to the chronicler Wace, the lords agreed to accept William as Robert's lawful successor and 'went to the youth and became his vassals; they took many oaths and swore fealty and alliance to him' (Burgess 2004, 124). He then had the bequest confirmed by his overlord, the French king, Henry I (1031–60). Thus, the stage was set for Robert the Magnificent to embark on his fateful journey.

Before undertaking a major pilgrimage it was the practice to visit local cult centres in order to enlist the support and prayers of the community for a safe journey; therefore, before Robert left Normandy for Jerusalem he visited the abbey at Fécamp, which was a centre for the veneration of Christ's blood. From there he appears to have travelled south-eastwards from Normandy, through Paris, Langres and Besançon. He then crossed the Alps by way of the St Bernard Pass into Lombardy. After this the duke followed the route regularly taken by Norman pilgrims making their way to the eastern Mediterranean, through Italy to Rome and on to the Adriatic port of Bari.

It was at about this time, in 1035, that the first three of Tancred de Hauteville's sons, William, Drogo and Humphrey, travelled south from Hauteville-la-Guichard in the Cotentin to Italy. They joined the forces of Count Rainulf I, who had acquired Aversa on the Campanian Plain a few years earlier. This was the first Italian territory to fall into Norman hands. There is no suggestion that there was any direct link between Duke Robert and the Hauteville sons, but in its way their journey was to prove as momentous in the long run as his own. It was two of the younger Hauteville brothers, Robert and Roger, who later in the eleventh century would become rulers of the Norman territories of southern Italy and Sicily.

After the sea crossing from Bari to *Dyrrachium* (now the port of Durrës in Albania), Robert travelled to Constantinople by the old Roman road, the *Via Egnatia*. Leaving Constantinople, we know that he joined forces with the fearsome Fulk of Anjou and they travelled together along the old imperial highway which ran to Antioch, from whence the pilgrims would have travelled south down the Syrian and Palestine coast. According to William of Jumièges, Robert travelled in style and scattered alms along his route. Later, the story developed that because the Franks had a reputation for meanness in Constantinople, Robert had his mule shod in gold before entering the city. However, Wace, writing a century and a half after the event, claims that 'barefoot and in rags, he made a pilgrimage to Jerusalem, with great devotion' (Burgess 2004, 7). William of Jumièges also records that as a sign of his humility Robert refused precious gifts from the Byzantine emperor. When in Jerusalem it is said that Robert acquired one of St Stephen's fingers. Stephen, referred to as a protomartyr, had been stoned to death as early as c.AD 34; the eastern gate of Jerusalem, close to where he died, is named after the saint. The relic was sent back to Normandy and subsequently formed the basis of a major cult, not only in Normandy but throughout the rest of France, and when William, as duke, founded his abbey in Caen, it was dedicated to St Stephen in veneration of the saint and the memory of his father, Robert.

Robert died from unknown causes on the return journey in Nicaea (now Iznik) in Asia Minor early in July 1035. Robert's death was followed by the usual stories alleging that he too had been murdered; according to Wace, 'A young boy poisoned him on the advice of a wicked relative'. The story was elaborated by William of Malmesbury, who made the unlikely claim that Robert died 'by poison administered to him by an official named Ralph Mowin. This Ralph committed the crime in the hope of obtaining the dukedom, but when he came home his offence became known, and, shunned by all, he departed into exile' (Douglas 1964, 409). Duke Robert was interred in the cathedral at Nicaea 'in the manner befitting such a noble lord'. The speed with which Robert appears to have managed this journey is rather suspicious. He did not leave Normandy until late 1034/early 1035 and yet he managed to travel to Jerusalem and Bethlehem and return as far as Nicaea, which is less than 100km to the east of Constantinople, within six months. It would have been impressive if he had made even the one-way journey to Jerusalem in so short a time. It is, therefore, possible that Robert actually died *en route* to Jerusalem and that the stories told about him in Palestine are a later fabrication. Indeed, one story tells that he was about to leave Constantinople on his journey to the Holy Land 'when an illness, which lasted for two weeks or more, overtook him' and he was then carried

9 Duke Robert at the gates of Jerusalem from a nineteenth-century drawing. Having fallen ill en route the duke is being carried on a stretcher towards the Holy City; because several of the porters were black, Robert is reported to have joked that he was being carried to paradise by devils. *Lacroix, P.,* Vie militaire et religeuse du Moyen Age, *1877*

shoulder-high on a bier by Saracens. Could it be that it was really at this point that Robert died and not on the return journey? In 1086 William the Conqueror arranged for his father's remains to be returned to Normandy, but the king died before the mission was completed and, consequently, Duke Robert was reburied in Apulia by the envoys that had been charged with returning the duke's remains to the duchy. The death of Duke Robert in 1035 meant that his young son William's life was about to be transformed as was that of his half-brother, Odo.

3

• The Boy Bishop and Bayeux •

Odo was appointed Bishop of Bayeux on the death of Abbot Hugh in 1049/50, when he was somewhere between the ages of 14 and 19 (dependent on his birthday). In any case, he was well below the canonically required age of 30 for promotion to a bishopric. There is no record of where the ordination occurred, but since all other episcopal consecrations were held in Rouen, it is reasonable to assume it was in the ducal capital. It has been suggested that it might have coincided with Duke William's re-entry into Rouen, following the suppression of an uprising there early in 1050. Odo's appointment was part of a deliberate policy to extend ducal influence in western Normandy after the Battle of Val-ès-Dunes (1047); it would, therefore, also have been appropriate to hold the ordination in Bayeux, which itself had recently been in revolt against William.

Despite the great secular positions he was to acquire and important roles he performed, Odo was to remain Bishop of Bayeux until his death almost fifty years later. Odo's investment as bishop at such a young age was of course entirely due to William, but as none of the contemporary observers raised any objection to Odo's youthful appointment we can conclude that he was thought suitable for the position (Bates 1975). William of Poitiers claimed that Odo was elected to Bayeux because of his exemplary 'probity', but such politically motivated appointments for the close male kinsmen of Norman dukes were common. Although Odo appears as a witness to charters from the early 1050s onwards, it is unlikely that he had much initial impact on the diocese, and he was presumably being politically steered by the duke and his counsellors.

It is possible that William had identified character traits in Odo which marked him out as a future baron/bishop – characteristics that meant that he would support the duke and extend ducal authority in the Bessin but that he would also create a strong bishopric in the duke's image; Odo's success in developing Bayeux financially, architecturally, intellectually and spiritually was a reflection not only of the bishop, but of the duke as well. The ties of ducal authority were strengthened as a result of Odo's achievements and it was, therefore, an appointment which paid dividends at many levels, at least until the early 1080s.

• Duke William and the Church •

At about the same time as Odo's appointment, William was stamping his authority on the Norman Church with other family appointments. Several of Odo's contemporary prelates were part of or closely linked to the ducal family. William's cousin Hugh d'Eu had already been made Bishop of Lisieux (c. 1046), while Geoffrey de Mowbray, who may also have been a distant relation, became Bishop of Coutances (2 March 1049). These men were chosen for their loyalty and played a fundamentally important role in the government of the duchy. William's grandfather Richard I had appointed Hugh, son of his own half-brother, Count Rodulf, to the See of Bayeux (1015–49). Another of Count Rodulf's sons, John, became Bishop of Avranches in 1060 and subsequently Archbishop of Rouen. Before 1055 the See of Rouen was held by two sons of Norman dukes, Robert (990–1037) and Mauger (1037–55).

However, William needed bishops who were closer to him both in age and in disposition than the old guard. His appointment of men such as Odo and Geoffrey of Coutances created a Norman Church with strong ties to William. By 1066 William's control of the Norman Church was virtually complete; the Norman bishops attended synods over which he presided and they acknowledged their obligation to support him militarily by providing him with soldiers from their estates. The two muscular bishops Odo of Bayeux and Geoffrey of Coutances were to dominate the Norman Church for a generation. They owed their positions and their allegiance directly to William, giving them the confidence and backing to re-establish episcopal authority within their dioceses and form the backbone of a revitalised Church in the duchy. Orderic Vitalis brings home the reality of William's power when he writes, 'If any monk from his duchy dared to bring a plea against him [Duke William], he would ignore his cloth and hang him from the top of the highest oak-tree in the wood near by' (OV, iii, 94).

William's other half-brother, Robert, was also given a position of authority, but probably not until the late 1050s, when he became Count of Mortain. Mortain lay on the frontier with both Brittany and Bellême and close to the ecclesiastical centres of Avranches and Coutances. William of Jumièges thought these appointments reflected William's desire 'to raise up the humble kindred of his mother' while 'he plucked down the proud kindred of his father'. Although some chroniclers threw doubt on Robert's abilities, William had trusted him with the important task of protecting a volatile border of the expanded duchy, where he built castles along the south-western Norman frontier with Anjou at Mortain, St Hilaire-du-Harcouët, le Teilleul and Tinchebrai. Robert created markets and probably laid out new towns at these locations – a policy that was designed to combine commercial prosperity with security, and a strategy which Robert and other Normans were to bring over to England with great effect after 1066. Robert strengthened his position further through his marriages to Matilda, daughter of Roger de Montgomery, and then to Mabel de Bellême.

• Odo the Ecclesiastical Lord •

Although Odo was appointed as an ecclesiastical lord, he along with the other bishops played a role in the governance of Normandy and was expected to act at ducal level as well in his own diocese. Bishops played an overtly political role and provided a link between the faithful and the duke. His presence was required at court and at synods and he had to be ready with advice and support for the duke (and later, king), both of a practical and of a financial nature. One of Odo's first recorded acts as bishop was to witness a charter of St Evroul on 25 September 1050. He was also present at ecclesiastical councils held at Rouen in 1055, 1061 and 1063. Odo's importance in pre-Conquest government is demonstrated by his prominence among the witnesses to these charters, and it is clear from his subsequent role in the Conquest of England and his eminent position in the government of England that he had already reached a position of considerable power and influence by 1066.

As a major landholder, the Bishop of Bayeux was expected to provide knights for William's various military activities. The military role of the bishops was as important as their pastoral obligations and the bishop's knights owed specific obligations to their lord. These military obligations became particularly important at the time of the Conquest, when the duke needed to know what resources he could call upon both for the invasion of England and for the defence of the duchy in his absence. In a survey of the Bishop of Bayeux's lands of 1133 the extent to which Odo built up his military complement is made clear. The bishop was obliged to provide twenty knights to the duke from his episcopal estates; but in fact, the diocesan estates brought the service of 120 knights, six times the number required. Although Odo did campaign on occasion, both in England and in Normandy, and most notably at the Battle of Hastings, this number was far in excess of his normal needs. There was a financial gain to be had from such an arrangement in the form of feudal revenues. The bishop was entitled to 20*s* per knight when he went to Rome on Church business, whenever it was necessary to repair the cathedral, or when it was necessary to repair episcopal buildings damaged by fire. He also received what were known as reliefs; for instance, when a vassal died without heirs his property would revert to the bishop, or if a minor inherited an estate the bishop could take the revenues until the heir came of age. Such reliefs were valued at £15 per knight, although later bishops had some difficulty in collecting reliefs and had to depend upon the duke for help (Gleason 1936, 48–51).

The bishop's military vassals included nobles such as the *vicomte* of the Bessin. Below these were the 'vavassors', some of whom performed a modified form of military service, while others were little more than peasants. It was this category of vassal that 'undoubtedly formed the main basis of the bishop's wealth' (Gleason, 53). Several of Odo's tenants, such as Wadard and Vital, went with him to England and continued to benefit from the bishop's support. Odo clearly enjoyed having people around him who were dependent upon him, both secular and clerical.

Although there were such financial implications for the bishop to have land held under military tenure, Bates has argued that the reasons are more likely to have been political (Bates 1970). Land held in this way was probably part of a ducal policy to reward the bishops with land whose holders could be used for the duke's own ends and to maintain a strong ducal presence in the Bessin. Such arrangements meant that the bishops would have felt that it was much more unlikely that the duke or anyone else would seize land that was held by military tenure.

Although Odo belonged to a new generation of Norman bishops, he was not associated with the ecclesiastical reform movement which was gathering pace, particularly after the Conquest of England. The bishop was expected to enhance his cathedral by increasing its wealth and prestige. The prelate's role was to glorify the cathedral and to provide a strong influential figurehead. Odo and his contemporaries built great basilicas, assembled large bodies of clergy and enthusiastically collected saints' relics, but they were not expected to undertake pastoral work or even to provide spiritual leadership. Gilbert Maminot, Bishop of Lisieux (1077–1101), a devotee of hunting and gambling, enjoyed a life of ease and luxury, but there was no suggestion that he was a bad bishop (Bates 1970, 44).

Later, William did appoint men of learning and who had received an adequate ecclesiastical training, to high church offices. As such, these prelates were much closer in temperament to the ideal set out by the English bishop Wulfstan of York and Worcester (d. 1023), who declared in rhythmic prose, that a bishop should think hard on peace and concord, how he might further Christendom and reduce heathenism. He followed this with a stream of observations, how a bishop should look after his household, be not too eager for song or hounds or hawks nor worldly wealth, should live in seemly fashion, be prepared to turn the other cheek, to excommunicate only for great causes, should see to book learning and proper instruction for his household, exercise his talents in good handicrafts and see that his household was kept busy in the same way, keep his hours properly and instruct men in the folkmoots with godly instruction (Loyn 1991).

• Bishop Odo's Wealth •

Odo's appointment brought considerable power and wealth to the young bishop. Bayeux was a rich diocese; work on its reorganisation had begun under his predecessor Bishop Hugh and estates lost during the period of Viking incursions had been partly recovered. The income from diocesan holdings was large. Bayeux was second only to Rouen in both status and wealth in Normandy, and Odo acquired a reputation for gathering wealth. Odo's 'remarkable and outrageous' career had resulted in great wealth and a claim by Marbod of Rennes that Bayeux was so rich it could have supported three bishops. Before 1066 the bishop is known to have possessed houses in Caen, Lisieux and Rouen as well as the bishop's palace in Bayeux (Bates 1982, 130–1). He also had a castle at Neuilly l'Évêque and fortified manors at Douvres-la-Délivrande and Cambremer (Casset 2007, 243–50, 279–91, 363–406).

The bishop also had urban property held by *burgenses* or burgesses. These were merchants, traders and craftsmen who lived in towns or in recently created *bourgs* – satellite urban centres attached to places like Caen, where the Bishop of Bayeux had tenants living in the duke's *bourg*, or Bayeux, where the bishop had his own *bourg*. Such burgesses were free of dues payable at the bishop's markets and fairs. Their *raison d'être* was to develop commercial activity through markets, from which the bishop would receive tolls from those coming to buy and sell from outside. Tolls were levied on goods bought and sold at the markets and fairs of the bishopric. Markets were held in the churchyards of many parishes, while important episcopal fairs were located at Neuilly, Isigny, St Clair (Manche), Tilly, Plessis, St Vigor and Cambremer. At the great fairs of Neuilly and Isigny, barons, knights, clerics and officials of the king and bishop were exempted from tolls as well as specified individuals, such as the gatekeeper of the bishop's castle of Neuilly and an unnamed onion seller, who provided the bishop with a supply of garlic. The value to the bishops of such tolls is demonstrated by the vigour with which they opposed attempts to establish rival markets. In the twelfth century one bishop of Bayeux even appealed to the pope in an effort to stop the establishment of a new market at Crèvecoeur, sited near to his market at Cambremer, but in the neighbouring diocese of Lisieux (Gleason, 63).

It is not known if Odo was as fond of hunting as his half-brother William, who, it was said by the *Anglo-Saxon Chronicle*, 'loved the deer as though he were their father', but he did have his own deer parks at Bayeux and Neuilly and he created others at Wickhambreux, to the north-east of Canterbury, and at Eridge Park in Sussex. Theoretically, bishops were canonically prohibited from hunting, but as it was an integral component of the aristocratic lifestyle enjoyed by men like Odo it seems probably that he did participate in hunting parties. We know that the Bishop of Lisieux was an enthusiastic hunter and that Geoffrey of Coutances imported deer from England for his Norman parks. The bishops of Bayeux also had their own 'forests'. As with the royal forests in England, hunting was restricted to the bishop or his nominees, and the taking of deer, timber and other items was strictly

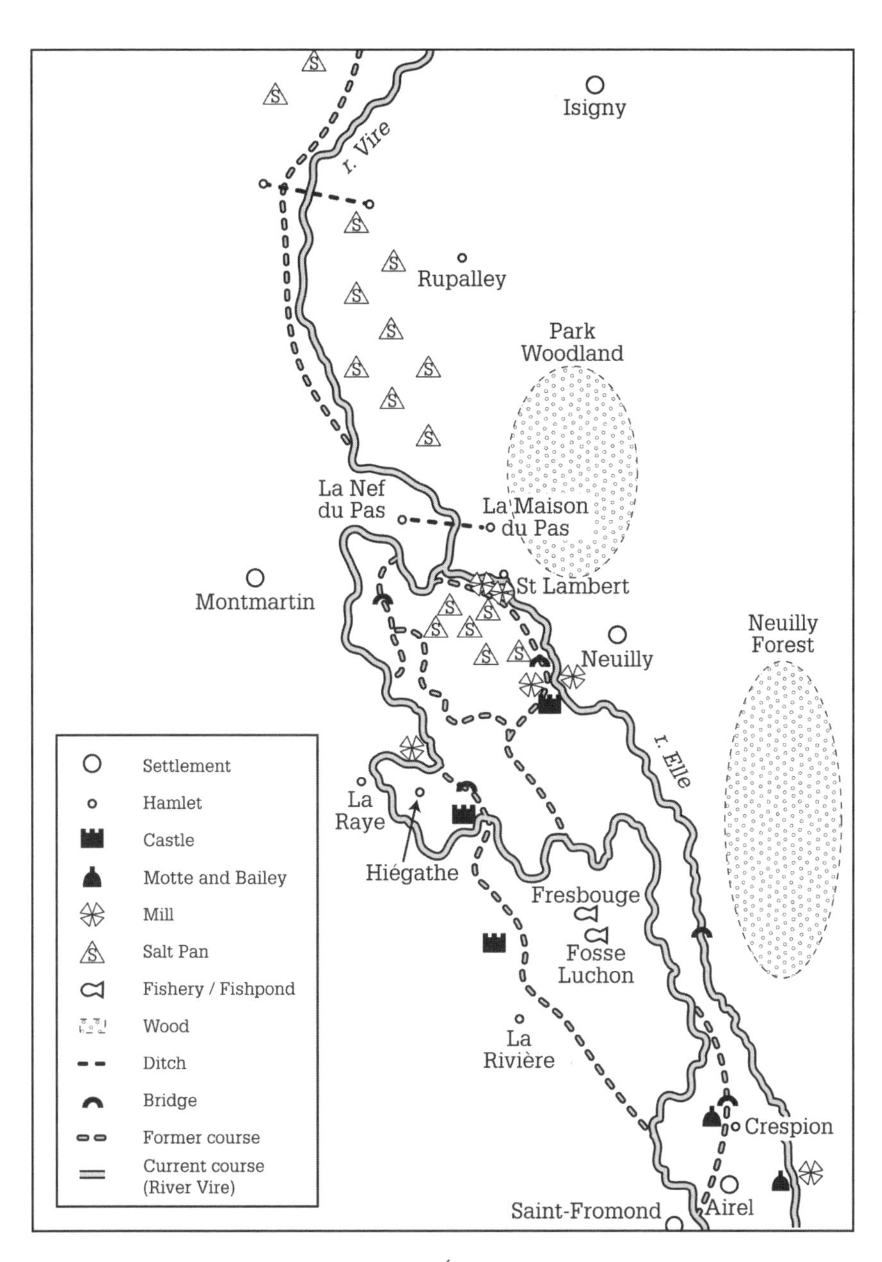

10 The Bishop of Bayeux's estate at Neuilly l'Évêque.

controlled. New enclosures were still being made in the eleventh century, when areas of former woodland were taken over for partial cultivation. The forest of Neuilly, for instance, once covered a considerably larger area than it did during the twelfth century and had originally been joined with the Cérisy forest to the south-east. Those tenants who pastured their animals within the limits of the forest were charged a fee called a *herbagium*. The administration of the diocesan forests was in the hands of foresters who collected forest revenues and policed illegal hunting.

The bishop also had access to sea-fishing revenues. He held an estate at Port-en-Bessin where the fishermen paid a fee called *aquagium* to the bishop. The size of the fee depended upon whether or not nets were used for the catch (Gleason, 61). Along the coast and in the estuary of the River Vire there were many diocesan salt pans and in some areas the bishop enjoyed a monopoly of salt production. In addition, the bishop would have controlled stretches of river fishing and would have had his own fish ponds for freshwater fish farming, normally located close to his castles and palaces. The bishop also had fish ponds on the River Aure at Bayeux. At Neuilly, close to Odo's castle in the Vire Valley, there was an integrated economy, with fish ponds, dovecotes, apiaries, fisheries, salt pans, mills, marsh and reed beds, woodland and parkland operating under the bishop's control. There were extensive water-management schemes and the bishop also controlled navigation on the River Vire (Casset). Another lucrative area for the bishop was milling, as he enjoyed a monopoly of corn milling in Bayeux where everyone using the bishop's mills was liable for a fee called a *multure*. If the bishop's tenants were found grinding their grain elsewhere, they forfeited the flour to the miller and the horse which carried it went to the bishop.

Such a wide-ranging economic enterprise required a large group of administrators. The oversight of the administration was in the hands of dapifers or seneschals, who supervised port reeves, toll receivers, tithe collectors, foresters, millers and revenue collectors. Thus, the diocese had its own administrative structure, which had to be cared for in addition to the cathedral chapter and the upkeep of all episcopal buildings, including the cathedral.

• Bayeux •

In the eleventh century there was a bridge over the River Aure, which ran immediately to the east of the walled town; the bridge led directly to

St Martin's Gate. There were four other bridges in 1100, but several were destroyed in the fire of 1105. The river was used intensively for milling, fishing, tanning, the provision of drinking water and to fill the city's defensive ditches (Neveux 1997). By the eleventh century Bayeux was expanding again, as witnessed by the establishment of new parish churches and of four or five satellite *bourgs*, one of which was *burgus episcopi*. Such *burgi* were often relatively small, but laid out in a planned design, sometimes enclosed within their own defensive circuit. It was a feature of ducal Normandy that burghal privileges were accorded to some of these settlements, such as that sited around Odo's new abbey of St Vigor (Clout, 340), where four burgesses were recorded in 1098. The other *bourgs* recorded at the end of the eleventh century were Bourg

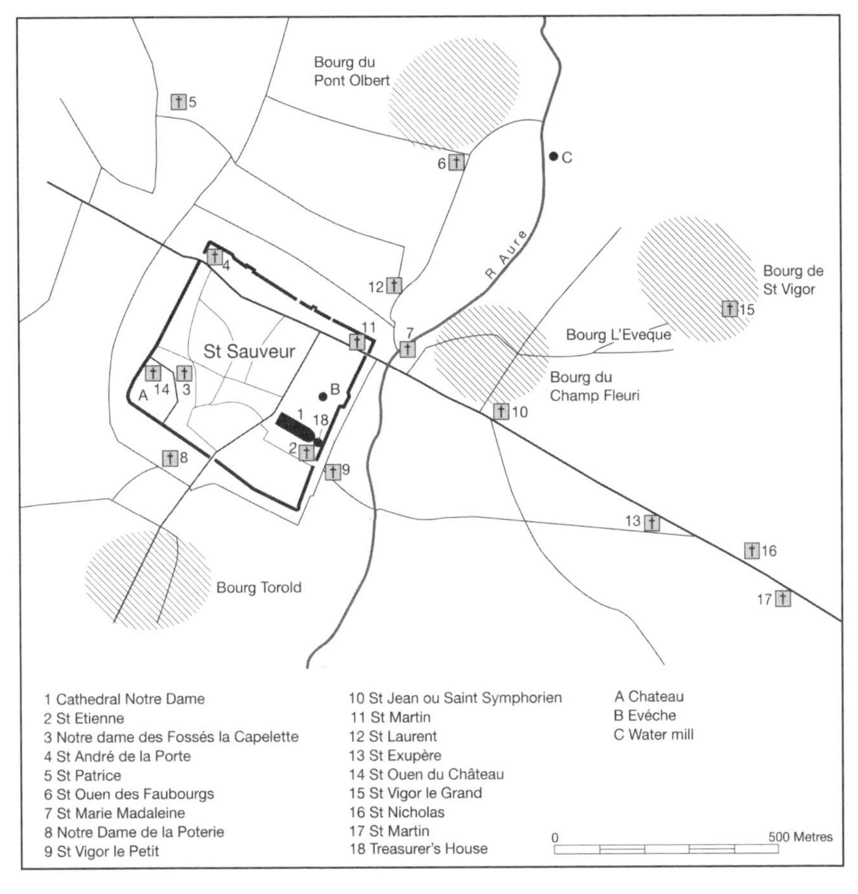

11 Plan of Bayeux and immediate surrounding area in the eleventh century. *After Neveux, 1996*

Turold, to the immediate south of the city, the Bourg du Champ-Fleuri, to the north-east of the city on the road leading to St Vigor, the Bourg du Pont Olbert and the Bourg l'Évêque, between Champ-Fleuri and St Vigor. Several of these *bourgs* disappear after the 1105 fire which destroyed much of Bayeux, although most have reappeared by the late Middle Ages (Neveux 1997).

The presence of financiers and property dealers in Bayeux, particularly from 1050 onwards, is noticeable and linked to the developing organisations of the cathedral chapter and ducal government. Only Rouen and Bayeux in Normandy had mints and Bayeux continued to produce coin in an archaic Carolingian style into the eleventh century. Descriptions of Bayeux in the early twelfth century emphasised the magnificence of the town and the cathedral with shining rooftops and soaring towers. Serlo, the canon/poet, described Bayeux as a town with a population of 3,000 and at least ten parish churches; in addition to the cathedral and the bishop's palace there seem to have been many stone buildings, including some Odo built for the canons close to the cathedral. In 2003 excavations immediately to the south-east of the cathedral uncovered the lower part of a high-status dwelling, believed to have belonged to the Treasurer of the cathedral. A contemporary of Odo's called Conan was a member of the chapter and Treasurer in 1092 and must have occupied this building. He is recorded as having a stone house and a small wood on the outside of the city wall next to the bishop's gate. The poet Serlo described his house as being 'a remarkable residence'. It was destroyed in the 1105 fire and rebuilt by Conan, but he appears to have fallen into debt as a result. It later passed into the hands of the cathedral's clerk of the works. The excavations here also demonstrated that the city walls had been restored during the Carolingian era (Delacampagne 2006, 159–76).

Tortaire, a monk from Fleury, was particularly impressed with the cathedral, although with characteristic regional bigotry he condemned the local cider as unpalatable and the inhabitants as distastefully coarse. Warming to this theme, Serlo accused the citizens of Bayeux of counterfeiting coins, theft, the oppression of widows and orphans, and cowardice (Bates 1970, 149). Serlo saw the fire of 1105 as divine retribution for the evils of the townspeople. Nonetheless, Bayeux in the second half of the eleventh century appears to have been a 'prosperous and busy community, elevated a little above its station by the exuberant extravagance of bishop Odo' (Bates 1982, 129–30).

Odo was perhaps trying to emulate his half-brother, William, who at the same time was busy developing Caen as a ducal capital city, quite distinct from the ancient regional capital of Rouen. Caen had the advantage of lying in the Jurassic limestone belt with ready access to a plentiful supply of excellent building material. Caen also had the benefit of being located on the River Orne, which provided adequate access to the sea, but compared to Rouen it was much less vulnerable to attack from the river. Caen was also chosen in order to provide William with a powerful base in Lower Normandy, where the duke's control had always been at its weakest. The rise of Caen would also deprive Bayeux of its claim of being the second city of Normandy.

Caen was growing as an important trading centre before William's ambitious development plans; around 1025 William's grandfather Richard II had included the *villa* of Caen, with its churches, toll, fair and markets, in his wife's dowry (Gibson 1978, 99). By 1060 William had a stone castle built at Caen on a rocky spur overlooking the Orne and had founded the abbeys of St Stephen and the Trinity. These were created in part penance for his marriage, which the pope deemed uncanonical and led to his excommunication for a while. The new foundations were particularly important for William as they provided a strong ducal ecclesiastical presence in a town which had no cathedral. St Stephen's was designated as William's burial place, thus, effectively designed to replace Fécamp as the ducal monastery. The new abbeys provided a supply of literate men and written documents, a means of control over a complex of estates, a source of ready cash, communities to pray for the duke and his family, and an impressive mausoleum. The first abbot, installed here in 1063, was the Italian cleric Lanfranc, who in 1070 went on to become Archbishop of Canterbury. Although the abbey lay within the diocese of Bayeux it was specifically placed under papal protection and the rights of the Bishop of Bayeux in relation to St Stephen's were strictly limited. Nevertheless, bishop and abbot seem to have worked in harmony and there is no suggestion of a strained relationship between Odo and Lanfranc before 1066, although in England after the Conquest they were to cross swords on several occasions (Cowdrey 2003, 25–7).

• Odo and Bayeux Cathedral •

Odo was not only the wealthiest of the Norman bishops, he was the first in precedence after Rouen; but the Bessin was still a border region, and a highly conservative area. The Church had suffered badly and traces of

Viking paganism survived well into the eleventh century. Cerisy, founded by Duke Robert in 1032, was the first monastery in the diocese to be re-established after all the earlier institutions had been broken up during the Viking era. Religious differences between Upper and Lower Normandy were one of the principal causes of the 1046–47 revolt, which was focused in the Bessin.

According to William of Poitiers, Odo played a major role in the ecclesiastical revival of Lower Normandy. In addition to acquiring estates for the cathedral he encouraged the establishment of new monasteries. There were six new foundations in his diocese between 1050 and 1066; these included the two ducal monasteries in Caen, and St Martin's in Troarn, reputedly consecrated by Odo in 1059. In addition to Odo's own foundation of St Vigor in Bayeux, Duke William endowed the hospital of St Nicholas as part penance for his marriage to Matilda. Bishop Odo continued the work of diocesan reform and on the new cathedral at Bayeux. The Carolingian cathedral had been destroyed by the Vikings and a replacement or restoration, about which we know little, was destroyed by fire in 1046, after which Bishop Hugh began work on the building which was completed by Odo

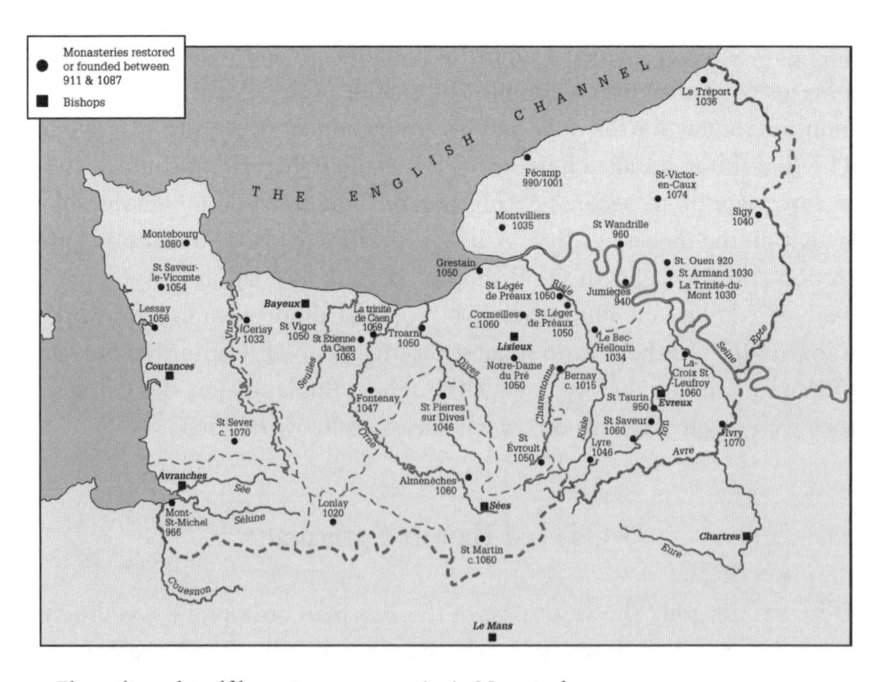

12 Eleventh- and twelfth-century monasteries in Normandy.

(Neveux 1996). Orderic Vitalis observed that, 'After his consecration Odo built a new cathedral in honour of Mary the holy mother of God, where he increased the number of able clerks and which he admirably enriched with many ornaments.'

Other Norman churches, such as the abbey at Jumièges and Coutances Cathedral were being built at the same time that Odo's cathedral of Notre Dame was being constructed. Bayeux Cathedral was particularly significant in the contribution that it made to the development of Norman Romanesque architecture. Like Coutances it had five bays, but it was a larger building than its contemporaries and integrated the nave with the western towers to give a new, unified composition to the church. New methods of construction included the use of ribbed vaulting in the towers – its first application in Normandy. Other innovations included the use of great arcades with high

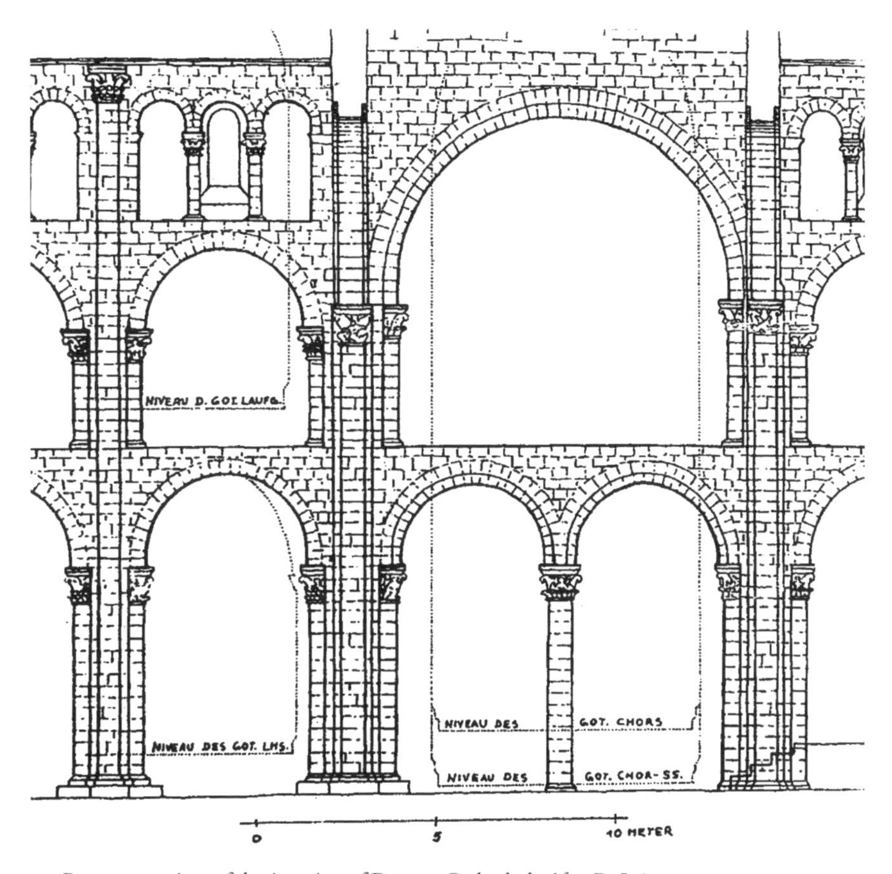

13 Reconstruction of the interior of Bayeux Cathedral. *After R. Leiss*

windows and the lavish use of Corinthian capitals as at Rouen. Perhaps the most audacious feature was the great west front, which may have been the inspiration for the grand west façade at Duke William's St Stephens in Caen (Gibson 1978, 101). Perhaps because relatively little of Odo's work survived the 1105 destruction and the twelfth-century rebuilding, he is not normally portrayed as an architectural innovator. Methods of construction and design used at Bayeux had an influence which extended far into Normandy and England after 1070 and Odo the 'prelate enjoyed an important role in the evolution of eleventh-century architecture' (Bayle 1995, 167–72).

Odo's new cathedral incorporated elements from an earlier group of Carolingian churches that had made up the pre-Viking cathedral. The choir was dedicated to Notre Dame and the nave to St Saviour, the latter also gave his name to the cathedral parish. A third sanctuary, adjacent to the cathedral, was dedicated to St Étienne; this church survived until the seventeenth century (Neveux 1996). In 1856 numerous capitals carved before the Conquest were found below later masonry at the crossing in the cathedral; opinions on their quality vary, but they represent an important link with the earliest years of Odo's bishopric. The most unusual of the capitals is that which is believed to be one of the earliest representations of the Incredulity of Thomas (Allen 135). The sculptors came from outside the duchy and were

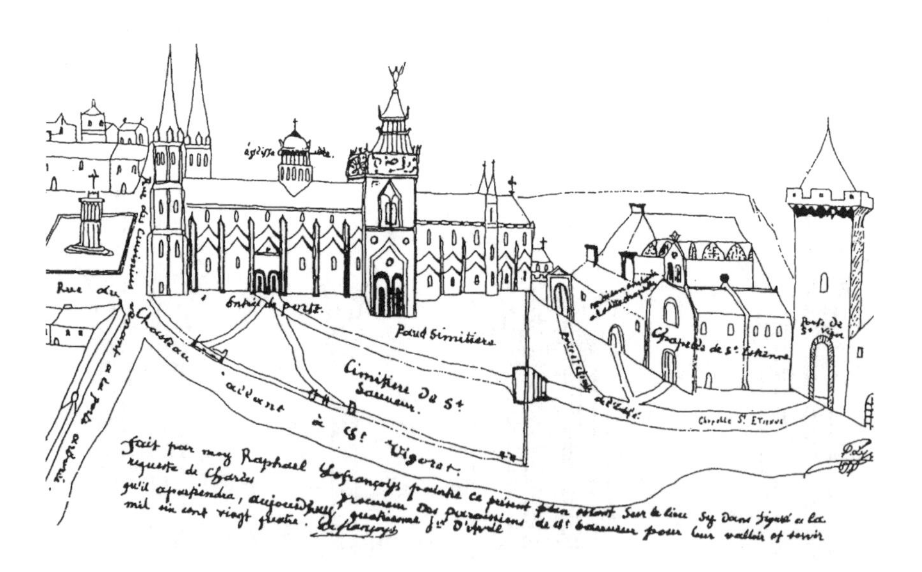

14 Drawing showing the south side of Bayeux Cathedral in 1664. *Neveux, F., 2007.* A chapel dedicated to St Stephen and the St Vignor Gate are on the right.

influenced by a variety of styles found from Provence to England. The presence of a cosmopolitan group of craftsmen confirms twelfth-century opinions of Bayeux 'which paint the city created by Odo as a sophisticated centre of international trade and commerce' (Allen 2009, 128). An early twelfth-century writer, Rodulf Tortaire, a monk of Fleury-sur-Loire, claimed that the cathedral was covered with statues. Although there is no other evidence to support this statement, it is possible that the exterior had a Romanesque frieze similar to that which survives at Lincoln Cathedral. The Lincoln frieze is, however, somewhat later than Odo, dating from Bishop Alexander's episcopacy (1123–48), although it is tempting to view the cartoon designs of the frieze in the context of the Bayeux Tapestry. The surviving work from Odo's time shows that he operated on a grander and more lavish scale than his colleagues and 'indicates a monumentality, ambition, and stylistic range of reference of a quite remarkable kind' (Bates 2004–11).

Odo was responsible for other buildings associated with the cathedral, notably, the bishop's palace and canons' houses. After its destruction by fire in 1046 the bishop's palace was moved to the north of the cathedral, where it has remained ever since. It seems to have been rebuilt at the same time as the cathedral as it was on the same alignment as the western towers. There are twelfth-century references to an *aula* (hall) and a *camera* (bishop's lodgings) in Odo's palace, and the palace appears to have had an L-shaped plan. Odo's palace was rebuilt after the 1105 fire (Renoux 195–6). Serlo described the 'precious chapter house' damaged by Henry I in 1105 (Bates 1975). In the eleventh century the cathedral served the only parish within the walls. There were a number of chapels, such as St Ouen in the castle and St Martin by the east gate, as well as the extramural suburban parish churches.

• Treasures and Holy Relics •

The cathedral was generously endowed with treasures during Odo's time as bishop, but it is only possible to obtain a glimpse of the true extent of these riches, as many were lost during the Huguenot uprisings in the sixteenth century. Tortaire was particularly impressed by the great gilded crown that hung at the crossing, which was said to be 5m high and almost wide enough to touch the cathedral walls. It was made of copper gilded in silver and carried ninety-six candles as well as verse inscriptions which included a prayer in Odo's honour. The monk also commented on the amount and quality of the cathedral's plate and vestments. Close members of Odo's family are known to have donated precious gifts to the cathedral; for example, William gave a gilded casket as well as the cloaks that he and Matilda had worn during their wedding service. It is possible that these gifts were donated when their daughter Agatha was interred in the cathedral in 1068 (Allen, 139), at a time when Odo's standing with his half-brother must have been at its highest. Odo and his half-brother Robert gave two enormous vessels to the cathedral, each in the form of a unicorn's horn. It is not clear what their function was, but a cathedral inventory of 1476 records that they measured 3m and 5m in length and were 'very precious'. Items crafted to represent 'curious creatures' such as whales and crocodiles were commonly found in other cathedral treasuries in medieval France (Allen, 137).

In the eleventh century holy relics represented the most precious possessions of a church. There was a hierarchy in the importance of relics and those associated with the bodies and lives of Jesus Christ, the Virgin Mary and the Apostles were the most highly prized. Such relics gave those cathedrals, abbeys and churches holding them enormous status and created a powerful attraction for pilgrims. Below these were the relics of local saints, whose potency increased in proportion to the number of miracles associated with them. Although it was believed that saints might offer protection and perform miracles wherever they were venerated, their primary loyalty belonged to the places where their bodies were preserved. As cathedrals and monasteries were being re-established in the wake of the Viking era in Western Europe there was a scramble to reclaim dispersed relics or obtain new ones. This was particularly true of Normandy, where during the ninth century many relics had been moved, broken up or lost as a result of Viking attacks. There followed a tussle for relics, land and influence between the revived monasteries of Upper Normandy, led by the ducal monastery of Fécamp, and those of Lower Normandy. By 1027 Jumièges, St Wandrille, St Ouen, Fécamp and Mont-Saint-Michel all possessed lands, churches and privileges in the Bessin. These were largely acquired by ducal grants as the dukes

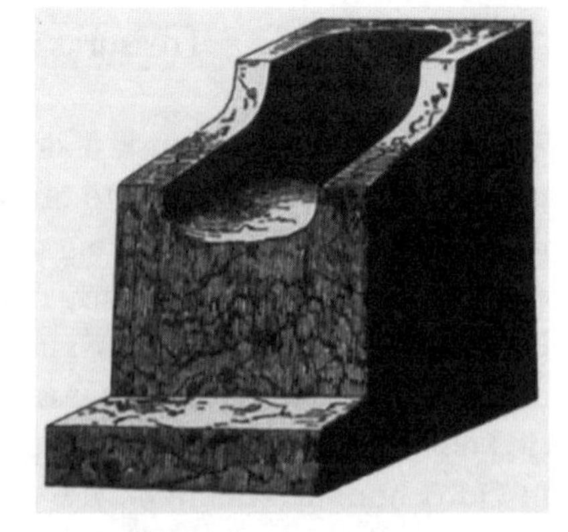

15 Bishop's throne Bayeux, probably contemporary with Bishop Odo.

16 Eighteenth-century drawing of the Carolingian Abbey of St Riquier, Somme, where the relics of St Vigor were kept in the eleventh century.

attempted to re-establish control in the region. There was rivalry not only over the merits of different relics, but even concerning the relative sanctity of neighbouring cathedrals. For example, Coutances Cathedral claimed that its dedication to the Virgin Mary was more sacred than that at Bayeux and, therefore, more worthy of veneration. There was also rivalry between institutions in the same city; for example, competition between the abbey of St Ouen and Rouen Cathedral over the relative sanctity of their relics sometimes led to violence (Herrick, 39).

This competition was illustrated by the case of St Vigor, a sixth-century bishop of Bayeux, whose relics were the source of considerable contention. The remains of St Vigor were mainly held at St Riquier in Ponthieu, where they had been taken in the tenth century after being displaced from Bayeux during the Viking period. According to Hariulphe of St Riquier (d. 1143), a cleric from Bayeux took St Vigor's relics from Bayeux around 987 and sold them to the abbey of St Riquier, where they remained and enjoyed considerable veneration. This story appears in various forms and confirms that Bayeux was not securely in ducal hands at the end of the tenth century. The monks of St Ouen in Rouen also claimed a jawbone of the saint and by diplomatic means had gained control of the cult of St Vigor, that is, appraisal of relic claims and dissemination of the *vita*. When Duke Robert founded a monastery at Cerisy he dedicated it to St Vigor as a political move to consolidate ducal power along what was essentially a frontier region at the time. He also placed it in the charge of St Ouen, the leading monastery in the capital, Rouen (Herrick, 43). The first abbot of Cerisy and probably the monks accompanying him came from St Ouen. It appears that Vigor was also being commemorated at Fécamp from the second half of the eleventh century, as part of what has been called the 'monastic reconquest' (Potts 1997), and it may have been as a response to this that Odo founded the monastery of St-Vigor-le-Grand just outside Bayeux (c. 1066), as an affirmation of the saint's ties to his episcopal city. Odo made strenuous efforts to have the relics of St Vigor translated from St Riquier to Bayeux, but his petitions were of no avail. The abbey of St Riquier was in Ponthieu, which, although subject to Duke William's overlordship, was not under any obligation to Bayeux, and the abbey argued that Bayeux should have taken better care of its relics in the first place. It has been claimed that the St Vigor episode was an exercise in control by Rouen, tying the people of Bayeux and the archiepiscopal capital. Vigor's relic lodged in Rouen directed the veneration of the Bessin faithful towards the ducal capital and sanctioned the submission of Odo's abbey and region to Rouen. 'By implication, the saint likewise approved the authority emanating from Rouen, and accepted the duke as his distant successor to control the Bessin' (Berkhofer III et al., 20).

There was a legend recounted in his *vita* that St Vigor had founded a monastery at a place named as *Mons Chrismatum*, where there had been a pagan temple, just outside Bayeux. Odo claimed that his later foundation was on the same site, but no archaeological evidence for this earlier monastery has been found (Herrick 2007, 169). Work on Odo's own abbey just outside Bayeux at St-Vigor-le-Grand began in 1050, but may not have been completed until after the Conquest. The church of St Vigor was intended to have been Odo's own mausoleum as well as that of future bishops of Bayeux.

17 The ruined Romanesque church of St Vigor, from a drawing of 1889.

As part of his efforts to establish a relic cult at Bayeux, Odo attempted to bribe the sacristan of Corbeil, south of Paris, to give him the bones of Bayeux's first bishop, St Exuperius (c. 390–405), which, apart from the head and a tooth, had been moved from Bayeux. This shabby tale was related by Guibert of Nogent in his *Treatise on Relics* of 1106:

> Odo, Bishop of Bayeux, eagerly desired the body of St Exuperius … He paid, therefore, the sum of one hundred pounds to the sacristan of the church which possessed these relics that he might take them for himself. But the sacristan cunningly dug up the bones of a peasant named Exuperius and brought them to the Bishop.

The custodian swore an oath that these were the authentic bones of the saint, but Guibert records how the townspeople were incensed by what they saw as a betrayal of their patron saint, 'See now what disgrace this Bishop's bargain brought upon religion when the bones of this profane peasant Exuperius were thrust upon God's holy altar, which perchance will never more be purged of them' (de Nogent 1910, 15–22). Guibert was making a broader point about the danger of dealing in fragmented holy bodies, as whole corpses were more difficult to fake. Complete bodies were rare and were prized for their rarity; Odo would, therefore, have been motivated by his desire to reconstitute the highly prestigious body of St Exuperius in its entirety.

More successfully, between 1050 and 1060 Odo commissioned a new shrine for the relics of the brothers St Rasyphus and St Ravennus. These were two fifth-century British martyrs who were at the centre of the most popular cult at Bayeux in the mid-eleventh century. According to later sources, the two Christian brothers fled from England during the early phase of incursions by the pagan Anglo-Saxons to Macé on the south-eastern boundary of Normandy. Here, they became hermits and were later martyred, perhaps by Arian Goths. One version of their deaths claims that they were thrown against a large block of sandstone, but although their heads dented the stone they were not harmed; two indentations found in the church of St Aubin of Macé are reputedly the result of this incident. Subsequently, they were decapitated and buried near the church. The saints were venerated as great healers who were responsible for many miracles, particularly in the diocese of Sées (www.catholic.org). Their relics were moved to St-Vaast-sur-Seulles, about 5 miles to the south of Bayeux, during the Viking invasions and forgotten about, but their location was miraculously revealed to Hugh, Odo's immediate predecessor as Bishop of Bayeux (1011–49). The relics were then returned to Bayeux Cathedral, where the cult of Rasyphus and Ravennus flourished (Overbey 2009, 39–43). Odo's new reliquary was designed to impress and was described in a fifteenth-century inventory as being 'made of fine gold, with raised golden images, and decorated with large and expensive enamels and precious stones of various kinds …'. Odo's efforts to promote the importance of these relics were obviously successful as, shortly after their re-enshrinement in Bayeux, the popularity of the cult of Rasyphus and Ravennus was second only to that of the Virgin Mary, to whom the cathedral was primarily dedicated. It has been argued that the cult of these rather obscure saints was in its 'fullest bloom at the time of Harold's oath' and that it was on these relics that Harold swore the infamous oath depicted so graphically in the Bayeux Tapestry (Musset, 150). The 1476 inventory indicates that Odo may also have secured some of the bones of St Aubert, an eighth-century Bishop of Avranches. Odo's preoccupation with relics for his cathedral and abbey appears to have survived until the end of his life. There is a reliquary used

18 Earl Harold being handed the crown by English nobles, from the Bayeux Tapestry.

to hold the chasuble of St Regnobert which is still to be found in Bayeux Cathedral's Treasury. It is Arabic in origin and Odo may have obtained it in southern Italy or Sicily just before he died (Allen, 159, 297) (colour plate 4).

There does not seem to have been a collection of miracles associated with the cathedral, and the cult of the Bayeux saints had only limited popularity outside the city; for instance, there is only one church dedicated to Ravennus and Rasyphus in the whole of Normandy. Conversely, there are several records of the citizens of Bayeux travelling out of the city to be healed at St Ouen, St Wandrille, Mortain, Countances and Fécamp (Bates 1970, 157–8). Despite his best efforts, Odo failed to establish a successful relic cult in Bayeux and his disappointment at this failure may have stimulated his desire to succeed in other spheres such as becoming pope.

• The Chapter and Cathedral School •

Despite his frequent and prolonged absences from Bayeux, particularly after the Conquest, and whatever his character deficiencies in other areas, Odo's commitment to Bayeux Cathedral was never doubted. His posthumous reputation at Bayeux was excellent, as witnessed by the celebration of a mass for his soul during the Lenten processions right up until the eighteenth century (Bates 1975, 12). The size and constituency of the body of clergy – the chapter – was a reflection of the power and prestige of a medieval cathedral. Odo appreciated the importance of cultivating men of high intellectual ability, who he realised were indispensable for a successful bishop's entourage. He aimed to create a court of the same quality as those of the duke and the archbishop of Rouen. The successful operation of Bayeux Cathedral during Odo's long absences in England was a reflection of the bishop's accomplishment in fostering a prestigious, well-educated and well-trained chapter. Odo wasted little time in building up the number of men who served his cathedral, based on a network of endowments throughout the diocese. By 1092 there were nine dignitaries of the chapter and over thirty canons. In comparison, Coutances only had fourteen canons. Odo steadily acquired land for his cathedral to support the chapter and by the early twelfth century Bayeux could boast of having three times as many knights as any other Norman bishopric.

Prior to the Conquest, Odo built himself a reputation as a strong defender of monasticism and a patron of learning by encouraging the advanced education of young clergymen. By the 1050s there were already small schools attached to Norman cathedrals for the training of parochial clergy for their own diocese. However, Odo sent his most promising clerks to study at cities outside Normandy, including Paris. Odo appears to have been in touch with all the important intellectual centres in northern France where, according to Orderic Vitalis, 'he knew that philosophic studies flourished, and supported them generously so that they might drink long and deeply from the springs of knowledge' (OV).

In particular, Odo appears to have favoured the cathedral school at Liège, which became a nursery for future abbots and bishops in Normandy and in England. Liège was known for its excellence in the teaching of 'moral discipline', liberal studies and the study of virtue. Ironically, by the 1050s scholars were already complaining about the collapse of discipline and the lost golden age of the Liège School (Jaeger 1994, 54–6). Two young brothers from Bayeux, Thomas and Samson, initiators of a dynasty of English prelates, were sponsored by Odo and sent to Liège to study in the 1050s. They both returned to Bayeux, where Thomas became Treasurer of Bayeux, and subsequently they became royal chaplains, positions that often led to bishoprics. Thomas went on to be appointed Archbishop of York (1070–1100), while Samson, who some historians have suggested might have been the scribe who undertook the mammoth task of writing out Domesday Book, became Bishop of Worcester (1096–1112). Samson appears to have enticed Norman scribes, presumably from Bayeux, to Worcester Cathedral, where a copy of the *Registrum Gregorii* was written in both English and Norman hands. Samson had two sons: Richard, who became Bishop of Bayeux (1108–33) and Thomas, who like his uncle became Archbishop of York (1108–14). Samson also had a grandson called Richard, who was Bishop of Bayeux from 1135 to 1142 (Galbraith 1967). The school at Bayeux seems to have increased in importance in the decades after the Conquest as the cathedral chapter grew in size and status. Training at Bayeux or Odo's sponsorship at another institution usually led to a bishopric or a post in the government of the duke or the king. It is an endorsement of the quality of the training these men received that many of them were appointed after Odo's fall from grace. No other cathedral produced as many men of distinction as Bayeux, and 'its contribution to the practical government of conquered England and of its bishoprics and monasteries was fundamental and unrivalled' (Bates 1975). The intellectual clerical network that Odo had established throughout western Christendom must have been on his mind in 1082, when he was attempting to make a bid for the papacy. No doubt he had important strategic positions in mind for many of his protégés if he had been successful.

• Bishop Odo's Patronage of the Arts •

Odo's patronage of scholars, poets and theologians established Bayeux as an intellectual centre. Odo also sponsored a number of the most significant contemporary poets, including Marbod, Bishop of Rennes who wrote lyric poetry covering a wide variety of topics, both sacred and secular. His erotic love poems have predictably received some of the most attention. Some of these works deal with male and female desires, while others are concerned with same-sex romance, although they fall short of endorsing homosexual physical relationships. Marbod wrote a verse life of St Thaïs, a fourth-century Egyptian who finished her life as a recluse prostitute, which inspired a novel by Anatole France and an opera by Jules Massenet (Boswell 1981).

Marbod has been described as 'surely the most unjustly ignored theorist and poet of the entire Latin Middle Ages'. Marbod later became Bishop of Rennes but he seems to have maintained his links with Bayeux throughout his life. He was widely thought of as being an eloquent writer, who once spontaneously composed a hexameter when handed a silver drinking vessel at a dinner party with Odo and William the Conqueror; but the resulting line, 'this silver vessel needs neither pitch nor nails', seems to have lost something in translation (Bond 1995, 70, 232). Marbod wrote to Odo reminding him of a previous favour and asking for another; in an age of sycophancy his poem might not have sounded as unctuous as it does today:

> But good Fortune has bestowed upon you all that Man seeks for himself;
> Riches, a good life, an excellent character,
> A tongue with which to speak, a mind which can think,
> Impeccable morals, the favour of the people, and of the Fathers.
> (Bates 1970, 195)

The cathedral's most prolific author, the poet/canon Serlo, wrote 'satire in a glutinous Latin, which can have given pleasure to few' (Bates 1975). Eight of his poems have survived, six of which are concerned with regaining property he has lost because he was a priest's son and his appeal to Odo to help him; one of them carries the wistful title, 'On the Defence of the Sons of Priests'. He also wrote on the fine qualities of the secular clergy and its Bayeux members, of which he was one. His poems on the deficiencies of the reformed papacy and the new monasteries were also motivated by a strong dose of self-interest. His poem describing the assault on Bayeux in 1105 by Henry I provides a description of the city which contained eleven churches, Bishop Odo's beautifully decorated court, the house of a rich burgess called Conan (the treasurer), the chapter house and the ducal castle (van Houts 2004–11).

If we look at the *curricula vitae* of the *alumni* of Bayeux, it would appear that Odo also supported grammarians, dialecticians and musicians just as Bishop Geoffrey did at Coutances Cathedral (Bates 1970, 198; Gazeau 2007, 244).

4

• The Duke Becomes a King •

Duke William of Normandy sailed an invasion fleet across the English Channel in late September 1066 and on 14 October defeated the English army led by King Harold at the Battle of Hastings. Two distinct but very simple versions of the events of 1066 soon emerged: the Norman claim, articulated by William of Poitiers and other Norman chroniclers, that William gained the crown legitimately by defeating the usurper Harold, and the English account, expressed by the *Anglo-Saxon Chronicle*, that William unlawfully seized the throne by killing King Harold.

William's close family were at the heart of the Norman campaign. They were present at the council called in response to Harold's accession to the throne, and they provided much of the invasion fleet and many of the men-at-arms. It was the three brothers – William, Odo and Robert – who held a council of war just before the battle and who appear on the Bayeux Tapestry as supreme commanders poised to strike (colour plate 14), like General Eisenhower and Field Marshal Montgomery meeting on the eve of D-Day in June 1944. In another very important way Odo's contribution was fundamental to the story. If the Bishop of Bayeux was responsible for creating the Bayeux Tapestry, a visual record of the Conquest, his fingerprints are all over Anglo-Norman history between 1064 and 1066. Our perception of almost every aspect of the Conquest of England is coloured by the images on the Bayeux Tapestry, which often provides primary evidence for details of the campaign. If there was a detailed chronicle of the Norman Conquest of England written by Odo, it could not have provided as valuable an historical source as the Tapestry.

• The Oath •

During his minority, William's court still included the two exiled English princes Alfred and Edward, sons of Ethelred II and Emma, daughter of Duke Richard II. In 1036 the brothers returned to England and Alfred was captured by Godwin, Earl of Wessex, who handed him over to Harold Harefoot, who was acting as regent for his brother King Harthacnut. Edward returned to Normandy after Alfred was blinded and died from his wounds. According to tradition, it was at about this stage that Edward first promised the English crown to Duke William. In 1041 Edward had been invited back to England by Harthacnut and became king the following year. William believed that Edward had confirmed his promise of the throne in 1051–52 at the time the Godwines had been banished from England. According to one version of the *Anglo-Saxon Chronicle*, William sailed to England 'with a great force' at the end of 1051 and was received by Edward, entertained honourably and returned laden with gifts. This story does not appear elsewhere and is largely discounted. Nonetheless, William did expect to be King of England on Edward's death, and the origins of that expectation lay in the period of Edward's exile in the Norman court.

William was in possession of English hostages, Harold's brother Wulfnoth and nephew Hakon, who had probably been taken to Normandy by Archbishop Robert of Jumièges on his enforced return to the duchy in 1052. According to English sources, Earl Harold's journey to the continent in 1064 was undertaken to negotiate their release. Norman sources claim that Harold went with the intention of confirming Edward's promise to William. William of Poitiers relates that Edward sent Harold:

> To confirm his former promise by a further oath he sent to him [William] Harold, of all his subjects the greatest in riches, honour and power, whose brother and nephew had previously been accepted as hostages for the duke's succession.

Harold's journey takes up much of the first half of the Bayeux Tapestry, but the visual narrative does not make the purpose of that journey clear. It has been argued that William's policy for many years had been directed towards his acquisition of the English throne; in particular, his enlistment of Harold in his 1064 Breton campaign and his holding of the English hostages are explained in terms of that strategy. Eadmer, in his *Historia Novorum in Anglia* (c. 1124), writes that William sought Harold's active support for his bid to be King of England and asked for the stronghold of Dover (with a water well) and a marriage alliance; Harold's sister was to be married to a Norman noble, while Harold would marry Agatha, one of the duke's daughters. Harold was to retain his prominent position in England, but under the rule of King William. The hostages would be released on William's accession to the throne. Harold was required to swear a solemn oath on holy relics supporting William before he was allowed to leave Normandy. It was the breaking of this oath that justified William invading England and removing the perjurer Harold from the throne that he had illicitly seized. Whatever the truth of this version of events, it was the one which the Normans repeatedly used to validate William's accession to the English throne.

There has been considerable debate about where Harold's oath was sworn. The Norman chroniclers identify Rouen or Bonneville-sur-Touques as its location, but the Tapestry indicates that it was at Bayeux. The capital of Normandy would have been a natural location for such an important event, but logistically Bayeux or Bonneville would have made more sense as they were both closer to the Channel ports which would have taken Harold back to England. The imposing ducal castle at Bonneville overlooking the Seine would have been a fittingly dramatic place for the oath. Alternatively,

19 The ducal castle at Bonneville-sur-Touques. One of the locations where Harold's infamous oath could have been sworn.

the cathedral at Bayeux was second only to Rouen in status and would have provided a suitably sacred environment for the oath. Odo is not shown on the Tapestry at the time of the oath, but he would not need to have been depicted if the oath had been given in his own diocesan cathedral, where his presence would have been taken for granted. It would have been characteristic of Odo to have provided the collection of holy relics on which this declaration was made and to have placed himself at the centre of the events which were critical for the future of Normandy and of Odo and his family in particular.

Harold may have thought that as he was a virtual prisoner of William's in Normandy he had no option but to agree to William's terms, and he may also have felt that because there was implicit pressure to swear, his promises were not binding. Indeed, he was not actually in a position to offer the English throne to William – that remained the prerogative of Edward and the English *witan*. Events in England on his return did little to improve Harold's position. A rising in the north in the autumn of 1065 succeeded in removing his brother Tostig as Earl of Northumbria; up until that point, with the exception of Edwin of Mercia, the Godwines had held a monopoly of the English earldoms. Harold's failure to maintain the Godwines' stranglehold on regional power weakened his position; not only had a member of the house of Wessex been removed from the northern earldom, but he was substituted by Edwin's brother, Morcar. Furthermore, Harold had made an enemy of Tostig by the ambivalent way he had dealt with the Northumbrian crisis and his brother would return seeking retribution.

• The Death of Edward the Confessor •

In England, no sooner had the dust begun to settle on the Northumbrian crisis than the question of Edward's successor became a real issue, as the king fell ill towards the end of 1065. Duke William and his Norman court would have been aware of King Edward's failing health and would have been monitoring events across the Channel closely. Although there is no direct evidence that the duke was anticipating the king's death by making any specific preparations to launch an invasion of England prior to Edward's death on 5 January 1066, it has been suggested that the presence in his army of troops from Flanders, Brittany and even Aquitaine indicates that a campaign had long been planned. It is, nevertheless, possible that William was taken by surprise by the speed of King Edward's demise. Edward's new Westminster Abbey was due to be consecrated on Christmas Day 1065 while the court was assembled. Edward became unwell on Christmas Eve and, although he still made appearances in public over the next three days, the consecration was delayed until 28 December, by which time the king's condition had worsened and he had taken to his bed. Just before he died, Edward took counsel with his immediate advisers and bequeathed the throne to Harold, with the stipulation that he should protect Queen Edith and her lands, saying, 'I commend this woman and the entire kingdom to your protection.' Edward also provided for those Frenchmen who had remained with him after the Godwines had regained influence in 1052. He instructed Harold to accept an oath of loyalty from those who wanted to stay in England and retain them in his service. Those who wished to return to France should be allowed to do so, taking their possessions, under safe conduct (Higham 1997, 174).

Edward's options in his choice of successor were strictly limited. According to Saxon tradition, the new king should be a blood relative, however remote, and should have sufficient support within the *witan*, that is, the leading *eoldermen* in the kingdom. There was only one serious legitimate English blood contender, the 14-year-old Prince Edgar, known as Edgar Aetheling, who had little support at the English court despite his credentials as Edward the Confessor's grand-nephew. By offering the crown to someone outside the royal lineage, Edward opened the way for Duke William's interference in the process. In addition to the old king's nomination, Harold required the support of the nobility and the clergy. It is the Bayeux Tapestry which provides the most detailed portrayal of Harold's takeover with the consent of the secular and ecclesiastic community. Harold is shown holding a battle axe and being offered the crown by a secular figure, with the caption, 'And here they gave the king's crown to Harold'. This version of events is supported by the account of John of Worcester, 'After the burial the underking Harold, Earl Godwine's son, whom the king before his death had appointed successor to the kingdom, was elected to the royal dignity by the magnates of the whole realm and on the same day was honourably consecrated king by Ealdred, Archbishop of York' (Higham, 175). The Norman chroniclers William of Jumièges and William of Poitiers both contest this version of events, claiming that Harold seized the throne unlawfully and, furthermore, that he was crowned by the discredited Archbishop of Canterbury, Stigand. On the Tapestry it is implied that Stigand alone crowned Harold. The archbishop had been excommunicated by several popes and was guilty of simony and pluralism as he held the See of Winchester at the same time as Canterbury.

Edward died on either 4 or 5 January and was buried in his newly consecrated abbey on the morning of 6. Harold was crowned king the same afternoon, probably by both Archbishop Ealdred of York and Archbishop Stigand of Canterbury. The Bayeux Tapestry shows a shooting star, believed to be Halley's Comet, appearing when Harold is sitting on the throne; but the comet actually appeared on 20 March 1066. The *Anglo-Saxon Chronicle* also reported the appearance of the comet, concluding that it would bring ill fortune for some. The caption on the Tapestry reads, 'Here resides Harold King of the English', and it has been suggested that the building in which Harold is sitting was a palace, rather than Westminster Abbey and that this was a Crown Wearing ceremony. If so it could have been at Easter, which fell on 16 April in 1066 (Higham, 184). Whatever the precise nature of the occasion, it was meant to demonstrate that Harold was now firmly enthroned as king.

• The Invasion Fleet Sails •

According to the Tapestry, Harold sent a messenger to Normandy taking news of Edward's death and at the same time the more unwelcome information that Harold had acceded to the throne. William would have been acutely aware that Harold was in a strong position. He had been nominated by Edward and supported by the English magnates, which meant that the only way to replace him would be by force. William would also have been well aware of Harold's problems with his brother Tostig, who in late 1065 had moved to Flanders, where he had been welcomed by his brother-in-law, Count Baldwin of Flanders. Baldwin made Tostig his deputy and settled him and his family in St Omer, where he was able to attract the support of mercenaries, drawn by the possibility of loot and land in England in the event of an invasion. Orderic Vitalis claimed that Tostig travelled to Normandy to offer William his support in his bid for the English throne, but this is not mentioned by any of the other commentators writing closer to the events of 1066. There would, nevertheless, have been close communication between Tostig, Baldwin and William which would have been maintained right up to the time of Tostig's unsuccessful invasion of England in September 1066.

Duke William's response to Harold was little more than a formality, in the form of a protest to the English court asking Harold to step down in his favour. William convened a series of councils aimed at maximising support amongst the Norman nobility and named his wife, Matilda, as his regent in Normandy. The duchess was to be supported by Roger de Beaumont and Roger de Montgomery, and it was accepted that Robert (Curthose), his 12-year-old son, was his heir. Odo was at these meetings and according to the Bayeux Tapestry appears to have played a significant role in persuading William to assemble an invasion fleet. During the first half of 1066 William travelled throughout the duchy, visiting his palaces at Rouen, Fécamp, Caen, Bayeux and Bonneville-sur-Touques, and met with his chief vassals; there were a series of rallies to encourage and organise the preparations. He had meetings with the rulers of those territories who were planning to join him as allies, notably, Eustace, Count of Boulogne and Aimeri, Vicomte of Thouars in Poitou. William also sent emissaries to obtain the support of Pope Alexander II, who, after some hesitation, blessed the mission and granted William the right to carry the papal banner. 'Through it he achieved a remarkable coup which immediately transformed a buccaneering enterprise into a legitimate enterprise against a usurping king' (Bates 1988, 85).

According to the chroniclers, William's main advisers were William fitz Osbern and Roger de Montgomery. Odo only appears with William occasionally, but it is difficult to believe that the man who was to wield such immense powers after the Conquest did not play a significant role in these preparations. The Tapestry conspicuously shows that Odo played a seminal role in the decision making both before and after the invasion fleet sailed. It is only the Tapestry that implies that it was Odo who advised William to build an armada and it is only the Tapestry that tells us that William took counsel with his half-brothers, Odo and Robert, on the eve of the Battle of Hastings. The preparations for the invasion culminated with the dedication of Matilda's abbey of La Trinité in Caen on 18 June. It was a grand religious occasion attended by Archbishop Mauritius of Rouen and at least four bishops and eight abbots. No description of the ceremony survives, but we can be sure that as the abbey lay within the diocese of Bayeux, Odo would have participated fully in the day's events.

In England, Harold's troops were deployed along the south coast from the Isle of Wight to Dover in anticipation of William's invasion. However, by early September it looked as if the long anticipated attack was not going to take place and on 8 September Harold dismissed the Wessex militia and with his housecarls he returned to London. The English fleet, which had been patrolling the south coast, was also disbanded. On 18 September a Scandinavian army led by Harald Hardrada, King of Norway, with the assistance of Tostig, landed at Riccall on the Yorkshire Ouse. Two days later, Harald, a seasoned warrior, decisively defeated an English army led by the

20 La Trinité, Caen in 1819, known as the Abbaye aux Dames and the burial place of Queen Mathilda. It was consecrated just before the invasion of England. *After Cotman, J.S.*

Earls Edwin and Morcar at Gate Fulford and subsequently negotiated the surrender of York. In response, King Harold assembled an army, marched it north and surprised Harald and Tostig on 25 September, defeating them at the Battle of Stamford Bridge. The king's overwhelming victory at Stamford Bridge would be seen as one of the greatest battles in English history, were it not for what followed. There is no reference to Harold's northern campaign on the Tapestry.

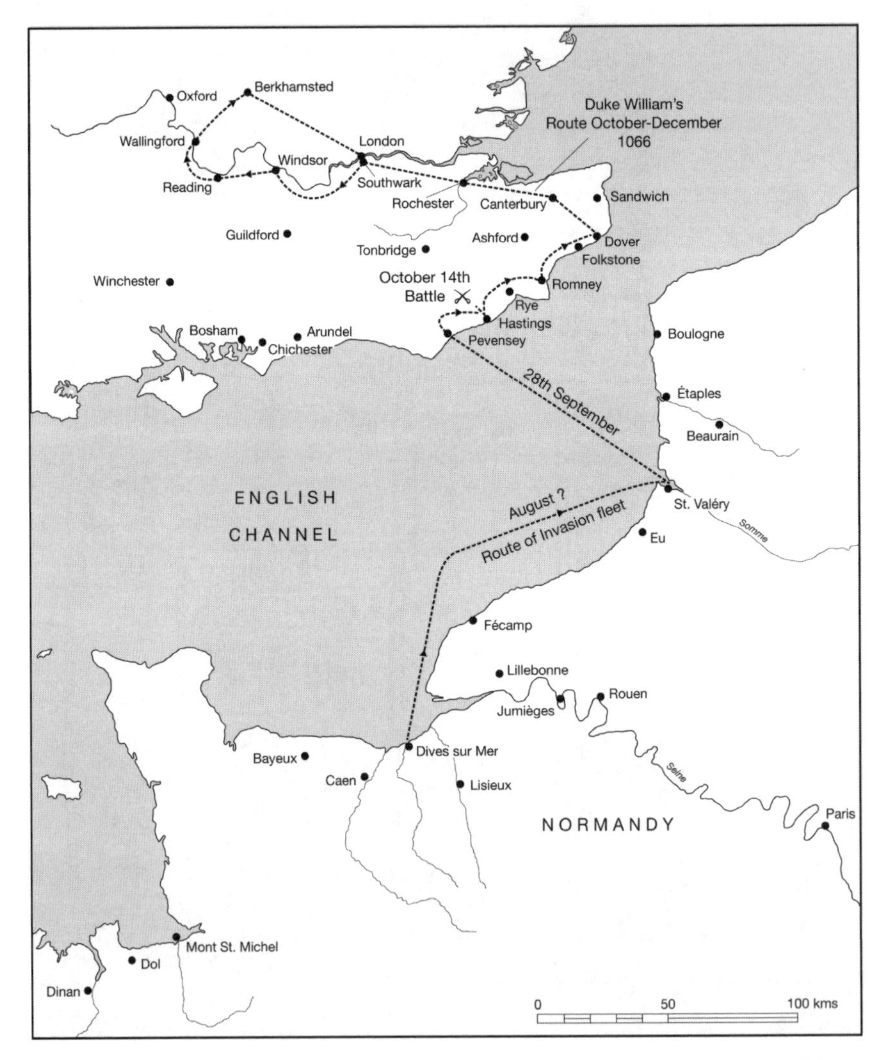

21 The route of the invasion fleet in late summer 1066 and William's journey to London after the Battle of Hastings.

In July 1066 the Norman invasion fleet was assembled at the mouth of the River Dives, about 20km to the north-east of Caen. It stayed there for about a month before being moved up the coast to St-Valery-sur-Somme in Ponthieu. The conventional story was that William was delayed, waiting for a favourable wind, before sailing and that there were prayers for the wind to change. The chroniclers imply that he was waiting the whole summer for this change to take place; in fact, it may only have been a few weeks. In any case, the news William was waiting for was of a military rather than a meteorological nature. The religious underpinning of the venture was emphasised when William ordered that the relics of the local saint, Valery, be taken in procession around the town, prior to the departure of the fleet. It has been suggested that Odo may have led the pre-invasion ceremonies at St Valery. After the Conquest, William endowed the church of St Valery with lands that he had promised in the event of a successful campaign.

It would seem that William was aware of Harold's movements and timed his sailing to coincide with the Scandinavian invasion in the north of England, and the fleet sailed to England on the night of 27/28 September. The Norman ships landed in Pevensey Bay, close to the Roman fortifications at Pevensey Castle (*Anderitum*). It is difficult to believe that William landed here by accident; if he did it was great good fortune for him. The heavily defended walled enclosure, covering almost 4ha, provided a ready-made stone castle which would have given protection to much of his army. It had been garrisoned by Harold's men before they had dispersed, but there was no opposition waiting for the Norman forces and they were able to dig in without any hindrance.

• Pevensey and Hastings •

The geography of the coastline on which the Normans landed has changed dramatically over the last millennium. Several watercourses flowed into Pevensey Bay and then into the sea, having passed through the low-lying marshy area now known as the Pevensey Levels. The levels were open water in Roman times and the distribution in Domesday of dozens of saltworks in what are now inland areas shows that tidal water still covered much of the area in the eleventh century. References to Pevensey during the eleventh century are normally linked to ships taking refuge in a harbour there. There has been a great deal of drainage, canalisation and river diversion as well as woodland clearance in the surrounding Weald, which has resulted in the silting up of Pevensey Bay. Consequently, *Anderitum*, which lay on a narrow peninsula at the mouth of the bay in 1066, is now separated from the sea by a swathe of marshland about a mile wide. The conventional story told by the chroniclers, which appears to be confirmed on the Bayeux Tapestry, is that after landing at Pevensey William built a castle. The next day he moved his fleet and troops eastwards to Hastings where he built a second castle. Yet topographically this is distinctly odd. Saxon Hastings was little more than a small fishing village, which is not recorded in Domesday Book, with a harbour that would have been quite inadequate for a fleet the size of William's. It would have made little sense to move from the safety of *Anderitum* and Pevensey Bay, with all its safe inlets, until such time that the army needed to move on.

An intriguing, somewhat heretical, suggestion that requires further investigation is that in the late Saxon period the place-name 'Hastings' covered the whole region which included Pevensey and the later town of Hastings (Combes and Lyne 1995). It can also be argued that the name Pevensey was used in connection with the bay and river rather than specifically with the fort at *Anderitum*. The use of the place-name suffix *ceastre* is invariably associated with Romano-British sites and there is no evidence of any significant Roman or Saxon occupation at Hastings. As many other Alfredian *burhs* were sited within former Roman fortifications, at places such as Winchester, Chichester and Porchester, it is possible that the place name *Haestingaceaster* was applied to the Roman fort at *Anderitum*. If this is the case, then William landed his fleet in Pevensey Bay on 28 September and moved his forces the short distance to *Anderitum* the following day. On the Tapestry he is later seen supervising his troops building a castle at *Hestinga*, which might have been an earthwork constructed within the Roman fortifications. In logistical terms this seems more likely than William moving his recently landed troops 10km to the east across the difficult terrain of the Pevensey Levels and the Sussex Weald to a smaller harbour with far less capacity than the one he was leaving.

Within a few years of the Conquest, Sussex was organised into north–south corridors, called rapes, which were placed in the hands of some of William's most trusted magnates. Pevensey was in the hands of his half-brother Robert of Mortain; Robert's father-in-law, Roger de Montgomery, held Chichester and Arundel; William de Warenne (1st Earl of Surrey), a distant relative of

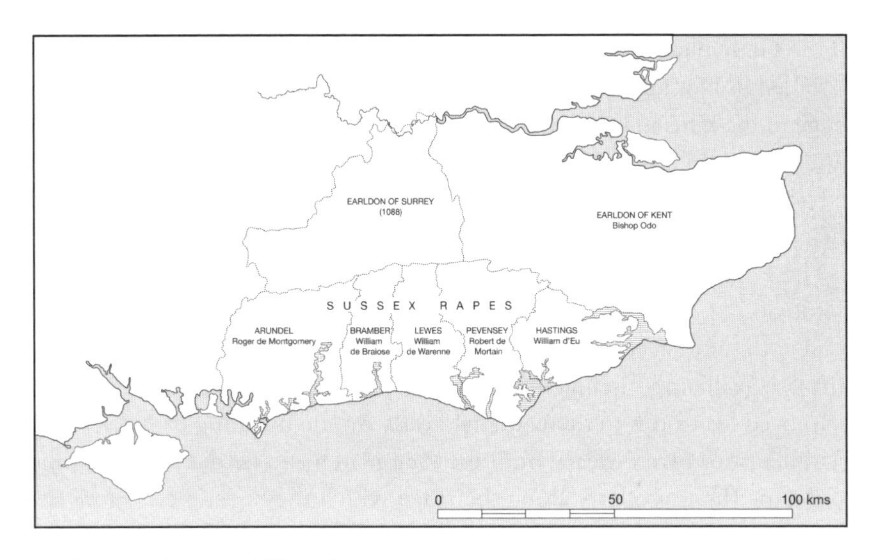

22 The Sussex Rapes and Kent after 1066.

the Conqueror, held Lewes; Robert, Count of Eu held Hastings; and William de Braose held Bramber. Odo held the strategically vital county of Kent, immediately to the east of the Sussex rapes. Although rapes existed in some form before the Conquest, as compact semi-autonomous power bases they were a post-1066 creation, centered on castles, similar to the *castleries* found in Normandy. Each of the rapes had its own sheriff, who answered to the tenant-in-chief, not to the Crown. The rapes had an artificial profile, running in roughly parallel strips between the coast and the northern boundary of Sussex, each controlling a corridor of communication between London and the Channel. The vital routes between England and Normandy were thus in the hands of six (or seven, with Odo in Kent) of William's most trusted relatives or lieutenants; but no one or two of them could conspire against the king and block his way southwards to the coast (Cownie 1998, 111–22).

• The Battle •

Having landed successfully William's troops set about the systematic raiding of the countryside around Pevensey and Battle. This was essential to keep his forces properly fed, but was also undertaken to provoke a hurried response from Harold. The coastal area of Sussex involved was at the heart of the Godwines' territory; most of the land terrorised by the Normans was recorded in Domesday as having belonged to Harold. This was a direct challenge to the king and one which he must have felt it necessary to respond to. With hindsight, it would have been better to have allowed the Normans to exhaust local supplies and be forced to move away from the coast and from their ships which provided them with a lifeline in the event of military defeat.

The English army moved quickly from London and reached present-day Battle on 13 October. Harold's strategy appears to have been the one he had used with such success at Stamford Bridge, which was to take the enemy by surprise. William's intelligence was good and anticipating Harold's arrival he moved his troops to the battlefield early on the morning of 14 October. Harold's troops were weary from the long march and he did not have time to deploy them properly along the ridge which they occupied before the Normans were upon them. During the battle William is said to have worn the relics from Bayeux Cathedral, on which Harold had sworn his oath, on a string around his neck. The battle lasted the whole day, during which the English army was progressively weakened by the Normans' mobile and well-organised cavalry. The end came late in the day with the death of King Harold. The *Anglo-Saxon Chronicle* laconically observed, 'And the French had possession of the place of slaughter, just as God granted them because of the people's sins' (Higham, 213).

• Odo at Hastings •

According to the Norman historian Wace, Norman priests set up portable chapels amidst the soldiers and spent the whole night before the battle praying, fasting and giving penance. Odo and Geoffrey, Bishop of Coutances, who was chief chaplain to the army, spent the time hearing confessions and giving blessings. This was in contrast to Wace's account of the English army, who he recounted spent the night eating, drinking and dancing. He went on to explain that Odo, 'who conducted himself very nobly', and his brother (Robert) 'brought a great force of knights and other men, being very rich in gold and silver'.

Three of Odo's definite four appearances on the Bayeux Tapestry occur in the immediate run-up to and during the Battle of Hastings. After the Normans forage for food in the Sussex countryside, there is a feast, at which a bishop, believed to be Odo, is seated at the head of the table. This is followed by a scene in which William is seated with his two half-brothers, Odo and Robert, who are named, in a council of war. Odo is talking animatedly to an attentive duke, presumably laying out the battle plan. Finally, Odo is pictured at the height of the battle in a quasi-military role encouraging the flagging troops.

The bishop is shown carrying a mace-like implement, which has been variously interpreted as a club or a commander's baton. No other contemporary source gives Odo such a prominent place in the proceedings and none records him actually participating in the fighting. There has been much dispute over the role of the Norman clerics at Hastings. As a priest, it was forbidden for him to spill blood, but the Tapestry shows Odo in the midst of the battle, and significantly a later papal enquiry into the slaughter at Hastings required the Norman clerics to give penance for shedding blood in the battle. William of Poitiers comes closest to claiming that Odo joined the fighting when he explains that Odo 'helped in war by his most practical counsels as far as his religion allowed … and was most singularly and steadfastly loyal to [William], whom he cherished with so great a love that he would not be willingly separated from him even on the battlefield'. In the battle scene on the Tapestry, Odo is wearing a gambeson – a padded jacket – over his hauberk, which is short compared to the longer version worn by the

23 Bishop Odo 'encouraging the boys' at the Battle of Hastings from the Bayeux Tapestry.

fighting soldiers. It is argued, therefore, that as he was dressed defensively, he was a non-combatant (Legge, 84–5). It is true that Wace, writing a century after the events of 1066, records that, 'The Bishop of Bayeux … conducted himself very nobly' when hearing confessions and giving blessings before the Battle of Hastings. He also writes of an incident reminiscent of the one depicted on the Tapestry, where Odo urges the flagging soldiers back to fight and then goes back to the thick of battle where he makes the reluctant cavalrymen turn, stop and attack. Wace reported that Odo addressed these young noblemen, whose task it was to guard equipment, by saying, 'Stand still, stand still! Calm down and do not move! Do not fear anything, for, please God, we will win the day.' Wace continued:

> Odo went back to where the battle was at its fiercest; that day he had truly shown his worth … he sat on an all white horse and everyone recognised him. He held a club in his hand, made the knights head for where the need was greatest and brought them to a stop there. He often made them attack and often made them strike.
> (Burgess, iii, 8121–8)

Although Wace was writing much later than Hastings, he was a canon of Bayeux and would have been familiar with the Tapestry and with the other principal sources. Therefore, his account cannot be totally discounted and perhaps the best way to describe Odo's role at Hastings is 'support and command'.

Odo's actions at Hastings may have been the factual basis for Archbishop Turpin of Rheims in the *Song of Roland*, but it could also work the other way round and Odo's story may have been influenced by the *Song*. 'To some degree the Tapestry might seem a *Song of Roland* without its hero … There is no Roland but there is a Turpin. Archbishop Turpin … was … Roland's companion at Roncesvalles, and it is in at least a comparable role that bishop Odo is depicted' (Dodwell 1966).

• The Aftermath of Battle •

Deprived of their king and leader, the English troops had no reason to continue the fight and began to leave the battlefield, pursued by the victorious Normans. Although the Bayeux Tapestry ends at this point, writers such as

William of Poitiers record the movement of William's army along the south coast wreaking havoc on its way, sacking Rye and Romney, and making camp at Dover. This must have been an awkward journey as in Norman times there were a series of tidal inlets penetrating well inland, today represented by the Brede and Rother Levels. William's army appears to have avoided these hazards by taking an inland route, as reflected in the line of waste and semi-waste manors depicted in Domesday Book. This move into Kent was significant as it was not only a highly important strategic region, but Canterbury was also the centre of the English Church. Movement was slow, hampered by sickness amongst the Norman troops; nevertheless, it gave time for the English to come to terms with the unpalatable truth that they had been soundly defeated and, what is more, they lacked a credible leader. One by one the Kentish regions surrendered to William and, more importantly, the city of Winchester to the west, held by Edward's widow, Edith, and home to the English Treasury, submitted to the duke.

We do not know the movements of William's senior lieutenants such as Odo during this period, when south-east England was being brought under Norman control. It is reasonable to assume that the king delegated the control of towns to men he could rely on as soon as possible and that individuals were being identified for specific tasks during the interregnum. Odo's practical support for William's campaign alone would have guaranteed that he would be richly rewarded in the event of victory and his main prize was to be made Earl of Kent. This was a prestigious appointment and with it went large swathes of the Kentish countryside; Odo became second only to the king in the extent of his English lands. According to the Ship List, William was going to give Kent to his wife, Matilda, in return for her gift of the *Mora*, the ship which brought the duke to England (Van Houts). Even if this had been William's intention, it would clearly have been impractical for Matilda to have played an active role in ruling this critical corner of England. Although he was not formally named earl until 1067, it is likely that Odo was left in charge of Dover and Kent as the army moved on. He would have made profitable use of his time by laying claim to estates, beyond those of the defeated Godwines and others who had fought for the English at Hastings, whose land would automatically have been confiscated.

There may have been a late Saxon *burh* in the Iron Age fort at Dover. All the sources talk of a *castrum* here, which probably referred to the refortified prehistoric fort. The Roman lighthouse still sits within the enclosure, as does the late Saxon church of St Mary in Castro. William of Poitiers records that when William entered the *castrum* of Dover, he commanded that the English inside had to evacuate their houses. Apparently, William spent eight days constructing defences here, while many of his troops were suffering from dysentery. A ditch 8.2m wide and 5.5m deep cutting through a Saxon cemetery has been interpreted as part of William's fortifications. In 1067 Dover was in Odo's hands and it is quite probable that he remained here with a garrison while William moved towards London (Allen Brown 1985, 5–6).

There was a ten-week gap between the Battle of Hastings and William's coronation in Westminster Abbey on Christmas Day 1066. During this period the Normans subdued and intimidated towns on their circuitous journey to London. The Normans would have seized the food they needed for men and animals as they progressed through the English countryside. Additionally, whenever William encountered opposition he pursued a 'scorched earth' policy, pillaging and burning communities indiscriminately. In the words of the *Anglo-Saxon Chronicle*, 'they [the Normans] harried everywhere they came'. Many of the settlements which were adversely affected by the passage of the Normans had still not recovered by 1086. In addition to the damage caused by the movement of the main army, which itself was probably broken into contingents, there were also reinforcements from Normandy coming into the southern coastal ports. Additionally, there would have been many sorties by smaller groups of Normans to collect food and subdue strategic and political targets. The routes that all these groups took can be traced from those manors which are recorded still as 'waste' or 'part waste' in Domesday Book (c. 1086) (Darby 1971, 570–3).

William seems to have made use of Roman roads wherever possible and the Norman army then made its way to London, by way of Rochester, along the Roman Watling Street. Significant surviving Roman fortifications would also have been available to him and he adopted them for his use at *Anderitum*, Dover and possibly Richborough. There are no records of what happened to William's fleet after the initial landing; some of the ships would have returned to Normandy to collect reinforcements and ordnance, while others would probably have moved along the coast keeping in close touch with the army. The fleet could have sailed around Kent into the Thames estuary, and may well have sailed as far as London or even further upstream to provide support. The fleet could also have been used to ferry troops, particularly on difficult sections of their route, for instance, around Romney Marsh (Rowley 1985).

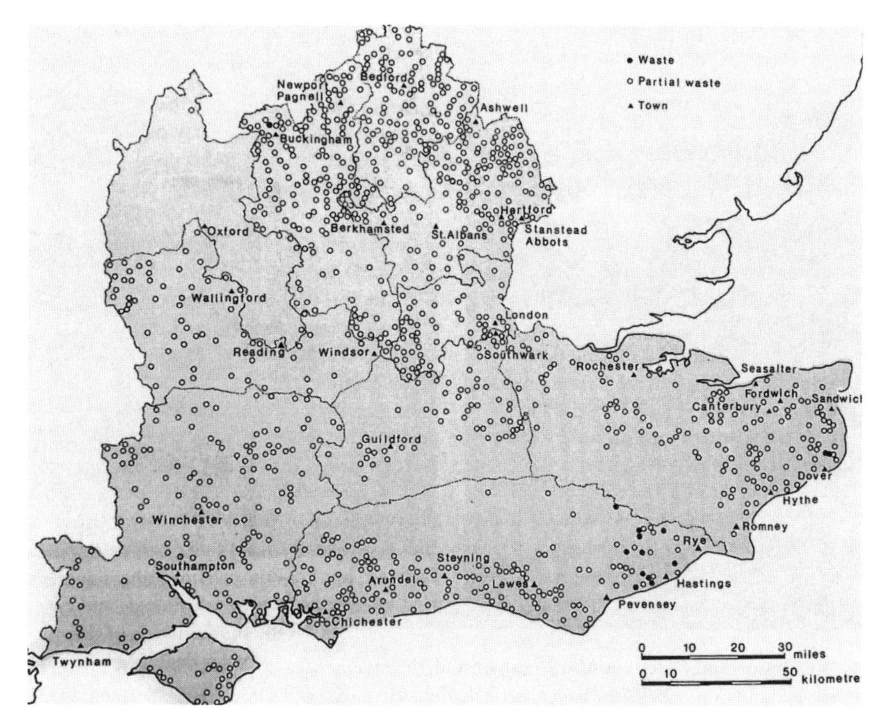

24 The distribution of waste manors in the south-east of England at the time of the Domesday survey. The straight lines of waste estates marks the movement of Norman troops at the time of the Norman invasion and immediately afterwards.

When William reached the outskirts of London he stopped at Southwark on the south side of London Bridge. Here he met a force of English led by Edgar the Aetheling, who was effectively the English king at this point. The Normans drove the English back across the bridge, burning all the buildings south of the river, and in doing so 'dealt a double blow on the pride of [William's] stubborn foes', giving Edgar 'a bloody nose'. Despite such bluster from his hagiographers, William obviously did not feel strong enough to take London at this point and continued westwards along the Thames Valley, taking Windsor and Reading before crossing the Thames at Wallingford. From here he may have taken control of Abingdon Abbey and of the strategically important town of Oxford. While at Wallingford, the most important cleric in the land, Archbishop Stigand, travelled from London to transfer his allegiance to William.

From Wallingford William marched north-eastwards along the Icknield Way, the ancient track at the foot of the Chilterns which meets the Roman

25 The motte and bailey castle at Berkhamsted, thrown up soon after the Battle of Hastings. It was from here that William negotiated the final surrender of London. Berkhamsted was in the hands of Odo's brother, Robert, soon after William's coronation.

Akeman Street at Tring. The Normans then followed the Roman road through the Chilterns, along the Bulborne Valley, towards London and made camp at Berkhamsted. At this point William had subdued much of south-east England and effectively cut off the capital. Bowing to the inevitable, the English leaders met with William and offered him the throne. The *Anglo-Saxon Chronicle* gloomily reported that, '[William] was met by Archbishop Ealdred, and the Aetheling Edgar and Earl Edwin and Earl Morcar, and all the chief men of London, who submitted from force of circumstances, but only when the depredation was complete ... They gave him hostages and swore oaths of fealty, and he promised to be a gracious liege lord.' William now felt confident enough to enter London with little or no resistance and was crowned King of England in the newly consecrated Westminster Abbey on Christmas Day 1066.

5

• Bishop Odo and the Bayeux Tapestry •

The Bayeux Tapestry is the greatest surviving document of Anglo-Norman history. 'As a large-scale picture of warfare at the close of the Dark Ages it stands alone,' observed the doyen of Saxon historians Frank Stenton. 'But its ultimate distinction lies … in the artist's grasp of his theme, his skilful arrangement of contrasted scenes, his mastery of the technique of composition, and above all, the curious air of vitality … that runs throughout the whole long work' (Stenton 1957, 23). It is an invaluable source of information not only about the Norman Conquest of England, but also about eleventh-century weaponry, clothing, buildings and ritual. The Tapestry provides a clear exposition of the justification for Norman rule, yet embodies recognition of the valour of King Harold and the English defenders. Some scholars have suggested recently that the Tapestry is not a piece of Norman propaganda, but if analysed closely presents a balanced representation of events, others have gone further and claim that it carries a subversive English message. In reality, the Tapestry is capable of being interpreted in many ways and most scenes are ambiguous in some aspect of their meaning. 'Was it made so that Normans could impress the subjugated foe? Or so that the English could flatter, yet secretly insult the victors?' (Hicks 2006, 32).

The hanging is not a tapestry at all, but embroidery of coloured wools on a linen background consisting of eight separate panels joined together. It is 50cm wide and just under 70m long and the final section, having been partly destroyed, is now much shorter than the others. The central section of the Tapestry depicts the main narrative of the Conquest; at the top and bottom are narrow borders which are basically decorative, but occasionally complement the main action in the central narrative. In scenes of heightened tension, the central story spreads out into the borders. The border decoration consists of birds, beasts and fish, some of them mythical in character, as well as scenes from fables and portraits of agriculture and hunting. There are also nude figures and others of a ribald nature that comment on events in the main story. Some features, such as moustaches for most of the English figures and shaven backs of heads for many of the Normans are probably based on authentic characteristics, but are exaggerated to provide a convenient visual grammar to aid reading the Tapestry.

The colours are not used naturalistically; thus, horses are blue or buff, with legs and hooves portrayed in different and arbitrary colours. The use of unnatural colouring gives an element of caricature which, together with lively outlines, is articulated with great skill. Despite such variety there is a remarkably uniform design throughout and because of this consistency it is believed to have been devised by a single artist working to the instructions of a patron, like Bishop Odo. The designer was familiar with illuminated manuscripts, sculpture, frescoes and oral sources. The visual flow of the narrative is controlled with devices such as trees and buildings used to separate scenes. No evidence of an outline drawing or cartoon which was transferred on to the linen base has been found, although one must have existed. According to the Life of St Dunstan, as a young cleric Dunstan was required to draw up designs for a young noblewoman to embroider. There are historical mistakes, which suggest that the artist/designer was not fully aware of the history, but was working with instructions, information and possibly some written phrases provided by his patron, which he formulated into the Tapestry design (Caple, 84).

There are fifty-eight captions above the main part of the Tapestry; these are brief notes pointing out the names of some people and places. The captions are in abbreviated Latin and may have been added after the pictorial narrative had been completed. Several words which appear on the Tapestry suggest an English origin, for example, *Aedwardus* rather than *Edwardus*, *Ceastra* rather than *castra* and *Franci* rather than *Normani*. In a world where literacy was restricted largely to the clergy, visual imagery was of great importance in the telling of stories and of history. The use of hands, facial expressions and body language are vital to the telling of the story and contribute to the appeal of the Tapestry in surviving as a much admired artefact over 900 years after it was produced.

Roman and Carolingian rulers recorded their victories as historical narratives in wall paintings and hangings, which decorated their halls and palaces. The use of long strips of illustration was popular in early medieval Scandinavia and Germany. Examples are to be found on the eighth-century Frankish casket and remains of a hanging found in the ninth century Oseberg ship burial. There are references to tapestries in contemporary French epic poetry, for instance in the *chanson* of Girard of Roussillon the guest chamber of a count's palace was 'everywhere spread with tapestries and hangings'. Chroniclers also record that after William the Conqueror's death dishonest servants carried off hangings from his palace in Rouen (Dodwell 1966, 49). Hangings had been authorised, even encouraged, by the Council of Arras (1025) as one of the means of edifying and informing the Christian faithful (Caple 2006, 80). The depiction of military scenes was not seen as unsuitable for places of worship, as demonstrated by a reference in the *Liber Eliensis*, compiled in the mid-twelfth century. Aelfleada, the wife of an English chieftain killed by Danes at the Battle of Maldon (AD 991), 'at the time her husband was killed and buried, gave to this church [Ely] his demesne lands and a necklace of gold and a coloured woven wall-hanging showing his deeds, in memory of his greatness'. There would therefore have been no objection in showing the fighting at Hastings, which had been blessed by Pope Alexander II.

• The History of the Tapestry •

Since at least the fifteenth century, when it was first recorded, the Tapestry has been housed in Bayeux. An inventory of Bayeux Cathedral furnishings dating from 1476 records, 'Item, a very long and narrow hanging, embroidered with images depicting the Conquest of England, which is hung around the nave of the church on the day and throughout the octaves of the relics (1–14 July)' (Caple 2006, 80). That is, during the second week of July, which included the anniversary of the dedication of the church, the Tapestry would have provided a suitable backdrop for the feast of the relics. Its existence became more generally known only in the eighteenth century, when it was called Queen Matilda's Tapestry because it was believed that King William's wife, Matilda, was involved as either the Tapestry's patron, designer or embroiderer. Early scholars also considered that the work was executed in Normandy.

It is not surprising that the Tapestry's characteristics which most appealed to the Norman victors – a successful invasion and military victory over the English – also attracted the attention of later military despots. The cult of Matilda and the Tapestry reached its height during the early nineteenth century as a result of patriotic fervour built up by Napoleon, who projected himself as a reincarnation of William the Conqueror. In November 1803 Napoleon visited his troops assembled in Boulogne in anticipation of the invasion of England, where the building of the invasion fleet was progressing erratically. Napoleon observed that the Tapestry 'records one of the most memorable deeds of the French nation and preserves the memory of the pride and courage of our ancestors'. In order to boost morale, Napoleon had the Bayeux Tapestry transported to be exhibited at the Palace of the Louvre (then called the Musée Napoléon). As a result of this exhibition and Napoleon's involvement there was extensive press coverage, which prompted the composition of a one-act musical comedy called *La Tapisserie de la Reine Mathilde.* The play opened at the Théâtre du Vaudeville on 14 January 1804 and according to the stage instructions, 'When the curtain rises, we see Matilda, surrounded by her women, all busy embroidering. A portion of the tapestry is hung around the stage' (Hicks, 108). There is

26 The opening scene of the operetta *La Tapisserie de la Reine Mathilde* composed by a Mr Wicht and performed in 1804. *Hicks, 2006*

no record of the play having been subsequently revived! Undoubtedly, such events cemented the popular belief that the Tapestry was the work of Matilda and in the following decades there were several paintings and prints which portrayed Matilda at work on the embroidery. For instance, the frontispiece of Ducarel's *Anglo-Norman Antiquities* (1823) shows Matilda supervising her ladies embroidering the Tapestry in the nave of Bayeux Cathedral. In 1849 Alfred Gaillard completed an oil painting entitled *La Reine Mathilde travaillant à la Telle du Conquest* which now hangs in the Musée Baron Gérard in Bayeux. The Tapestry was extensively restored in 1842 using machine twisted thread instead of the original hand-spun wool.

The Tapestry was intended to be used for more sinister propaganda purposes during the Second World War. The Nazi ideas for the Tapestry went far beyond its appeal as a depiction of a successful invasion of England. After the German occupation of France a systematic multidisciplinary analysis of the Tapestry was planned. This was motivated by the belief that the embroidery demonstrated the superiority of the Aryan spirit and that Duke William represented a Germanic prince. A unit of the SS established by Himmler was called the '*Ahnenerbe*' (Ancestral Heritage), part of whose remit was to study, reclaim and confiscate culturally significant monuments for display

27 Nineteenth-century impression of Queen Matilda and her ladies creating the Tapestry in the crossing of Bayeux Cathedral. The frontispiece to the French edition of *Ducal's Anglo-Norman Antiquities* (1823).

in a triumphant post-war Germany. It rested on the premise that the Normans were directly descended from the Vikings and had inherited many of their characteristics, notably, 'the joy of fighting, the love of war and the chivalric respect of the enemy' and the Tapestry proved that 'the Viking heritage and Viking customs lived on in Normandy in a relatively pure form'. To Himmler, the heroism displayed on the Tapestry was central to his vision of the SS, and the Tapestry represented a 'magnificent example of Germanic, Aryan art and deserved to be recognised as such'. The project, which included a scheme to print a life-sized copy of the Tapestry, was never completed, although after the D-Day landings in Normandy, Himmler made an unsuccessful attempt to have the Tapestry moved to Berlin. As part of the French Liberation celebrations in November 1944 the Tapestry went on display at the Louvre once more before being returned to its pre-war home of the Hôtel du Doyen in Bayeux (Hicks 2006, 205–31).

As a result of increasing visitor numbers in the 1960s and 1970s, it was decided to provide a new, more spacious home for the Tapestry. There is now a dedicated Musée de la Tapisserie in Bayeux, occupying the Grand Seminary, opened in 1983, where the Tapestry is on permanent display. The move provided an opportunity for a full examination of the Tapestry from the back as well as the front and initiated its reassessment at many levels (Bouet et al. 2004).

• The Narrative •

The story told in the Tapestry falls into two distinct parts. The first half is largely devoted to Earl Harold: going to France, being captured, campaigning with Duke William, swearing an oath, returning to England for King Edward's death, and being crowned. The second part concentrates on William and the Normans: hearing the news of Harold's coronation, preparing the fleet, sailing for England, foraging and feasting, and finally a long account of the battle itself. The oath is seen by most scholars as the important junction, when Harold, swearing on holy relics, makes a sacred promise which he subsequently breaks. The real change in the direction of the Tapestry actually comes with the appearance of Halley's Comet immediately after Harold's coronation. In the previous scene, Harold appears to be regally in control of the situation; it is when he is told of the comet's appearance that the new king visibly crumples, as if he knew that the journey to his destruction had started.

It is generally accepted that the Tapestry starts in 1064 with Edward the Confessor sending Earl Harold on a mission to France. Edward is identified by his regalia and by the first caption, which states simply – *King Edward*. The nature of Harold's mission is not stated but its significance is emphasised by the body language of the participants. Norman sources claim that Harold was going to pledge his loyalty to William as Edward's designated successor to the English throne. On the other hand Eadmer, the Canterbury chronicler, writing in the early twelfth century claimed that Harold's mission was to secure the release of his kinsmen that William was holding hostage. William of Malmesbury even casts doubt on whether Harold was on a diplomatic mission at all, and suggests that the earl was enjoying a pleasure cruise in the Channel, when he was shipwrecked off the coast of Ponthieu (Brooks & Walker 1979, 86, 92).

Earl Harold and his men, accompanied by hunting hounds and a hawk, make their way to his manor at Bosham in Sussex. Here, on the south coast of England they pray in the church (which survives), feast and set sail for Normandy. The winds blow the English contingent off course and they land by mistake in the territory of Guy, Count of Ponthieu, a vassal of William's. Harold is seized by Guy and his soldiers, who take the earl's sword, symbolising his vulnerability as a captive who could be ransomed. Harold is taken to Beaurain to meet Guy, and two of Harold's men ride to inform William of the earl's plight. William is seated immediately next to a formidable fortification which, although it is not named, is generally believed to be the 'Tower of Rouen' where, ironically, Odo was to be imprisoned in 1082 (Musset, 118). It has been argued that fortification was Guy's castle at Beaurain and that the stone structure was a gatehouse for a motte, the top of which is visible behind the entrance structure (Taylor 1991). This claim is based partly on the assumption that the Tapestry is providing an accurate topographical representation of the castle as it was in 1064. In the case of this and the other castles depicted on the Tapestry, such a degree of accuracy seems very unlikely. It is much more probable that the images of castles are ingenious symbols for those fortifications.

William sends messengers to Guy ordering him to release Harold, which he does eventually. William then accompanies Harold back to Rouen holding the hawk, which together with the hounds may have been brought as a gift for him. During the exchanges between Guy and William the name *Turold* is inscribed either next to one of the duke's messengers or above a dwarf holding the Normans' horses. Turold was a common Norman name, but here it

28 The tower of Bosham church, Sussex. The Saxon church, of which parts survive, was depicted on the Bayeux Tapestry. It lay on Godwinson land and Earl Harold prayed here before undertaking his journey to France in 1064.

28a Earl Harold entering Bosham church, from the Bayeux Tapestry.

has been taken to refer to one of Bishop Odo's vassals who accompanied him to England. At this stage there is a curious incident where a woman, one of only three depicted on the Tapestry, with the English name of Aelfgifu is seen with a gesticulating cleric who, touching her face, seems to be chastising or blessing the woman. The incomplete caption above simply reads, '*Where a certain clerk and Aelfgyva*'. This scene must have had a clear meaning to eleventh century observers, possibly relating to a well-known contemporary scandal, but although it has been interpreted in a variety of ways it remains the most baffling episode on the whole Tapestry (Stephenson 2011, 71–4).

Subsequently, Harold joins William in a military campaign against William's enemy Count Conan II of Brittany. At the start of the Breton campaign Mont-Saint-Michel is prominently displayed, possibly to highlight the change in location from Normandy to Brittany. Another suggestion is that Mont-Saint-Michel is emphasised because Abbot Scotland, the first Norman head of St Augustine's, Canterbury, came from the monastery there, where he had been a scribe. Furthermore, Mont-Saint-Michel was recognised as having 'the most decoratively active Norman scriptorium' (Gameson 1997, 172). Abbot Scotland provides another indication that St Augustine's was where the Tapestry originated. Bishop Odo also had links with Mont-Saint-Michel, as it was from here that he recruited monks to house his own foundation of St Vigor, Bayeux. On their way past Mont-Saint-Michel some of the Norman cavalry become mired in quicksand by the mouth of the River Couesnon and Harold is shown as a hero on this occasion by rescuing two of the drowning men himself. One of the mounted onlookers wears the chequered costume worn by both William and Odo at Hastings and carries a baton. While the figure is most likely to be the duke, it is possible that it could also be Bishop Odo. It has been suggested that the bishop's attestation of a charter at Domfront between 1063 and 1066 could have been linked to his presence on the 1064 Breton campaign.

The Normans besiege a motte and bailey castle at Dol; this and the other earthwork castles on the Tapestry are graphically and uniquely illustrated. The designer of the Tapestry was obviously familiar with motte and bailey castles, probably from England during the first phase of the Conquest. Earth and timber castles were built quickly following Hastings in order to secure strategic positions as Norman rule was imposed. However, it seems that they are being used as a symbol rather than as a realistic depiction of the Breton and Norman castles, which probably would have been built of stone. Conan escapes to another castle at Dinan but is forced to surrender before the town is burnt. It is possible that after the Breton campaign was over Duke William and Earl Harold led a triumphal march from Domfront to Bayeux, prior to Harold swearing his oath of allegiance to William (Bates 1970, 11).

In the next scene William ceremonially gives Harold a helmet, coat of mail, sword and lance. William is reinstating Harold to the status of a full knight, a status of which he had been deprived by Guy of Ponthieu. Thus, Harold becomes William's vassal, a further obligation of the earl to the duke. This scene has variously been interpreted as William 'dubbing' Harold as one of his knights, as a symbolic recognition of William's future overlordship of England, or as recognition of the military prowess shown by Harold during the Breton expedition (Musset, 142). Its occurrence, just before the oath scene, might suggest that it is confirming Harold's military obligation to the duke.

The 'arms' scene leads on to '*William came to Bayeux*', where Bayeux is depicted by a splendid turf and timber motte castle. However, we know that the castle in Bayeux had been built in stone by William's grandfather Richard II in around 980. There is no evidence of there ever having been a motte and bailey in Bayeux. Indeed, all the castles depicted on the Tapestry – Dol, Rennes, Dinant, Bayeux and Hastings – are shown as mottes. Only the Tower at Rouen is clearly built of stone. Next Harold unarmed and bareheaded, is seen taking an oath of loyalty on two shrines containing sacred relics

29 Duke William handing arms to Earl Harold after the Breton campaign in 1064, from the Bayeux Tapestry.

before the seated William. This ritual act completes a sequence binding Harold to William by both custom and law. The central location of the scene is intended to make the faithful reflect on the sanctity of oaths sworn in the presence of relics. It would also have emphasised the importance of the Bayeux relics. The only onlookers are ordinary soldiers and servants; such an event would normally be witnessed by clerical and secular lords. It seems, therefore, that the Tapestry wanted to stress that this was a sacred bond between the two men and thus emphasise Harold's perfidy when he breaks it.

Following a series of conspiracies and rebellions in the 790s, feudal oaths of loyalty were instituted by Charlemagne, where all men were required to swear an oath of allegiance to the king upon relics. The king's inner circle swore an even stronger oath of vassalage, committing them to obedience and military service. This was a binding covenant and breaking it was perjury. The details were unimportant; it was the oath itself that was sacrosanct (Brown 2009).

After sailing back to England, Harold, appearing submissive, reports back to a markedly older Edward who appears to be remonstrating with the earl. The next scenes are in reverse chronological order: the shrouded body of Edward is carried in a funeral procession to Westminster Abbey before the deathbed scene where Edward '*speaks to his faithful followers*' as Harold's fingers touch those of the dying king. The next caption states that, '*Here they gave the king's crown to Harold*'. In other words, Harold had been bequeathed the crown before witnesses. Harold's coronation immediately follows on and the new king sits in splendour on the throne with orb and sceptre while he receives the sword of state. Prominently standing next to Harold, arms outstretched, is Archbishop Stigand, who has been excommunicated and is regarded as a usurper by the Normans – the implication is that the ceremony is invalid. This is borne out by the next episode with the appearance of a star with a streaming tail. Such cosmic events were regarded as bad omens in the Middle Ages and the significance of the appearance of Halley's Comet coinciding with his coronation was not lost on Harold, who visibly crumples on the news of its sighting. (The comet actually appeared later in the spring of 1066.) At this stage the lower border, which up until now has been largely given over to decoration, echoes the bad tidings with the appearance of the ghostly outlines of the boats of the future invasion fleet.

The story then moves back to Normandy, where William, sitting together with his half-brother Odo, receives the news of Harold's coronation from

30 The new king, Harold, hearing the news that Halley's Comet has been sighted. In the bottom frieze the ghostly outline of the invasion fleet is depicted. From the Bayeux Tapestry.

England. A conference is called, and Odo and William are shown seated on a bench. The caption reads, '*Here Duke William ordered ships to be built*'. Odo, who is the larger of the two men, is pointing onwards to the felling of trees. The bishop has an open hand, indicating that the two men are talking, and William's hand on his hip indicates that he is being persuaded. The graphics of the Tapestry here, as elsewhere, depict Odo as a proactive figure, but this is not always reflected in the captions (Lewis 2007, 100–20).

The next scenes show the Norman preparations for the invasion with tree felling and boat building. The contemporary cleric, Baudri de Bourgueil describes woodmen felling timber at the command of the prince and shipwrights who fashion oars, masts and other components from oak, holly, ash and fir (Musset 2002, 186). This is followed by the loading of boats with grain, wine, chainmail suits, helmets, swords, arrows and spears. The care with which the Normans are preparing for battle is emphasised by the diligent loading of the cavalry horses into the boats. The Norman fleet then sails across the Channel and lands unopposed at Pevensey, where they set up camp in the third-century Roman fort. The Norman troops under the command of Wadard, one of Odo's men, are then shown foraging and looting prior to a symbolic feast, where Odo presides over a semi-circular table, with fish, bread, knives and goblets, in a scene reminiscent of many depictions of Christ and the Last Supper. Odo's right hand is making a blessing over the food. The composition of this scene is similar to a Last Supper illustration in St Augustine's Gospels, which adds strength to the argument that the Tapestry was actually embroidered at St Augustine's Canterbury (Brooks & Walker 1979).

William then holds a final war council in a simple building before the battle, attended only by his half-brothers, Odo and Robert of Mortain; again, it is Odo who appears to be leading the discussion. This is the only time the three brothers are shown together. Orders are given for the building of a castle 'at Hastings', the construction of which is then portrayed, after which William receives news of Harold's movements. The next scene is one of the most poignant in the whole story; a mother and her son are shown escaping from what was clearly a grand house which is being torched by Normans – the caption reads casually, '*Here a house is*

31 Mother and child escaping from a substantial house that has been torched by Normans, from the Bayeux Tapestry.

burnt'. There are then some preliminary cavalry manoeuvres and William questions a mounted scout called Vital about Harold's movements. This is almost certainly Vital of Canterbury, one of Odo's vassals, who was a Channel merchant who would have had knowledge of the local geography and of the English language.

The final third of the Tapestry relates an account of the Battle of Hastings. To begin with, the Norman cavalry advance, first walking and then galloping; inspired by a speech from William they then charge the English shield wall. Despite the death of Harold's brothers Gyrth and Leofwine, the English continue to hold their hilltop position. The lower border joins in the general mayhem by depicting dead warriors and horses, dismembered limbs and corpses being stripped of their chainmail and weapons. When a rumour begins to circulate that William has been killed, Odo is once again portrayed in a favourable light, rallying and encouraging the troops. The caption reads, '*Here Bishop Odo, holding his staff, encourages the boys*'. The duke raises his visor to be recognised and the next scenes show first the death of Harold's personal guard and then of the king himself. The caption reads, '*Here King Harold has been killed*'; although this has generally been taken to mean the mail-clad figure with an arrow that has penetrated his helmet, it could equally apply to an adjacent warrior who simultaneously is being cut down. Effectively, the end of Harold is the end of the surviving Tapestry. A much repaired final section sees the unarmed English survivors making their way off the

32 The chest in which the Bayeux Tapestry was kept from the fifteenth century.

1 Bishop Odo's seal. On one side he is represented as a mounted soldier and on the other as a bishop holding a staff. It is a perfect representation of Odo's dual roles as a powerful prince/bishop. *Finch Hatton MS. 170, Northamptonshire Record Office*

2 The chapel at the gate and part of the perimeter wall of the Abbey of Grestain, founded by Odo's father Herluin de Conteville c. 1150. Odo's mother, Herleva, was buried here as was his brother Robert de Mortain as well as his father.

3 A surviving wall belonging to Odo's eleventh-century castle at Neuilly l'Évêque, which was built into a later farmhouse. The herring-bone masonry seen here was characteristic of Anglo-Norman architecture, both secular and religious.

4 A thirteenth-century reliquary dedicated to St Exupere, the first Bishop of Bayeux.

5 The crypt of Odo's Bayeux Cathedral, which was consecrated in 1077.

6 The Romanesque tower of the parish church of Cambremer, which formed a detached portion of the Diocese of Bayeux. The bishops of Bayeux held an important market here.

7 The gatehouse of the former abbey of Vigor le Grand. Little remains of the original abbey buildings created by Bishop Odo in the mid-eleventh century.

8 Earl Harold swearing an oath on two reliquaries in the presence of Duke William of Normandy in 1064, from the Bayeux Tapestry.

9 In this scene from the Bayeux Tapestry, Odo, seated next to William, appears to be ordering the construction of an invasion fleet.

10 A sandbank across the mouth of the estuary of the River Dives at Dives-sur-Mer. It was here that the invasion fleet was originally assembled.

11 Aerial view of Pevensey Castle, Sussex. This was the Roman Saxon-Shore fort of Anderitum, where Duke William established a base for his army immediately upon landing in England.

12 In this scene from the Bayeux Tapestry a mounted Norman soldier named Wadard is seen leading a foraging party before the Battle of Hastings. Wadard is believed to have been one of Odo's vassals, and his depiction on the Tapestry as evidence of Odo's close association with its creation.

13 In this scene from the Bayeux Tapestry a cleric, believed to be Odo, is blessing a feast after the Norman fleet landed in England. The crescent shaped table and the configuration of the diners is reminiscent of representations of the Last Supper. The soldiers to the left have to make do with a shield from which to eat their meal.

14 The three brothers, William, Robert and Odo, are depicted together before the Battle of Hastings in this scene from the Bayeux Tapestry. Odo is gesticulating and leading the discussion, William is listening and Robert is about to leave.

15 Turold, recorded on the Tapestry, was probably another of Odo's vassals. It is not clear if the name is applied to the dwarf holding the horse or, more feasibly, to one of the men on the left of the picture.

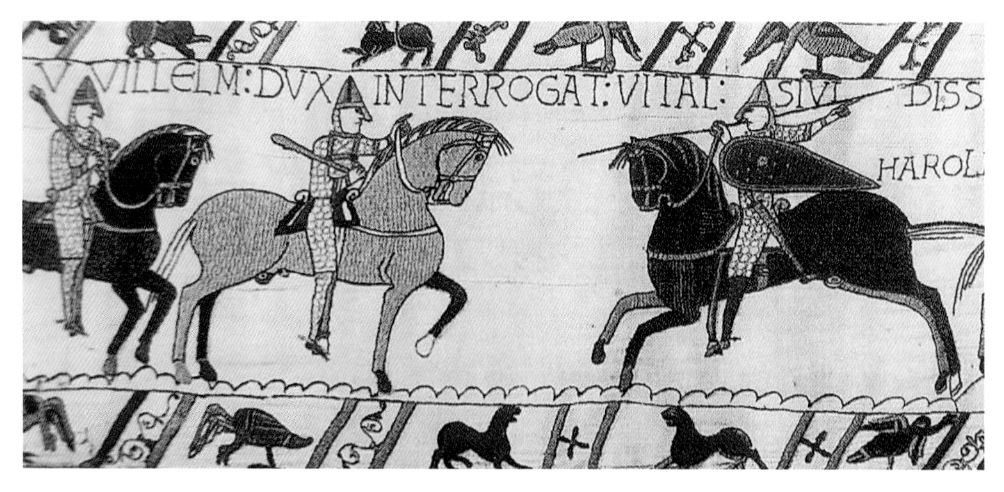

16 Vital is bringing news of King Harold's movements before the battle in this scene. It is likely that he was also one of Odo's followers. The specific naming of Vital, Turold and Wadard, all men with close links to Odo, provides a strong argument for Odo's involvement in making the Tapestry.

17 The battlefield at Battle. Harold and the English army were sited at the top of the slope where the remains of Battle Abbey can be seen. The Normans and their allies repeatedly attacked up the hill before eventually dislodging the English.

18 Bishop Odo wielding a baton or mace at the Battle of Hastings. This powerful image has been much discussed. Was Odo participating in the fighting or simply encouraging the Norman troops to victory?

19 A painting of Queen Matilda and her assistants working on the Tapestry from the oil painting, La Reine Mathilde travaillant a la Telle du Conquest, by Alfred Guillard (1849). It was popularly believed that Matilda was personally responsible for the Tapestry and there are several similar pictures from the nineteenth century.

20 Noah's Arc depicted on Aelfric's Pentateuch, a late Saxon manuscript, that shows certain similarities in design to the Bayeux Tapestry.

21 A section of Romanesque sculpture depicting a battle scene above the door to the cathedral at Angouleme. The portrayal of soldiers, horses and buildings is remarkably similar to that on the Bayeux Tapestry.

22 Penenden Heath, where the famous 'trial' of Odo took place, now sited on the edge of Maidstone in Kent.

23 Aerial photograph of Deddington Castle, Oxfordshire. The defences of a large outer bailey with massive earthworks are defined by their tree cover. It is probable that this was the *caput* or headquarters for Odo's Midland estates.

24 The fortified building depicted near the beginning of the Tapestry is probably the ducal castle at Rouen. Odo was imprisoned in the 'tower' here between 1082 and 1087.

25 Aerial photograph of Rochester Castle, Odo's stronghold in Kent. The siege of Rochester (1088) led to Odo's final banishment from England.

26 The motte at Tonbridge, Kent. The castle mound was probably erected soon after the Battle of Hastings and featured in the 1088 baron's rebellion.

27 A near contemporary depiction of Pope Urban II preaching the First Crusade at the great Abbey of Cluny in 1096.

28 Preparations for crusade from a twelfth-century manuscript.

29 A panoramic view of Palermo, Sicily, painted by E. Cremp in the nineteenth century. It was here that Odo died and was buried in 1097. *Chirico, 1992*

battlefield and a final caption, which is probably spurious, refers to the English running away.

Several authorities argue that the original was probably about 1.5m longer and portrayed William's triumphal entry into London and his coronation held on Christmas Day 1066. For centuries the Tapestry was folded and stored in a chest in Bayeux Cathedral, apart from eight days following the feast of St John the Baptist when it was probably displayed around the nave of the church. The uppermost part of the folded Tapestry would, therefore, have been the last panel, which would, therefore, have been the most vulnerable to damp and decay. The survival of the majority of the Tapestry in such relatively well-preserved condition resulted from the fact that it was folded and thus protected for most of the time, being brought out of its box for only eight days a year. Attention has also recently been drawn to the chest in Bayeux Cathedral that is traditionally said to have housed the Bayeux Tapestry. The chest is sufficiently large enough to have contained the Tapestry before it was lined in the eighteenth/nineteenth century and it has been argued that the Tapestry may have also been protected by the preserving properties of the box itself. The chest appears to be made of cedar and, if so, the Tapestry spent the first 600 years or so of its life carefully folded into a chest impregnated with cedar oil, a natural moth repellent (Hill & McSween 2011, 44–51).

• Odo's Role in the Creation of the Bayeux Tapestry •

The Tapestry was first attributed to Bishop Odo in 1824 by Honoré Delauney, but it was the seminal work of Sir Frank Stenton in 1957 which laid the foundation of modern Tapestry scholarship and where the responsibility for making the Tapestry was firmly placed on the shoulders of Odo (Stenton 1957). Furthermore, it was argued that the Tapestry was executed by English seamstresses in Canterbury and that it was probably completed in time for the consecration of Odo's new cathedral in Bayeux in 1077. An alternative theory, which has fewer adherents, is that the Tapestry was commissioned around the time of Odo's trial in 1082 or during his subsequent imprisonment, in an attempt to regain William's favour.

There are several compelling reasons to suggest that it was Odo who commissioned the Tapestry. Firstly, Odo appears on at least four occasions in the story – more than any other individual except William and Harold.

Moreover, his actions are emphasised as being central to the success of the Norman mission. It is also possible that an unnamed Odo appears witnessing Harold rescuing Norman soldiers at Mont-Saint-Michel. Odo's role in the Conquest is graphically highlighted in the Tapestry; for example, when he 'encourages the boys' at Hastings, the depiction of his horse is larger than any other on the Tapestry. The image stands alone and is not overlapped by other animals or riders, giving it a unique prominence in the whole of the Tapestry.

It is argued that there are strong similarities with Anglo-Saxon art, both manuscripts and reliefs. Canterbury was a celebrated centre for the production of illuminated manuscripts and artworks in the eleventh century, particularly pictorial narrative. Many aspects of the styles of depiction used in the Tapestry correspond to the artistic styles and traditions of Canterbury (Wormald in Stenton 1957). Scholars have identified exact parallels between some of the illustrations on the Tapestry and illuminations from St Augustine's Abbey, Canterbury, with which Odo, as Earl of Kent, had close associations. For example, the trees depicted have their closest parallel in the *Aelfric Heptateuch*, an English illuminated manuscript from Canterbury of the second quarter of the eleventh century. Also in a drawing of Noah's Ark from the same source the figures of men, women, animals and birds are similar to those on the Tapestry. The Viking-type prow of the ark is also reminiscent of those on the Norman invasion ships (see colour plate 20) (Williams 1997, 80–1). A Norman forager carrying a rope is almost identical to a figure in the *Psychomachia* of Prudentius, a manuscript found at St Augustine's.

Odo controlled the area around Canterbury and would have had the power and wealth to commission a lasting record of a momentous event, in which he played a leading role. In addition to celebrating William's victory, Odo may well have used the Tapestry to try to persuade surviving English nobles and clerics of the validity of the new Norman regime. Thus the Tapestry, while emphasising the legality of Norman rule, recognises the courage of the English troops.

• Turold, Wadard and Vital •

Besides the major historical characters, only four other individuals are mentioned by name, of which Turold, Wadard and Vital were Odo's vassals, holding large estates from the bishop both in Normandy and in post-Conquest England. The distribution of the lands of these three characters suggests that on the march to London, Duke William confiscated Godwinson family estates and passed them on to his own lords, including Bishop Odo, who, in turn, granted confiscated lands to his own followers, and they could also have appropriated land for themselves. Some of this land had actually been taken from monasteries by English magnates before the Conquest, but later gave rise to disputes involving the new Norman lords, such as that at Penenden Heath in the 1070s. Amongst the lands which Turold acquired were estates which had belonged to Aethelnoth Child. Aethelnoth was one of the wealthiest aristocrats in pre-Conquest England and appears to have been the leader of the Kentish contingent of the English *fyrd* at Hastings. He was taken as a hostage to Normandy with King William in March 1067 and never returned (Tsurushima 2011). Odo gave Turold the task of guarding Rochester, its hinterland, the Medway crossing and the route to Essex. The king built a castle at Rochester soon after the Conquest and trusted it, like Dover Castle, to Odo. In turn, Odo passed it to Turold, who had no major estates in Normandy and thereafter was called Turold of Rochester. After Turold's death, his son Ralph probably became constable of Rochester Castle.

Wadard has been identified as another of Odo's vassals, who he may have known from the Conteville area and who was an officer in the bishop's household. On the Tapestry he is depicted with a small military unit, looting and seizing provisions. Wadard appears to have been a provisions officer, following Odo's travelling episcopal household. He was amongst those of Odo's men who were trusted to guard Dover Castle and was one of the first knights to have been given houses in Dover town.

The third of the knights associated with Odo was Vital, who appears as a scout giving information to Duke William about Harold's location before the Battle of Hastings. Vital's estates were worth far less than those of Turold and Wadard. It has been argued that as his lands were largely on the Kentish coast his interests were those of a sailor and merchant and he was probably bilingual. The following account appears in *The Miracles of St Augustine*, according to Goscelin of St Bertin's (Tsurushima 2011):

> Under the first Norman king of the English, men from England, on business with fifteen ships landed at the market town of Caen. There having completed their trading, they were preparing to return, conveying stone to the

> king's palace of Westminster – for they were under contract to the Royal superintendent. This office was held by an upright man named Vital, who, having been received into fraternity by the Lord Abbot Scotland [abbot of St Augustine's, Canterbury], was proving himself most effective in conveying stone for the monastic building work of St Augustine's.

Tsurushima argues convincingly that not only were these three men closely associated with Odo, but they might have advised the Tapestry designer on military, maritime and architectural details, about which they were experts. Furthermore, they all had interests in Kent, which could support the claim that the Tapestry was made in Canterbury.

It has recently been claimed that many of the assumptions about the commissioning of the Tapestry are based upon the Renaissance concept of the artistic patron. It is unlikely that Odo or any other single sponsor would have micromanaged the production of the embroidery. If so, how does a work authored, designed and produced by others bear such a strong imprint of the author's agenda? The answer could be that it was an institutional production. While Odo was probably the Tapestry's benefactor, the nature of its contents, such as the inclusion of Turold, Wadard and Vital, are consistent with it being the work of St Augustine's Abbey (Pastan & White 2009).

It is widely believed that the setting for Harold's oath given before William, the critical point of the narrative, was in Odo's cathedral in Bayeux. Odo's central role in the English campaign depicted on the Tapestry is not repeated by contemporary accounts. Most descriptions of Odo at Hastings rely on the story told in the Tapestry, which is just as Odo would have wanted it to be. There is little other documentary evidence to suggest that Odo played any role at the Battle of Hastings. William of Poitiers, writing much closer to the events of 1066, mentions the presence of the two bishops, Odo and Geoffrey of Coutances, together with numerous clergy and a few monks, and that the assembly prepared for combat by prayer. He also states that Odo never took arms and never wished to. The *Song of Hastings* and Orderic Vitalis do not mention Odo at Hastings.

Similarly, there is conflicting evidence about where Harold swore his oath. It is the Tapestry which appears to place the oath in Odo's diocesan church at Bayeux, but William of Poitiers locates it at Bonneville, while Orderic Vitalis says that the oath was sworn in Rouen. The only near-contemporary document to connect the scene to Bayeux is a late twelfth-century life of

Thomas Becket, where the oath is taken in a hunting lodge near to Bayeux (Barlow 2003, 73–4). The depiction of the oath is probably the most important scene in the whole of the Tapestry and locating it in Bayeux was to place Odo and his cathedral at the very centre of the story. There was no need for Odo to be portrayed in this scene, which was, after all, taking place in Odo's own house.

Perhaps the most powerful argument for Odo's role in creating the Tapestry was the nature of his own ambitious personality. Odo was an enthusiastic and successful patron of the arts, and the development of Bayeux as an intellectual centre and the Conquest of England made him the second richest and second most powerful man in the Anglo-Norman world, with the capacity to call upon the artistic resources of the newly won kingdom. It is totally in keeping with Odo's disposition that he should commission a work which graphically told the story of how those riches were acquired and gave himself a pivotal role in the depiction of that achievement.

• The Other Candidates •

In 1982–83 the Tapestry was cleaned and conserved before being moved to its new home in the Musée de la Tapisserie de Bayeux. This allowed a detailed examination of the embroidery to be carried out. Since that time there has been a considerable amount of revisionary speculation about the Tapestry, both about its fabric and about its contents. The consensus is still that Odo was involved in some way with its creation, but several other candidates have also been proposed. These include Queen Edith, Edward the Confessor's wife; Eustace, Count of Boulogne; Wadard and Vital, the Loire Valley abbey of St Florent de Saumur and even Archbishop Stigand. Recently, the idea that Queen Matilda was responsible has been revived, but far more credible is the suggestion that Edith of Wessex was closely involved in making the Tapestry. She was both Harold's sister and widow of Edward the Confessor, placing her close to the centre of events in 1066. She is one of only three women depicted on the Tapestry, where she is seen sitting at the foot of Edward's deathbed. After the Conquest she moved into Wilton nunnery, but established cordial relations with King William and continued to be one of the most influential English aristocrats until her death in 1075, when the *Anglo-Saxon Chronicle* records that, 'The king had her brought to Westminster with great honour.' She is known to have been

33 Eustace of Boulogne depicted on the Bayeux Tapestry.

an accomplished needle worker and she ran a royal embroidery workshop, producing textiles for churches as well as Edward's robes of state. She was in a unique position to have sponsored the politically balanced Tapestry, as interpreted by some scholars, but as with all the candidates there remain, and will remain, many unanswered questions about Edith's possible involvement in the production of the Bayeux Tapestry (Hicks 2006, 29–39).

It has been argued that even if Odo was not the actual patron of the Tapestry, it could have been made as a gift for the bishop. Chief among those potential donors is Eustace, Count of Boulogne, who commanded the Flemish troops at the Battle of Hastings. Eustace's appearance in the Tapestry is problematic and his presence or otherwise depends upon a fragmentary inscription in the border which nineteenth-century restorers expanded into *Eustacius*. There is also a possible representation of the count leading the charge of the Norman cavalry. One recent commentator has suggested that this was not Eustace at all, but William's half-brother Robert of Mortain. There are also conflicting versions of Eustace's role at Hastings. William of Poitiers claimed that the count urged William to withdraw and was shamefully wounded in the back while retreating. On the other hand, the *Song of the Battle of Hastings* portrayed Eustace as a hero who saved William's life and gave up his own horse for the duke. In 1067, however, Eustace committed a cardinal error by attacking Odo's headquarters at Dover, after which he was outlawed and stripped of his lands; but a few years later, in the mid-1070s, he was reconciled to the king and his lands were restored. The pro-Eustace party argues that the Tapestry could have been a gift to Odo from Eustace, in order for him to regain favour with the king through his brother (Bridgeford 2004). An even less likely candidate, Archbishop Stigand, has recently been proposed as the creator of the Tapestry. Keats-Rohan suggests that it was the work of Stigand collaborating with Odo immediately after Hastings and before 1070 (Keats-Rohan 2012, 159–74).

Surviving contemporary narrative tapestries are rare but the closest comparable works come from the non-literate world of Viking Scandinavia. There is an intriguing reference to a near-contemporary tapestry in the work of Baudry de Bourgueil, who died as Bishop of Dol in 1130. Baudry, writing in verse form before 1102, described a hanging in the chamber of Adela, Countess of Blois and daughter of William the Conqueror. It told the story of William's Conquest of England, starting with the appearance of Halley's Comet and finishing with the Conquest of Kent. The author tells us that the hanging had captions and showed the construction of the fleet and the subsequent Channel crossing. On the face of it, this looks like a description of the Bayeux Tapestry being hung in the Loire Valley in the late eleventh century (Musset, 23–5), but Baudry was an imaginative poet as well as a cleric and may have been transferring knowledge of the tapestry he had seen in Normandy to Adela's chamber. One scholar has, however, recently argued that the Tapestry was actually produced in the Loire Valley at the monastery of St Florent of Saumur. He proposes that the work was commissioned by King William for propaganda purposes and managed by William, the abbot of St Florent, who was grateful to the king for coming to his father, Rivallon's help at Dol in 1064. It is argued that this would help explain the inclusion of the detailed coverage of the 'Breton Campaign' (Beech 2011).

Until recently, it was generally accepted that the Tapestry was designed to be installed in the nave of Bayeux Cathedral from the outset. There were objections which pointed out the lewdness of some of the border scenes and that the Tapestry had a violent secular theme which made it an inappropriate decoration for a church, but examples of similar hangings can be found in other churches dating roughly from the same period. It was also argued by some that the narrow strip of embroidery hung around the church would have been too small to have been appreciated. It was argued that the decidedly secular character of the Tapestry, which has 'no religious drift', meant that it was 'originally made for an extensive secular hall' and that Odo had palaces in England, Normandy and Rome, any of which would have provided a suitable home (Dodwell 1995, 14).

An alternative installation for the Tapestry has been suggested on the basis of a radical reinterpretation of its iconography. Whereas historically it was thought that the Tapestry was designed to be displayed in a rectangle, either in a church or a great hall, it has been proposed that there are symmetrical scenes in the hanging which mean that it was intended to be displayed in a square. This would have meant that there was a geometrical relationship between three scenes involving Harold or Odo: firstly, the feast at Bosham, secondly, Harold's oath and thirdly, Odo's blessing of the banquet before the Battle of Hastings (see colour plate 10). The two feast scenes would have been opposite each other and the oath would have been at the centre of the third wall; under this display scheme at the centre of the fourth wall would have been Odo wielding his baton triumphantly at the height of the battle. It is argued that behind this scheme was a rivalry between Harold and Odo and that there are a number of scenes which balance out the activities and fortunes of these two powerful men (Owen-Crocker 2005).

Additionally, it has been argued that, given this interpretation, an appropriate location for the Tapestry would have been within a square Anglo-Norman castle keep – and where better than at Dover? Although the great stone keep at Dover was not built until the twelfth century, there may have been an earth and timber castle built there immediately after Hastings which would have been under Odo's control in his role as Earl of Kent. Was the Tapestry designed to be hung within the square wooden tower of Dover Castle? (Henige 2005). There are, of course, serious objections to all these ideas, but they demonstrate that the Tapestry is still capable of radical reinterpretation which still gives Odo a central role in its creation and display. Other possible locations for the Tapestry include the church of St Augustine, Canterbury, as begun by Abbot Scotland (1070–87) and completed by Abbot Guy (1087–93). It is also possible that it was intended to be taken round ecclesiastical buildings in England and perhaps Normandy for set periods of public display. The Tapestry might also have been accompanied by guides and interpreters who offered a commentary on its details. It is possible that Odo's fall from favour in 1082 led to the Tapestry being sent to Bayeux from England along with his other chattels for storage (Cowdrey 1988, 49–65).

• The Song of Roland •

According to Wace, at the start of the Battle of Hastings, 'Taillefer, a very good singer rode before the duke on a swift horse, singing of Charlemagne and of Roland, of Oliver and of the vassals who died at Roncevales' (Burgess 2004, 181). This is a story which appears in various forms in other accounts of the battle and relates to the *Song of Roland*, the first *chanson de geste* (song of deeds), an epic tale which presents an account of Charlemagne's army in Spain in 778. Leaving Spain after a long campaign, the Frankish army is betrayed by one of Charlemagne's own lords, Ganelon. The *Song* concentrates on Roland, Charlemagne's nephew, who is bringing up the rearguard with his two companions, Oliver and Archbishop Turpin. They are ambushed by a Muslim (it was in fact Basque) force at the Roncesvalles Pass in the Pyrenees and fight to the death, protecting their honour and slaying all their attackers in the process. In revenge, Charlemagne returns to Spain with a large army and wipes out the opposing pagan kingdom.

The *Song* appears in the late eleventh or early twelfth century and it has been suggested that Odo was involved in its composition, as well as that of the Bayeux Tapestry. The *Song*, like the Tapestry, emphasises loyalty and feudal obligation as well as the dire consequences of treason and treachery. The heroes of both works have valour and common sense and have adversaries that are worthy, but are guilty of having broken codes and oaths (Caple, 82). There are several similarities between the *Chanson* and the Tapestry, notably, the role played by two clerics – Bishop Odo and Archbishop Turpin. Both are influential in the councils of war and both appear prominently in battle. In the *Song*, Turpin blessed the troops before the battle and offered martyrdom and instant salvation to those who fell fighting to 'help sustain the Christian faith' and fought to the end, and 'Archbishop Turpin goes throughout the field. No tonsured priest who ever sang a mass performed such feats of prowess with his body' (*Roland* v,

1129). Could Odo have consciously modelled himself on the Archbishop of Rheims from the *Song of Roland* in the Tapestry? Odo also blessed the troops before Hastings as well as presiding over the pre-battle banquet. In one specific area there is almost complete symmetry in the way the two men are portrayed: at the height of the Battle of Hastings, Odo is shown energetically rallying the young Norman knights who are showing signs of weakness, while at the height of the Battle of Roncesvalles, when many of the Franks have been killed, the surviving knights of the rearguard grow anxious and Turpin encourages them thus, 'My lords and barons, don't think shameful thoughts! I beg of you, for God's sake do not run, nor let proud men sing mockingly of you; it's best by far that we should die in combat' (*Roland* v, 1515–18). In both cases, the sight of a warlike man of God leading the charge served to embolden the troops whose morale was failing.

There is not enough evidence to be certain either that Odo was involved in the writing of the *Song of Roland* or that he used the model of Archbishop Turpin in the depiction of his own actions on the Bayeux Tapestry. There is, however, enough circumstantial evidence to persuade us to consider the idea seriously. It should also be remembered that Odo ended his days on the First Crusade, making his way to Jerusalem to fight Muslim forces, perhaps still motivated by the *Song* and a desire to emulate Archbishop Turpin.

The heroic figure of Archbishop Turpin, who died fighting valiantly at Roncesvalles, would have provided an appropriate model for Odo, the battling bishop.

> Archbishop Turpin rides about the field:
> Never has such a cleric sung a mass
> Who did so many deeds of gallantry.
> To the pagan he said: 'God's woes on you!
> You've slain a man for whom grief fills my heart.'
> Forward he launches his fine battle-steed
> And strikes him square on his Toledo shield
> To hurl him lifeless down on the green grass.
> (Owen 1990, 87)

6

• 'A Second King in England' •

The Battle of Hastings proved to be a major turning point in Odo's career. Although he had been 'a baron with the benefit of clergy', after Hastings he became first and foremost a powerful secular magnate (Dodwell 1966). Presumably, Odo was present at William's coronation, but he played no role in the ceremony; the Norman contribution was left to the other powerful baron-bishop, Geoffrey of Coutances, who, perhaps acting in his role of chaplain-in-chief to the Norman army, translated parts of the service. William was crowned king by Ealdred, Archbishop of York, who was acceptable to the papacy and he spoke in English, but the assent of the Normans was sought by Geoffrey speaking in French.

• Odo as Earl and Regent •

We begin to hear a great deal more about Odo after 1066 as he appears in a range of Anglo-Norman documents recording his various activities. William made Odo Earl of Kent late in 1066 or early in 1067 as part of his strategy to defend the south coast; he succeeded Harold's brother Leofwine, who had controlled a much larger region in the south-east. The reduction in the size of the earldom would have been part of a policy to limit the power of the new earl, but also recognising the importance of Kent in the defence of England. William had himself proved how vulnerable the south-east was to foreign invasion, and his creation of the

Sussex rapes and the earldom of Kent with a line of powerful castles running parallel to the coast was his response. Elsewhere in England, William largely took over and strengthened the English shire system for his local government, with county sheriffs acting as his representatives. Odo was responsible for choosing at least six of the new sheriffs, who were identified as his close allies (Green 1982). In the south-east and other sensitive areas the king adopted the Norman system of *casteleries*; these were well-defined districts 'within which the whole arrangement of tenancies was primarily designed for the maintenance of a castle' (Stenton 1961, 194). The intention was that these would form the front line of defence against an invading army trying to emulate William's own successful invasion campaign. It is probable that William intended sub-dividing Kent into *castleries* as well as Domesday Book talks of the *divisiones* of Odo of Bayeux and Hugh de Montford, the same term used for the Sussex rapes. Odo's base was at Dover Castle, which was the *castrum* Harold had promised to William in 1064; according to William of Poitiers. William had ordered the building of a castle here in 1066, work which had probably started as his forces made their way to London. Other major Norman castles in Kent were built at Canterbury, Rochester and Tonbridge and in total there were at least sixteen eleventh-century fortifications in the county. Some of these were motte and bailey castles, as at Tonbridge; others were large enclosure castles as at Rochester and Dover (Renn 1968).

In March 1067 King William felt safe enough to return to Normandy with hostages including Edgar Aetheling, Archbishop Stigand and Earls Edwin and Morcar. He also took money and items looted from English churches and monasteries; according to William of Poitiers, it was a virtuous act that large amounts of money were sent to a thousand churches in France and that the papacy received treasures worthy of Byzantium. Modern historians are less charitable, and describe the scale of losses from English churches as 'unparalleled since the days of the Danish predators ... in relation to the enormous losses of Anglo-Saxon objects in precious metal ... the replacements by the Normans themselves were simply derisory' (Dodwell 1982, 216). William then proceeded on a victory procession around the duchy during which the spoils of victory were displayed for the Norman people to see. During his absence William had appointed Bishop Odo and William fitz Osbern as his two regents. They were the most powerful men in the land, who were able to act without direct reference to the king, unlike other magnates such as Lanfranc who later acted as viceroys and undertook specific tasks allotted to them. No doubt they were given licence to take some English lands for themselves, and they started the process of piecemeal deprivation and demotion of the surviving English aristocrats and their families. Despite William's rhetoric about continuity and inheritance, his regents' actions spoke of high-handed superiority and dispossession.

Odo's initial responsibilities involved the defence and subjugation of south-eastern England. Odo would have inherited the prehistoric and Saxon fortifications at Dover, where the Norman army camped after Hastings. Two detached towers 'of Norman date' in the outer bailey of the later castle, destroyed in the eighteenth century, could have been Odo's work (Colvin 1963, 630–1). The *Anglo-Saxon Chronicle* for 1067 reported that Odo, with fitz Osbern based in Winchester, 'wrought castles widely through this country, and harassed the miserable people; and ever since has evil increased very much'. Orderic Vitalis complained that 'petty lords' oppressed both nobles and commoners with 'unjust exactions', while Odo and fitz Osbern, 'swollen with pride', ignored all complaints against the Normans. Such was Odo's power that Orderic called him, 'a second king in England'. Orderic stated that the two regents 'would not deign to hear the reasonable pleas of the English or give them impartial judgement'. Some of these complaints involved the treatment of English women, with whom illicit relationships were prohibited. The *Anglo-Saxon Chronicle* reported that William was 'stern beyond all measure to those that resisted his will … if any man had intercourse against a woman, he was forthwith castrated'. However, there are some indications that Odo may have condoned rape and forced marriage between Normans and English women. Orderic Vitalis reported that 'noble maidens were exposed to the insults of low-born soldiers and lamented their dishonouring by the scum of the earth' (OV, ii, 268–9). It was also recorded that Englishwomen were known to have taken refuge in nunneries, 'not for love of the religious life but from fear of the French' (Williams 1995, 12).

Predictably, William of Poitiers had a more charitable view of the regents' activities than the *Anglo-Saxon Chronicle*, 'Odo bishop of Bayeux, William fitz Osbern laudably performed their respective stewardships in the kingdom; sometimes they acted singly and sometimes together … Also the local governors, each placed in a castle, zealously administered their districts … But neither fear nor favour could so subdue the English as to prefer peace and tranquillity to rebellions and disorders …'. On his return in the autumn of 1067 the *Anglo-Saxon Chronicle* claims that William 'gave away every man's land'.

Explicit De Ricardo primo. Incipit De Secundo.
Quoniamquidem dignus preconiorum multis in precedentibus precio
[illegible] gemina Ricardus scilicet normannorum dux extiti
t [illegible] regisque; cum anulo decenter inseruimus. ope pretium [illegible]
ut celebrius ab ipso exorsus sectam sicuti [illegible] ita
[illegible] ingenuitatis eulogio. [illegible] teneat Ricard
us siquidem filius militaribus triumphis oppido conspicuus. et non
minora laudum preconio excoluerat. Qui sui fulgoris radios per diversos orbis car
dines glorioso nomine spargens. intra sui ducatus limites plurimum bonorum operum incrementis nor
mannicam pene patriam unam Christi insignivit ecclesiam. Hic in armis admodum strenuus.
ubique armatas militum legiones nobiliter rexit. de inimicis victoriam semper capere assuetus. Et
[illegible] seculari actu [illegible] tam fuit fide catholice. et erga dei cultores benivolus
ac devotus. Sub cuius moderamine plurima monachorum adoleverunt ovilia. que velud apes ex
multis [illegible] actuum canistris erumpentes: lucidissima in celestes thesauros intulerunt mella.
Cum igitur tante probitatis exuberaret copiis. in initio sue iuventutis intra normannicum ducatum
contigit quoddam pestiferi oriri seminarium discidii. Nam rustici unanimes per diversos totius
normannice patrie comitatus plurima agentes conventicula. iuxta suos libitus vivere
decernebant quatinus tam in silvarum compendiis quam in aquarum commerciis: nullo obsistente ante
statuti iuris obice. legibus uterentur suis. Que ut rata manerent. ab unoquoque cetu furentis
vulgi duo eliguntur legati: qui decreta ad mediterraneum ferrent roboranda conventum. Quod
ut dux agnovit. protinus Rodulfum comitem cum multa militum multitudine illis destinavit: qui agrestem comprimeret ferocitatem. et rusticam dirimeret contionem. Qui non morans iussa. cunctos
confestim legatos cum nonnullis aliis cepit: truncatisque manibus ac pedibus inutiles suis remisit.
qui eos a talibus compescerent: et ne deteriora paterentur suis eventibus cautos redderent. His
rustici expertis. festinato contionibus omissis: ad sua aratra sunt reversi.
Eadem tempestate. quendam ducis uno ex patre fratrem progenitum nomine Willelmum. quo
[illegible] tumidum et rebellem. Is enim fratris contubernio ex
[illegible] ab ipso accipiens, in munere comitatum. ut inde ei militie exiberet statuta: pra
vorum illectus calliditate. spreto ei domino: ab illius se cohibuit fidelitatis obsequio. Qui dum ple
[illegible] a duce Ricardo sepius obiurgaretur. et resipiscere ab obstinati animi nollet ausu: consil
[illegible] Rodulfi comitis captus. in rotomagensis urbis turre detruditur. [illegible] pen
[illegible] lucens. [illegible] satellitum in seditioni proposito [illegible]
crebris [illegible] tumultibus; [illegible] vita privavit: alios exules de suis finibus [illegible]
bavit. Willelmus tandem post quinquennium cuiusdam sui militis factione. longissimo fune pen
[illegible] fenestra a turre lapsus. fugam iniit. Qui diebus ne a querentibus repperiretur delitescens.
et noctibus iter carpens: novissime [illegible] apud se [illegible] illi fore cum vite discrimine

34 An extract from William of Poitiers' *Lives of the Norman Dukes*, written within a few years of the Battle of Hastings. *Art de Basse-Normandie, 1985*

• Odo – The First Justiciar? •

There has been some dispute about the precise nature of Odo's position in England between 1066 and 1082 and whether he can be described as England's first justiciar. Orderic Vitalis referred to Odo as *comes palatii* (count of the palace), the designation used for the most powerful official in the Carolingian court; this may have been because the term regent was not specifically applied either to Odo or to William fitz Osbern. Bates argues persuasively that Odo alone 'could act with the equivalent of royal authority when William was not in England' (Bates 2004–11) – an interpretation that appears to be confirmed in Domesday Book, which insisted that only Odo's seal had the same status as the king's. Clearly Odo was acting as justicias when he presided over pleas and mobilised shire courts.

The bishop's itinerary reflected his disparate activities as William's regent, as Earl of Kent, as a general, as a great landholder and as a bishop. Unlike other magnates Odo perambulated the country adjudicating small and large land disputes; he confirmed freehold tenure, decided between alternative claims and organised the royal demesne. However, his social status and his role as Earl of Kent would have prohibited him undertaking continuous administrative activity. Odo's chief residences in England were at Dover and Rochester in Kent, at Deddington in Oxfordshire and at Snettisham in Norfolk. He was present at Queen Matilda's coronation at Westminster on 11 May 1068 and at the primacy dispute at Winchester in 1072, where it was declared that Canterbury was the senior of the two archbishoprics. The main event in the court calendar, at which Odo was regularly present, was the Crown Wearing, where the king would ceremonially show himself to his people. These ceremonies were held on a regular basis at Easter, Whitsun and Christmas each year, taking place at Westminster, Winchester, Windsor or Gloucester. Odo witnessed the signing of Crown documents on thirty-four occasions; only Roger de Montgomery witnessed more, with forty attestations. Orderic Vitalis talked of a very small group of magnates like Odo as 'those wise and eloquent men who for many years lived at King William's court, observed his deeds and all the great activities there, were privy to his deepest and most sacred counsels, and were endowed by him with wealth that raised them above the condition to which they were born'.

One contemporary primitive form of justice, trial by ordeal, was applied by Odo, both in secular and ecclesiastical cases. According to custom the accused would normally be subject to ordeal by iron; the plaintiff would be obliged either to hold a red-hot iron or to walk across heated ploughshares. Their wounds would then be bandaged and if the injuries had healed or begun to heal within three days they were deemed innocent. However, if the wounds were festering then the accused was guilty and further punished accordingly (Bartlett 1986, 179–84). Ecclesiastical cases involving trial by ordeal had to be authorised by the appropriate bishop and before 1066 ordeal irons were held only by cathedrals in Normandy. Trial by ordeal was not only used to prove a man innocent or otherwise, it was also used as a means of confirming the honesty of jurors in a number of cases in England. In an infamous trial over landownership between Gundulf, Bishop of Rochester and Picot, Sheriff of Cambridgeshire the intrinsic unfairness and dangers of this system were graphically demonstrated. The county court, which was caught between a rock and a hard place, pronounced in favour of Picot but was reconvened on the intervention of Bishop Odo, who did not trust the judgment. Picot was the most famous villain in Domesday Book and known to the people of Ely as 'a ravenous lion, a prowling wolf, a cunning fox, a filthy pig, a shameless dog ...'. The jurors, all of whom were English, gave their judgement 'out of fear of the sheriff' and 'were struck with terror by a message from the sheriff'. Odo did not believe them and he presented the jurors to an assembly of 'the greater barons of all England', where it was judged that they had committed perjury. Consequently, twelve representatives of the shire were obliged either to recant or undergo an ordeal by red-hot iron. When the jurors who had not confessed to the crime protested, they were put to the iron and failed, as a result of which they were fined the considerable sum of £300 (Cooper 2005, 175–9).

• Rebellion •

The first few months of William's reign were relatively peaceful; the first signs of organised rebellion did not emerge until the latter part of 1067 when a revolt broke out in Odo's own backyard. According to Orderic Vitalis, the Englishmen of Kent, 'goaded to rebellion by Norman oppression', identified Count Eustace of Boulogne as a preferable alternative to William the Conqueror and invited him to attack Dover Castle. Earlier, Eustace had quarrelled with William and returned to Boulogne. With William away in Normandy he welcomed an opportunity to meddle in Anglo-Norman affairs. With the help of Kentish forces, Eustace attacked the castle. Odo and Hugh of Montford, warden of Dover Castle, together with most of the castle garrison, had travelled north of the Thames, where they were probably involved in land confiscation and transfer. The remaining defenders of the castle resisted fiercely and Eustace signalled to his men to return to the ships. As they did so they were pursued by the Normans and, believing that Odo had returned, they panicked, resulting in a rout. Eustace escaped, but many of his men were killed and his nephew was captured and presumably ransomed by Odo. This episode demonstrates the difficulty the English would have had in dislodging determined Norman defenders from their fortified castles. The scale of this uprising, and particularly the extent of involvement by English rebels, has been questioned. Eustace came with a force of chosen knights, but did not bring horses, which hardly sounds like a serious invasion attempt. Eustace's involvement with Dover went back to the early 1050s, when there was an abortive attempt by King Edward to install him perhaps as castellan of a projected castle. It is possible that Eustace was simply trying to gain that which he believed belonged to him, i.e. Dover Castle, while King William was away (Williams 1995, 14–16).

Odo does not appear to have played a major role in the suppression of the rebellions and invasions that were a major feature of the next few years of William's rule. The bishop's role was to facilitate the transfer or 'delivery' of land, while maintaining the peace in southern England; uprisings elsewhere within the kingdom were dealt with by others. William fitz Osbern and the king himself put down a northern rising in the autumn of 1068. Odo's brother Robert of Mortain and Robert of Eu led an army against a force of Danes who had landed at the mouth of the Humber and laid siege to York in 1069. The Danes retreated to the Fens but the Normans 'pursued them with great slaughter to their very ships'. Bishop Geoffrey of Coutances put down a rising in Dorset and Somerset in 1070, while the king was responsible for the most savage response to any of the disturbances. In 1069–70 William laid waste to large tracts of countryside in northern England, the Pennines and the Welsh borders in the 'Harrying of the North', the Conqueror's version of the 'final solution' for the troublesome north, so that it would not be able to support a rebellion again in the foreseeable future. The conventional interpretation of the 'harrying', based on the large number of manors in Yorkshire recorded as 'waste' in 1086 in Domesday Book, has been questioned. Such 'waste' entries may indicate a lack of information rather than estates still valueless almost twenty years after William's punitive northern expedition (Palliser 1993, 1–27). Yet the chroniclers were in no doubt about the damage caused by the severity of the Normans' treatment of the north-eastern counties in 1069. Simeon of Durham described how infected corpses were left decaying in houses and how survivors had to eat horses, cats and dogs and sold themselves into slavery. William of Malmesbury, writing of York, observed:

> As for the cities once so famous, the towers whose tops threatened the sky, the fields rich in pasture and watered by rivers, if anyone sees them now, he sighs if he is a stranger, and if he is a native surviving from the past, he does not recognise them.
>
> (*Gesta Regum*, i, 506–7)

Even Orderic Vitalis wrote magisterially about the brutal devastation of northern England. The 'Harrying of the North' certainly diminished the chances of a major successful rebellion in the north, but over the next few years the region continued to provide the most convenient route into England for a trickle of invaders from Scotland and Scandinavia.

When the king was in England, Normandy was under the control of Queen Matilda and their eldest son and heir, Robert, but William made frequent visits to the duchy and was sometimes accompanied by Odo. Normandy too had its share of problems, and in an attempt to solve a succession dispute involving Matilda's family in Flanders, William's most trusted colleague, William fitz Osbern, was killed in 1071. Odo's power and influence were inflated further by fitz Osbern's death and for a while his position as William's deputy was unchallenged. It is clear that until the early 1080s William relied heavily on Odo to govern England, and although he must have been aware of the bishop's weaknesses, he accepted them as a price worth paying, for the time being at least. In 1072 William took a large army across the Channel to Maine to restore Norman authority there. In 1074 the king spent much of the year undertaking regular governmental affairs in Normandy. Bishop Odo accompanied him from at least May to November, when presumably he was concerned with diocesan business, in particular, preparations for the consecration of his new cathedral in Bayeux which was now nearing completion. It was during this visit that William gave the cathedral the large estate of Le Plessis-Grimoult, confiscated from a rebel baron after the Battle of Val-ès-Dunes (1047), which Odo used to create prebendal estates for canons at Bayeux Cathedral.

In 1075 there was another serious rebellion, known as the Earls' Revolt, which took place against the background of growing threats from France and Denmark. Roger, Earl of Hereford; Ralph, Earl of Norfolk, who held land in Brittany; and Waltheof conspired against William but were put down by royal armies. John of Worcester reported that, 'Odo of Bayeux and Geoffrey of Coutances led a vast host … to attack the Earl of Norfolk', but other chroniclers do not mention Odo playing any role in the campaign. It is perhaps significant that it was Lanfranc and not Odo that was in charge of England at this point.

Nevertheless Odo was in charge from the latter part of 1077 to 1080, when William was preoccupied with the revolt of his eldest son, Robert, in Normandy. Robert, who had effectively been governing the duchy when William was in England, was in his late 20s and believed that he had the right to formally be recognised as Duke of Normandy. Robert quarrelled with his younger brothers as well as William, leading to an estrangement which developed into open rebellion, aided at times by the French king,

35 William the Conqueror, his wife Matilda and their two eldest sons William Rufus and Robert Curthose, from a thirteenth-century fresco in a chapel of St Stephen in Caen, which was destroyed in 1700. *Ducarel, 1767*

Philippe I. Several eminent emissaries attempted to heal the rift, including Pope Gregory VII, but Robert and William were not reconciled until Easter 1080 (12 April) when they attended a great assembly together in Rouen.

Almost immediately trouble broke out in England when the Earl of Northumbria, Bishop Walcher of Durham was murdered in a massacre at Gateshead on 14 May 1080. William's response was savage and intended permanently to emasculate the Northumbrians. There are no detailed descriptions of the campaign, but Odo, who led an expedition north to deal with the rebels, employed tactics similar to those used by the king in the 'Harrying of the North', creating areas where now, according to the monk Simeon of Durham, little grew except wolves and outlaws. The Normans slaughtered both the guilty and the innocent, laying waste the area to the north of the Tees and reducing the population and economic activity in the region for a generation or more. Odo weakened the local nobility by killing or driving many of them into exile, and 'there would be no more native revolts above the Tees, because in 1080 the Northumbrian nobility had joined the nobles of York' (Kapelle 1978, 142). Odo was accused of stealing treasures from churches, including 'a pastoral staff of rare workmanship' from Durham Cathedral. The staff was said to be sapphire encrusted and taken to the castle under guard of the soldiers, but soon disappeared; another source says that it found its way to Bayeux Cathedral (Aird 1998, 101, 4). William's son Robert, now fully absolved, then led an inconclusive campaign against the Scottish king, Malcolm, who himself had plundered Northumbria the previous year. It was as a result of this campaign that Robert built a castle on the Tyne, opposite Gateshead, and Newcastle was founded. This was to be the last expedition that Odo led on behalf of the Crown; thereafter he was to be part of the problem himself, engineering treasonable plots against two kings of England – his half-brother William I and his nephew William II.

• The Fruits of Victory •

After the Conquest, Odo became the wealthiest of the Norman tenants-in-chief in England. In Domesday Book he is credited with estates, chiefly concentrated in the south-east, valued at about £3,050. His lands far exceeded those of any other Norman's holdings; with 456 manors spread over twenty-two English counties. In all, these manors amounted to almost 1,700 hides, roughly the equivalent of 200,000 acres. Odo would have been delighted with an accolade he received in 2000 when *The Sunday Times* placed him fourth in a Rich List of non-royal Britons during the last millennium, with a fortune estimated at £43.2 billion (in 2000) – a dubious honour dubiously calculated. He would have been less pleased that curiously both his brother, Robert of Mortain and William of Warenne came in above him. Indeed, three out of the top four in the list were men who had accompanied William to England in 1066 (Bridgeford 2004, 209–10).

Odo appears to have acquired the bulk of his land in the five years after Hastings, but continued to accumulate assets right up to his fall from grace in 1082. He received his Kentish estates first of all. In terms of value he held almost half the land of Kent, more than that of the Archbishop of Canterbury. He then acquired his estates in Buckinghamshire, Bedfordshire, Surrey,

36 The distribution of Bishop Odo's estates in England from Domesday Book. *After Tsurushima, 2011*

Table1: The English Lands Held in Chief by Odo of Bayeux: By Counties (Ivens, 1984)

County	*Hides*	*Value*	*Demesne Hides*	*Value*
Kent	393	£1605 ls.	51.25	£201
Oxon.	307	£402 4s.	79	£160
Bucks.	223.75	£169 11s.	9.25	£5 10s.
Essex	191	£142 13s. 10d.	47	£47 5s.
Surrey	140.5	£148 13s.	56.5	£76 12s.
Lincs.	119	£112 9s.	6.75	£9 10s.
Herts.	66.3	£70 11s. 11d	12.5	£19 0s. 11d.
Norfolk	47	£100 15s. 2d.	?	?
Suffolk	39	£58 13s. 10d.	?	?
Hants.	34.375	£34 11s.		
Beds.	30.25	£40 6s. 8d.	12.25	£16
Warwicks.	18.625	£3 10s.		
Wilts.	18	£20 10s.		
N'hants.	13.85	£13 3s.		
Berks.	11.5	£8 10s.		
Worcester	10	£6 2s.		
Somerset	8	£10		
Cambs.	6.875	£16		
Notts.	6.3438	£10 2s.		
Dorset	6	£6		
Glouc.	3.875	£16		
Sussex	3	£30		
Total	1697.3	£3035 7s. 5d	274.5	£534 17s. 11d.

Hertfordshire and Essex, areas where he was active in the post-Conquest period. There was a direct link between his Kentish estates and those to the north of London. Wealthy tenants in Kent often held outlying estates in the second zone of acquisition. For example, Odo's richest tenant in Kent, Ralph fitz Turold, also held blocks of land in Essex, Hertfordshire and Oxfordshire, while another major Kentish landholder, Ansgot of Rochester had land straddling the Buckinghamshire–Bedfordshire border. The land Odo acquired in East Anglia (1068–70 and after 1075) and Lincolnshire (after 1075) he distributed to tenants who were prepared to take part in the colonisation of those counties. Men close to Odo, such as Wadard, had three bites of the cherry and gained land in Kent (valued at £42 16*d* in 1086) immediately after Hastings, in Oxfordshire (valued at £55 5*s*) in the late ten-sixties and in Lincolnshire (valued at £30 1*s* 4*d*) in the mid-ten-seventies (Tsurushima 2011).

The precise method used to transfer land from the English to the Normans varied in different parts of the kingdom. In the south and in the Thames Valley the main unit of land transfer seems to have been the Hundred, a subdivision of the Saxon Shire. In Kent, a county with over Sixty Hundreds in the eleventh century, Odo had control of thirty-one of them (Fleming 1987, 98).

In Oxfordshire Odo took over a large group of manors to the west of the River Cherwell, lying in Wootton Hundred. Almost half of the bishop's Oxfordshire holdings were located in Wootton; in all they comprised 161 hides, seventy-nine of which were in demesne, that were held directly by the bishop. It is probable that this nucleated group of manors represented a pre-Conquest estate, but Domesday Book only records a handful of the Saxon owners. Odo's estates were never organised into baronies as occurred with the estates of other great magnates, probably because the bishop was disgraced before this could be achieved. It does appear that in Wootton we can see a proto-barony based on the valuable manor of Deddington. Odo's three principal tenants in Wootton were trusted supporters with extensive estates elsewhere. Ilbert de Lacy, Wadard and Adam held more than eighty per cent non-demesne land of Odo's Wootton estate between them (Ivens 1980).

Much of the land Odo acquired had previously belonged to the Godwines and other English nobles who had fought at Hastings and accordingly forfeited their estates after 1066. These confiscations allowed Odo to install new tenants and reward his principal Norman followers. Surprisingly, many of these supporters did not belong to the Norman higher aristocracy and men of relatively humble origins became Odo's English barons. Tenants such as Ilbert de Lacy, Hugh de Port and Roger Bigot held very modest estates in Normandy yet were handsomely rewarded after Hastings and went on to found important English families. Other major English tenants, such as Wadard, Herbert fitz Ivo and Ralph de Courbépine, are not recorded as holding land in Normandy at all. A number of active followers were launched on prestigious careers by Odo; for instance, Adam fitz Hubert was appointed a Domesday commissioner and, significantly, Hugh de Port was one of those responsible for proscribing Odo and the other rebels in 1088 (Bates 1975).

• The Trial of Penenden Heath •

Odo gained a reputation for defrauding the Church and others of their lands – a reputation that was deserved – but he probably behaved no more badly than many of his peers. It is true that many of Odo's acquisitions were gained illegally; he was particularly aggressive in his procurement of land in Surrey where Domesday Book records many complaints, such as, 'the county states that he [Odo] had no right there' and 'he did not have livery or the King's writ for it' and 'the bishop himself seized Rodsell and Farncombe' (Bates 1970, 190). The *Liber Benefactorum* of Ramsey Abbey in Cambridgeshire complained that Bishop Odo had 'lawlessly' seized the abbey's lands or rights 'by violence'. After his death, several chroniclers commented on this avaricious aspect of his character which was embodied in Orderic Vitalis' account of his life. According to Orderic, Odo was a man of insatiable ambition and 'the greatest oppressor of the people and the destroyer of monasteries'. Proof of this was apparently provided by a significant event known as the Trial of Penenden Heath, which was probably held between 1075 and 1077. The term 'trial' in this context was a judicial examination of rival claims of land tenure, namely between Archbishop Lanfranc and Bishop Odo. The trial was held over three days near to Maidstone in Kent, where the Saxon moot (county assembly) had traditionally been convened. It was this continuity from Saxon to Norman that has made the Penenden Heath case of particular interest to historians, who for long have regarded it as evidence of Norman respect for Anglo-Saxon legal custom. More recently, historians have pointed out that there are several varying records of the trial and no agreement about which should be regarded as the definitive version of events (Le Patourel 1948). Indeed, some historians now argue that the trial demonstrated the undermining of Anglo-Saxon governance by the power of private interests rather than evidence of the continuation of Anglo-Saxon law and custom after the Conquest (Cooper 2001). This is not a universally held view and Bates has argued that Penenden and other pleas constitute evidence of the orderliness of the Norman settlement rather than the reverse, 'that the conquerors sought to resolve as peacefully as possible the resulting tensions … and that the ten-seventies and eighties in particular were a period of steady adjustment and integration' (Bates, 1978).

Lanfranc requested an enquiry into the activities of Odo, who he claimed had defrauded the Church and possibly the Crown during his tenure as Earl of Kent. Various eminent figures were present, including Geoffrey, Bishop of Coutances representing the king, Lanfranc representing the Church, Arnost, Bishop of Rochester, and Aethelric II, the former Bishop of Selsey, described as a 'very old man, very learned in the laws of the land', who was brought by cart 'in order to discuss and expound the ancient laws and customs'. There were also present a contingent of English witnesses as experts on ancient laws and customs as well as Norman representation. The trial ended with the partial recovery of properties for the Church from Odo and others; but most of the lands had not been lost to Odo, but to Earl Godwine and his family before the Conquest. Odo had simply succeeded to these encroachments and the conflict between Lanfranc and Odo was a rerun of that between Archbishop Robert of Jumièges and Godwine in 1051–52. One consequence of the trial was the realisation that there was a need to have a definitive record of the ownership and administration of Crown property – a need that was met by the commissioning of Domesday Book a decade later. It is also possible that this trial, which saw the first indictment of Odo, established the precedent for him to be stripped of his English properties entirely just a few years later. Domesday Book records several other disputes over land that Odo is claimed to have acquired illicitly, but also shows evidence of his work in allocating lands to their new owners after the Conquest.

Despite the Penenden Heath judgment, several of Odo's tenants were recorded in Domesday Book (c. 1086) as still holding the land that had legally been restored to Christ Church, Canterbury. The start of the often bitter rivalry between Odo and Lanfranc is normally attributed to Penenden Heath, exacerbated by Lanfranc's role in the arrest and imprisonment of Odo in 1082. It is difficult to disentangle the opinions of later chroniclers such as Orderic Vitalis who emphasised the antagonism between the two men. This may well have been exaggerated, although there is a curious

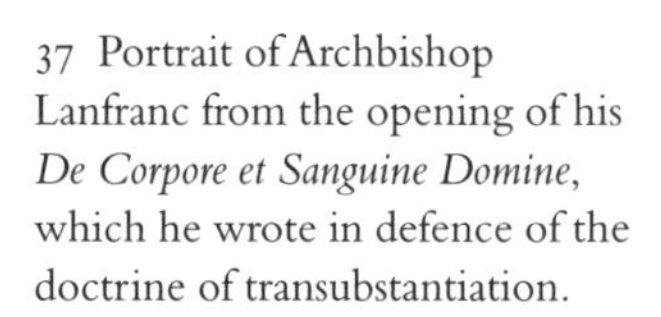

37 Portrait of Archbishop Lanfranc from the opening of his *De Corpore et Sanguine Domine*, which he wrote in defence of the doctrine of transubstantiation.

symmetry between their respective roles in the diocese of Bayeux and in Kent. In Normandy, Lanfranc was abbot of St Étienne in Caen, which lay within Odo's jurisdiction as Bishop of Bayeux, but enjoyed widespread exemptions from episcopal responsibilities; while in England, Lanfranc was Archbishop of Canterbury in the heart of Odo's secular estates. There seems to be little doubt that Odo took pleasure in devastating Lanfranc's estates during the Barons' Revolt of 1088.

• Bayeux Cathedral •

Some of the wealth Odo accumulated in England was transferred to Bayeux and the new cathedral benefited greatly from his benefactions. Odo is known to have visited Normandy, sometimes for several months at a time, in 1074, 1077, 1080 and 1082. On 14 July 1077 Odo's cathedral of the Holy Virgin at Bayeux was consecrated, although it may not have been complete as it was normal practice to consecrate churches before they were finished. The consecration ceremony was led by Archbishop John of Rouen and attended by King William, Queen Matilda and many other Norman notables. There were several other important consecrations in Normandy in 1077: these included the cathedral at Évreux, also dedicated to the Virgin Mary, the Abbaye aux Hommes and the Abbaye aux Dames in Caen, and the abbey church at the highly influential abbey of Bec. The cathedral was burnt and badly damaged by Henry I in 1105, when the poet Serlo records that 'thousands' of citizens sought refuge there. It was damaged again by Henry II in 1159 and, as a result, the only surviving sections of Odo's work are the crypt and the bases of the west towers, which incorporate semi-circular Romanesque windows. Even this section of Odo's work is concealed by later Gothic porches. The bishop employed the best available masons and sculptors in the construction of his cathedral; although the crypt capitals are mostly decorated with simple foliate designs they are of high quality. Something of the grandeur of Odo's work can be appreciated through two of the most impressive capitals from the destroyed eleventh-century transepts, which are now displayed in the crypt. One of the capitals has a representation of Christ after the resurrection with St Thomas the Incredulous and St Peter; the other portrays Christ holding a small figure, representing a departed soul, on his knee (Neveux 2007).

38 A maquette of Bishop Odo's Romanesque cathedral at Bayeux.

Despite the bishop's many and prolonged absences while performing the roles of Earl of Kent and regent of England, he maintained his involvement in Bayeux cathedral business as bishop. He continued to accumulate property for the cathedral and protected his clergy when necessary. Several members of the Bayeux chapter held land in England. Nine of Odo's protégés obtained bishoprics either in Normandy or in England and four became abbots. By the 1080s he would have had an impressive network of contacts spread across the Anglo-Norman Church and beyond. Charters also show that during the 1070s he made grants to abbeys within his diocese exempting them from some aspects of episcopal authority.

Perhaps the most unexpected aspect of Odo's work as bishop was his patronage of the arts, beyond the rebuilding of his cathedral. Undoubtedly, this sponsorship was undertaken in order to increase his prestige and that of his See, and perhaps it is overly sentimental to suggest that it shines a different light on the character of a churchman who was able to compartmentalise his activities to the extent of waging savage warfare at the same time as promoting artistic enterprise. By far the most important example of his artistic enterprises was the Bayeux Tapestry. It would have been in keeping with what we know of the man if it had been commissioned specifically to display at the consecration of his cathedral in 1077. In a year when there were several important consecration ceremonies it would have been a typically audacious stratagem to make Bayeux stand out conspicuously from the other Norman churches by producing his great hanging at the consecration.

Odo's Church activities extended to England; not so much in his role as bishop, but as Earl of Kent he protected and endowed St Augustine's Abbey in Canterbury, St Albans Abbey and Rochester Cathedral, all of whom acknowledged Odo as a benefactor. He also played an important role in the translation of relics of St Adrian at St Augustine's, with a care that is contrasted to Lanfranc's attitude to the relics of Saxon saints at Christ Church, which some historians characterise as cavalier. There is no evidence that Odo transferred his interest in education to England either, but his protégés from Bayeux were enthusiastic educators. For example, Archbishop Thomas of Bayeux established a schoolmaster at York between 1070 and 1100 and more generally schools were founded at many cathedrals in the following century (Orme 2006, 46–50).

• Odo's Castles •

Unlike the great Domesday holdings of other tenants-in-chief, Odo's estates were never formally arranged into baronies. This is probably because he built up his empire very quickly and his land was forfeited before 1086. Nevertheless, it is possible to detect the beginning of a geographical organisation around major central manors which can be seen as proto-baronies. A Kentish barony based on Rochester, a south-Midlands barony based on Deddington and an East Anglian/Lincolnshire barony possibly based on Castle Rising/Snettisham. The chroniclers attribute castles at Dover, Pevensey, Tonbridge and Rochester to Odo, and although he is associated in one way or another with all of them, this list is faulty. Dover Castle was granted to Odo along with his earldom of Kent, but although it was in his hands in 1067 during Count Eustace's abortive uprising, after that his name is not associated with the site. Indeed, records, both archaeological and documentary, for the castle in the century after Hastings are very elusive.

The great age of Norman keep castles came after Odo, and most of the castles he was involved with were neither keeps nor motte and baileys. They were large open enclosures, as they had been during the Carolingian era, capable of housing large armies. Dover Castle certainly fell into this category, although there may have been two early stone towers there which were demolished in the eighteenth century. Only Tonbridge seems to have originated as a motte and bailey, the construction of which was begun in 1067 by Richard fitz Gilbert. It occupied a strategic site to the north of a

39 Tonbridge Castle, a motte and bailey castle controlling the crossing of the River Medway in Kent. *Extract from the Ordnance Survey 2nd Edition, 1895*

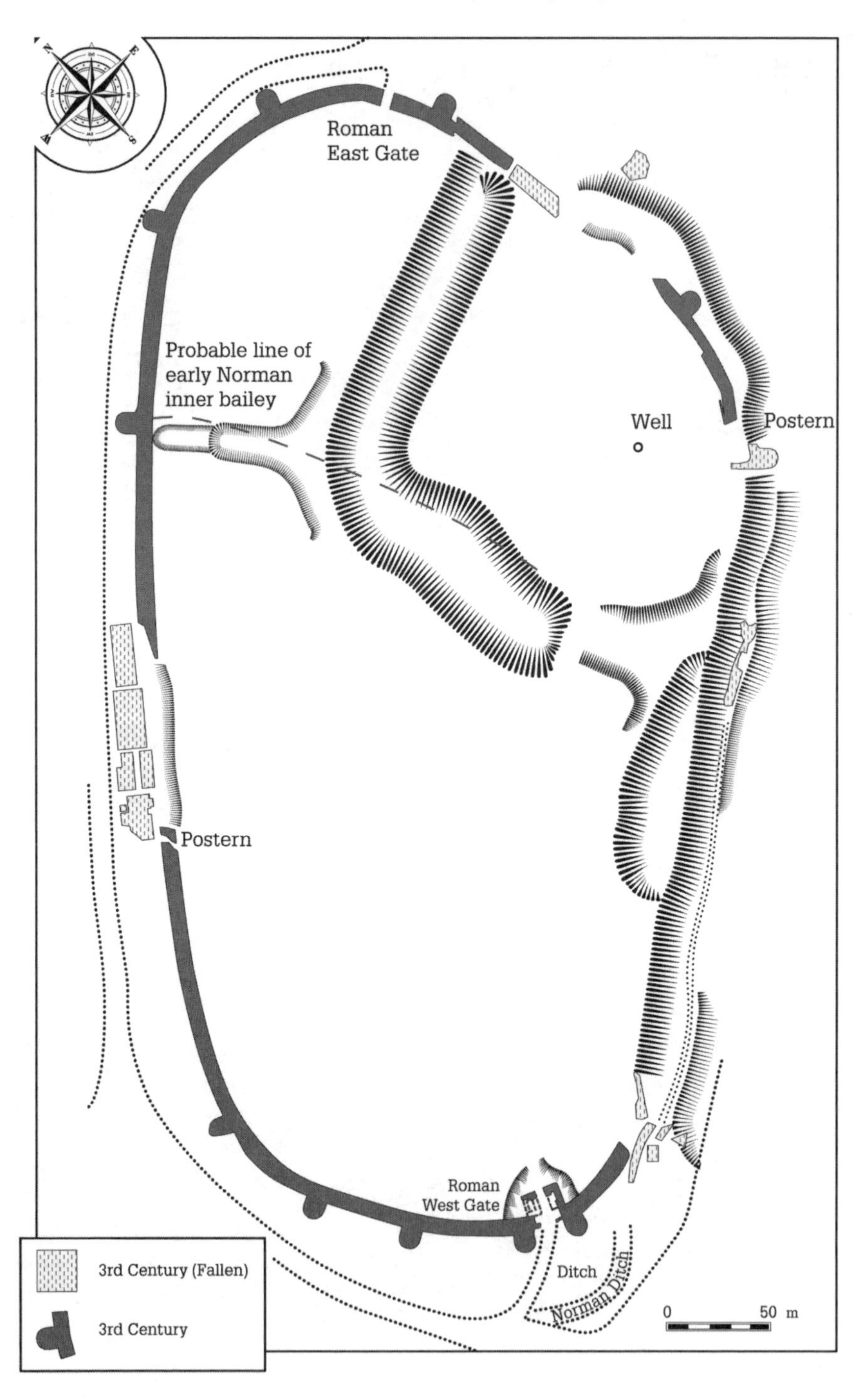

40 Plan of Pevensey Castle.

bend in the River Medway, overlooking an ancient river crossing. A flat-topped motte was surrounded by a circular moat, with one ditched bailey to the south-east and a second, slightly larger, bailey to the north. Tributary streams to the west of the castle were channelled and diverted to feed the moat. A triangular market place lay immediately to the north-east of the castle. It was this site that Odo held briefly in 1088, after which it was captured and burnt to the ground. Subsequently, fitz Gilbert was pardoned for his role in the Barons' Revolt and the castle was rebuilt, partly in stone (Kent County Council 2003).

William of Malmesbury claimed that Odo held Pevensey Castle, but it had actually been under the control of his brother Robert since 1067. Nevertheless, Pevensey Castle figures conspicuously in Odo's story – as the landing point of the invasion fleet, as the headquarters of his brother's *castlery*, and where Odo was besieged during the Barons' Revolt of 1088. A Roman fort was built here, with massive fortifications, in the late third century. There was more or less continuous occupation of the 4ha site up to the Norman Conquest, when there was a market town with fifty-two burgesses contained within the walls, a harbour and a considerable salting industry here. The defensive walls were probably strengthened and an earth and timber structure built at the eastern end of the enclosure, thus creating an inner and an outer bailey. This is likely to have been banked and ditched with a substantial timber palisade, which is indicated by the levying of regular services of 'heckage', due from local manors. There may have been an early free-standing masonry tower of possible eleventh-century date within the enclosure, but there does not seem to have been a motte here. The inner bailey area contained more than 1m's depth of dark earth midden deposits in the Saxo-Norman period, before the building of the keep (c. 1200), some of which can be attributed to the Norman invasion forces of 1066. There was evidence of concentrations of latrine waste, which reflected both a greater intensity of human occupation and the use of the general area for penning and stabling animals (Fulford & Rippon 2011, 1–3, 125). Pevensey appears to have suffered badly in the immediate wake of the invasion, and when it passed into the hands of Robert of Mortain in 1067, the number of burgesses fell by half. However, by the time of the Domesday survey it had risen to 110 and a mint had been established, reflecting Robert of Mortain's establishment of a planned borough here, outside the castle walls. It has been argued that this was the harbour settlement to the east of the fort, but it could also have been at

Westham, whose layout has all the characteristics of an early new town. In 1088 Odo and his brother Robert were besieged at Pevensey. The *Anglo-Saxon Chronicle* records:

> The king with his host … learnt that the bishop had gone to the castle at Pevensey; and the king with his host followed after, and besieged the castle on all sides with a very great host for fully six weeks … Thereafter food ran short inside the castle; then they asked for a truce, and surrendered it to the king. (Lyne, 42–3)

Only Rochester in Kent seems definitely to have been in Odo's hands. John of Worcester says that 'Odo carried off booty of every kind to Rochester' and other writers confirm that Odo swore to surrender his castle at Rochester to William Rufus in 1088. Rochester Castle was built soon after the Conquest, when the city was in Odo's hands. It stood between the River Medway and the Saxon cathedral on a slight hill, guarding the bridge over the river. The first reference to a castle here was in Domesday Book, which recorded that the Bishop of Rochester had been given land in Aylesford, 'in exchange for land on which the castle stands'. The *Textus Roffensis* (c. 1122) enigmatically noted that the land on which the castle stood was said to be 'the best part of the city'. The first castle was in the form of an earth and timber ringwork, which lay in the south-west corner of the Roman town of *Durobrivae*, and was comparable with the earliest phases of other important castles such as Exeter, the Tower of London and Winchester. The ringwork enclosed an area of around 1.7ha; there is no evidence of a motte here, although there does appear to have been a second, somewhat smaller, outwork or bailey to the south, known as Boley Hill. Excavations in the 1970s identified a massive rampart, incorporating a section of Roman wall and a ditch, which was almost 7m deep. Nothing is known of the internal plan of Odo's castle, but there would have been a wooden hall, numerous ancillary structures and possibly a timber tower (Flight & Harrison 1978). It would have been in this earth and timber castle that Odo and the barons held out against William Rufus in 1088. It was the site of Odo's last stand in England (Paul Drury Partnership 2009, 12–17). Odo's castle was replaced by a castle built by Gundulf, Bishop of Rochester in the late 1080s; this in turn was superseded by the great stone keep built by William de Corbeil, the Archbishop of Canterbury after 1127, which stands today.

Deddington Castle - 11th Century

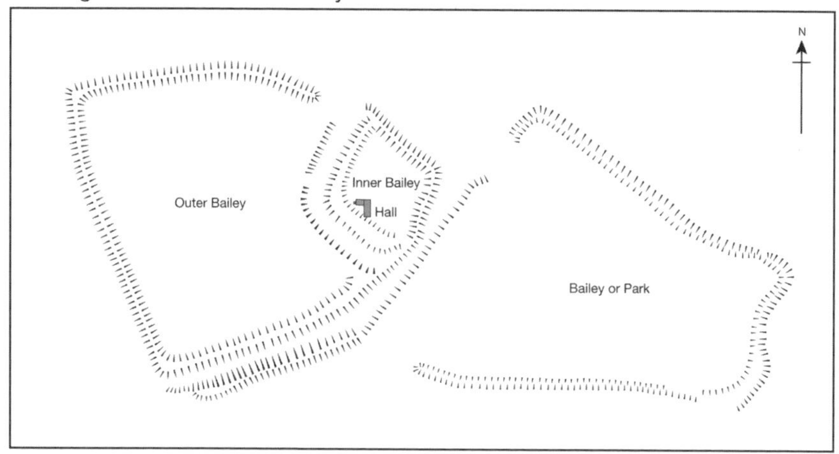

Rochester Castle - pre 1088

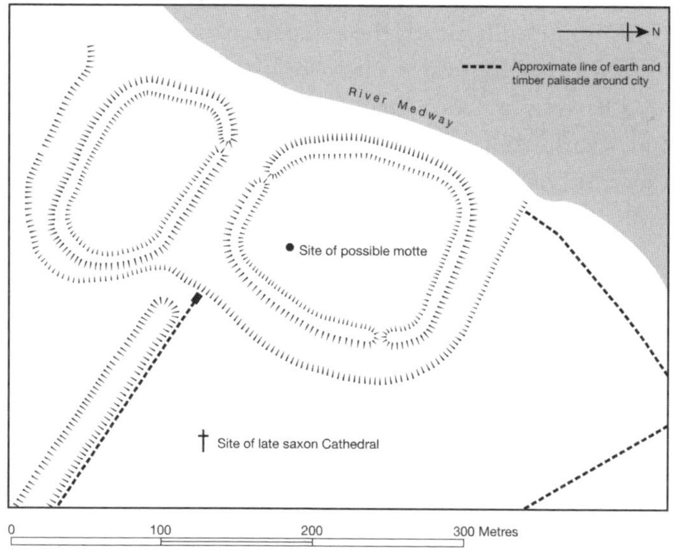

41 Rochester Castle in the eleventh century (*after Paul Drury Associates*) and Deddington Castle (*from Ordnance Survey 2nd Edition, 1895*). The eastern enclosure at Deddington is probably not contemporary with the main castle bailey, which appears to have been constructed by Odo.

It has been convincingly argued that another of Odo's castles was at Deddington in Oxfordshire (Ivens 1984, 118). Deddington lay at the centre of Odo's spread of Buckinghamshire and Oxfordshire estates (see colour plate 23) and within one of the most concentrated blocks of his holdings.

Furthermore, Deddington, along with Hoo (Kent), Bramley (Surrey) and Snettisham (Norfolk), was the richest of all Odo's manors, valued at £60 in 1086, and was maintained in demesne by the bishop. The castle lies on the eastern edge of Deddington village, about 100m to the east of the church and market place, which it clearly pre-dates. The layout of Deddington is that of a planned borough, which was laid out in the twelfth century on the line of the Oxford to Banbury road. The castle earthworks consist of impressive banks and ditches forming a sub-rectangular enclosure of about 3.5ha (8.5 acres) with an inner enclosure of about 0.4ha (1 acre) at the eastern end. The inner enclosure was subject to intensive excavation in 1947–51 and 1976–79, and although some initial results have appeared in print, a definitive report on this work is still awaited (Jope & Threlfall 1946–7; Ivens 1984).

The size of the earthworks of the large outer enclosure had led to speculation that they might be Iron Age or possibly late Saxon; however, as late Saxon pottery was found underneath the rampart at the eastern end an early Norman date for this impressive earthwork now seems most likely. Deddington could have been Odo's *caput* headquarters where he would have assembled his south Midland forces. The reports of the inner bailey excavations indicate a complex sequence of medieval structures which have been seriously disturbed by continual rebuilding and stone robbing. The earliest structure, dating to the eleventh century, is an earthen ringwork, inside which a small L-shaped stone hall was built, with a garderobe pit at its west end, all of which appear to be contemporary with Odo. A recent geophysical survey of the inner bailey indicates that the ringwork is a regular rectangle or square and calls into question a secondary motte postulated by the excavators. Traces of earthworks to the east of the castle may represent a second bailey or an enclosed park of similar size to the main enclosure, giving a butterfly shape in plan to the whole complex. There is evidence of a line of fish ponds of medieval date running to the south of the castle earthworks.

Odo's third possible *caput* castle lay at Castle Rising within the manor of Snettisham, close to the north coast of Norfolk. Snettisham had belonged to Archbishop Stigand before the Conquest and was one of the bishop's most valuable estates, worth £85 in 1086. In the mid-twelfth century the village of (Castle) Rising was chosen as the site of William de Albini's grand keep with its imposing ringwork defence and associated planned town. It is tempting but dangerous in the light of the incomplete archaeological evidence, to presuppose that Odo had an earlier enclosure castle on this

42 Aerial view of Castle Rising, Norfolk, the large outer enclosure could have been built by Odo and represent his headquarters in the east of England. *English Heritage*

dramatic site. Nevertheless, excavations in the 1970s did identify considerable pre-keep stratification dating from the eleventh century. This included what might have been a wooden bow-sided hall, which had been demolished well before 1140. The excavators reflected that 'it would not be surprising if part or all of the location was already set aside within a manorial *enciente*' – was it in fact Odo's East Anglian *caput*? (Morley & Gurney 1997, 133).

The two castles in England that are most closely associated with Odo, and which he was probably responsible for building, Rochester and Deddington, have somewhat similar designs. Both consist of large heavily defended earth and timber enclosures. Neither appears to have had a motte, but could have had stone or wooden towers. Both are capable of holding large numbers of soldiers and horses and of being used as a base for large-scale armed raids in the surrounding region or for garrisoning an army before a set battle. It is tempting to see them as the bases from which Odo won and controlled much of his English land. The absence of a third castle of similar design and dimensions in East Anglia or Lincolnshire may be because the bishop obtained these lands at a later date and did not have time to construct a major fortification here. It is possible that the earliest phases of Castle Rising performed the same role as a *caput* for the bishop as the enclosure castles at Deddington and Rochester.

Odo's early castles, along with those of the king and other magnates, played a decisive role both in achieving and consolidating the Norman Conquest. They were capable of withstanding a full-scale siege as well as delaying or blocking an enemy's progress. They acted as bases for controlling the surrounding territory, administrative centres, high-status dwellings, sites for dispensing justice and entertaining, and permanent demonstrations of power. Nevertheless the basic simplicity of Odo's castles compares strikingly with his cathedral and other contemporary ecclesiastic buildings. It was in the decades after Odo's death that castles became grand stone keeps and far more elaborate affairs. Castles and palaces grew closer together in design, as seen, for example, in the Bishop of Winchester's palace at Wolvesey.

• Robert of Mortain •

The Conqueror's other half-brother, Robert, also enjoyed considerable rewards in England after 1066. Henry of Huntingdon wrote that Roger [sic] de Mortain ravaged the country around Pevensey before the Battle of Hastings, and he was certainly granted the rape of Pevensey with its castle in 1067. He was also granted the castle at Berkhamsted, William's base before the surrender of London, which may have been his headquarters in England. After helping subdue some of the early attempts to unseat William, notably, his role in destroying Danish forces in Lindsey in 1069, Robert appears to have spent most of his time in Normandy. In England, Robert had estates valued at over £2,100, making him second only to Roger de Montgomery among the post-Conquest lay magnates. Most of his land was in the south-west, where he was by far the largest landholder in Cornwall and he is sometimes referred to as the Count of Cornwall. Robert also held extensive estates in twenty English counties, with concentrations in Somerset, Devon and Dorset. Unlike Odo, Robert held his English estates at the time of the Domesday survey and as a result it is a little easier to trace his activities, which show that he often acquired land in questionable circumstances.

Robert, like Odo, was no respecter of monastic lands and according to Domesday Book twenty-four institutions lost land to the count, notably, St Albans, Glastonbury and Christ Church, Canterbury. Robert acquired the most valuable estate in Sussex at West Firle from Wilton Priory. In Somerset he acquired the manor of Bishopstone, which had belonged to an English owner called Tovi, who had found a miraculous cross on a hilltop called St Michael's Hill on his estate. The cross was transferred to a new monastery that Tovi had founded in Essex at Waltham and became a sacred symbol for King Harold and the English at Hastings. Tovi granted Bishopstone to Athelney Abbey and after the Conquest Robert appears to have acquired the estate by sleight of hand. Robert built a massive castle on St Michael's Hill, which was perceived as a calculated insult by the English. The site, known as Montacute Castle, was besieged in 1068/69 as part of the western uprising, which was suppressed by Geoffrey of Coutances (Golding 1990, 119–44).

Robert had created new towns, markets and fairs in Normandy before the Conquest and he continued this activity on his English estates. Boroughs were established next to his castles at Pevensey, Berkhamsted, Montacute and Launceston. At Launceston Domesday records that, 'The count of Mortain took away a market from this manor [St Stephen's by Launceston] and put it in his castle.' Another Domesday entry, for St Germans, Cornwall, records that, 'In this manor there is a market on Sunday, but it is reduced to nothing by the Count of Mortain's market, which is nearby in his castle [Trematon] on the same day.'

If Robert had no reservations about depriving English monasteries of land, he was generous towards Norman houses. In particular, the family abbey of Grestain was favoured and granted ten estates in England by Robert with a value of more than £50. He also gave land to the priory within his castle at Mortain and to the abbey of Fécamp.

7

• Odo the Pontiff – A Step Too Far •

There are several purple patches in Odo's story, where the chroniclers have left a expanded, but still incomplete, record of events which enables a fuller narrative account of events to be compiled. It is particularly frustrating that there are yawning gaps between these highlights. The two events leading to the bishop's spectacular fall from grace were covered more fully by the chroniclers than the rest of his life story. In 1082–83 Odo raised a private army and as a consequence was imprisoned by King William, and in 1088 Odo stoked a rebellion against William Rufus and was banished permanently from England. In between, when the bishop was a prisoner in Rouen, the record is blank. The details of the timing and the precise nature of Odo's crime are uncertain; what is clear, however, is that Odo angered William so profoundly that the king was prepared to imprison his half-brother for the rest of his life. In 1082 the *Anglo-Saxon Chronicle* states simply, without amplification, that 'in this year the king arrested bishop Odo'. Later sources suggest that the arrest might have been made in the following year; if so, it would have been before William's return to Normandy for Easter 1083. Guibert of Nogent, writing in around 1108, was the first to suggest that Odo was planning to seize the English throne after William's death (Bates 2004–11, 10). Wace, writing a century later, reported that Odo coveted the English throne and had made covert enquiries about there being any precedent for a bishop becoming king; but long before this an alternative version of the story had emerged, according to which Odo had been attempting to buy the papacy in Rome for himself. Although both of these interpretations would have been consistent with Odo's reputation as an opportunist, neither is totally satisfactory, and they leave a trail of unanswered questions about the feasibility, timing and logistics of either scheme.

It was Orderic Vitalis who wrote an 'inflated and dramatic account' of how Odo had raised an army in England with the intention of taking it to Rome in order to seize the papacy. Bates articulates the general incredulity that this story tends to generate, 'The essential difficulty obstructing acceptance of this story is its basic improbability.' Nevertheless, he continues, 'It survives in three textually independent versions which have enough in common to suggest a well-founded and widely known source' (Bates 1975, 15). Orderic claimed that Odo determined on his bid for the Apostolic See on hearing that 'certain sorcerers [soothsayers] at Rome' had predicted that a prelate with his name would become pope (OV, vii). By the early 1080s Odo was immensely rich with powers second only to those of the king, but he knew that this was almost certainly the limit of his secular power and that it was virtually impossible for him to become king. He might have wanted to add the metropolitan See of Canterbury to the list of offices he held, but that position was already occupied by his rival, Lanfranc, and in any case would not have given him significantly more power than he already possessed. Odo was wealthy enough to have his own network of spies and informers in Italy and they would have brought him news that the situation was ripe for an opportunistic coup by the right man.

• The Normans in Italy •

Odo knew that the Normans had made great acquisitions in Italy and were now the most powerful force in central and southern Italy; he also knew that the papacy was in trouble and at the time dependent on Norman support for its survival. Odo could well have believed that with his wealth, his contacts and his cunning he was that right man. The Conquest of southern Italy by the Normans had mainly been the work of the Hauteville brothers from the Cotentin, with the support of many other minor nobles. Unlike the seizure of the English crown, which had been undertaken by William as a carefully planned military operation, successfully accomplished within the course of a few months, the Norman conquests in the Mediterranean were piecemeal and took over half a century to complete. Furthermore, the Conquest of England was undertaken by Duke William with an army specially recruited for the task, while the Mediterranean lands were won by miscellaneous groups of mercenaries under the control of minor lords often operating independently (Bouet 1994, 11–23).

The early Norman adventurers established themselves in southern Italy at the expense of local Byzantine lords. In his *History of the Normans* (c. 1080), the chronicler Amatus of Monte Cassino wrote a colourful description of Norman pilgrims riding 'through the meadows and gardens – happy and joyful on their horses, cavorting hither and thither' and added that 'the citizens of Venosa saw these unfamiliar knights and wondered at them and were afraid'. Amatus also recorded that the Archbishop of Salerno had a vision in which St Matthew proclaimed that 'this land has been given to the Normans by God'. It was an era of easy alliances and shifting loyalties, but by 1059 Robert Guiscard, one of the Hauteville family, had become Duke of Apulia and Calabria, and after the capture of Bari from the Byzantines in 1071 Norman control of southern Italy was virtually complete. There was significant contact between Normandy and the newly established Norman Italian lands which often sent money back to the homeland for religious endowments. Norman prelates such as Geoffrey of Coutances and perhaps Odo as well had called upon their kinsfolk in the south for money to help them fund their building activities at home. Many of the treasures that were sent back to Normandy were the result of looting from Greek churches in southern Italy (Douglas 1969, 111).

• The Normans and the Papacy •

The Normans were no strangers to papal politics. In Italy they demonstrated a cavalier attitude to allies and enemies alike and had fought their way to dominance in the south by frequently exchanging one for the other. Relations between the Normans and the papacy had been particularly volatile and they and their leaders had frequently been excommunicated. Despite the chequered history of their dealings with the papacy, in 1080 Robert Guiscard became the protector of Pope Gregory VII, viewing him as a buttress against the Holy Roman Emperor, Henry IV. Gregory is known to history as a great Church reformer, but for much of his time as pope he was deeply embroiled in the tangled politics of central Italy. The Holy Roman Empire controlled the Lombard states in the north of Italy and the Normans controlled most of the south of Italy and Sicily, with Rome and

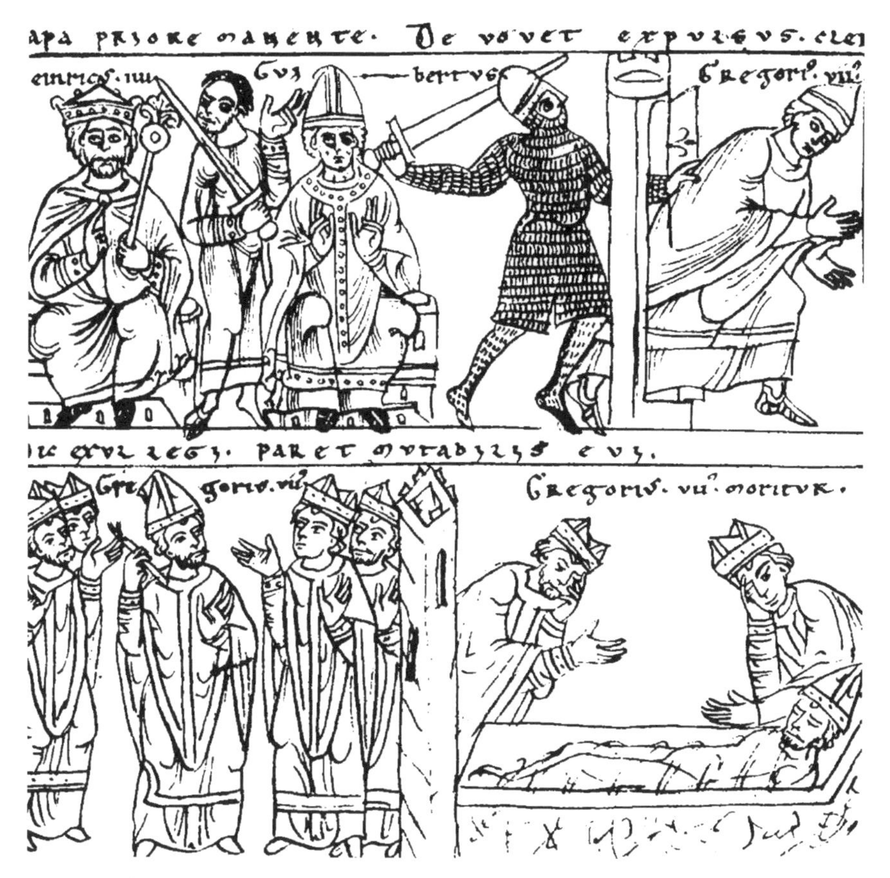

43 Scenes from the life of Pope Gregory VII from Otto, Bishop of Freising's *World Chronicle*, a twelfth-century copy of original illustrations in the manuscript presented by the author to his nephew, Fredrick I, in 1157. The top panel shows Gregory being expelled from St Peter's by Emperor Henry IV.

the Papal States lying between these two power blocks. Pope Gregory was involved in a bitter and prolonged dispute with Emperor Henry, which became known as the Investiture Conflict. At the heart of this quarrel was an argument over the primacy of popes, particularly in the question of who chose the bishops, and new canon law which proclaimed the exclusive right of the College of Cardinals to elect a pope. Matters came to a head in 1076 over the choice of a new archbishop of Milan, when Emperor Henry tried to appoint his own nominee and claimed that he had deposed the pope. In response, Gregory excommunicated the emperor, divesting him of his 'royal dignity' and freeing Henry's subjects of any oaths they had sworn to him.

Because he lacked sufficient support to force an armed confrontation at this stage, Henry was obliged to back down and there ensued an uneasy peace between the two, but four years later Gregory excommunicated Henry once more. This time it was the pope who was the weaker; thirteen cardinals deserted him and Henry pronounced Archbishop Guibert of Ravenna as the new pope. Guibert chose the title of Clement III and remained as an irritant anti-pope until his death in 1100.

In 1081 Henry arrived at the gates of Rome with his army and the anti-pope, but he had insufficient troops to take the city as to his surprise many Romans remained loyal to Gregory. In the spring of 1082 Henry made another unsuccessful attempt to enter Rome, but despite this setback his support amongst many factions in Italy was growing. Duke Robert Guiscard was on campaign in the eastern Adriatic and when he heard of the new threat to Gregory he returned in haste to Italy. When he arrived at Rome he found that Henry had retired to Tuscany and the anti-pope to Tivoli accompanied by a contingent of German soldiers. Consequently, the duke retired to Apulia to deal with an uprising of his own people. At the beginning of 1083 Henry returned to Rome with a larger army and began a serious siege of the city. Eventually, on 2 June the imperial troops breached the walls and entered the city; however, Gregory then took refuge in the heavily fortified Castel Sant'Angelo. There followed a period of stalemate between the two protagonists: Henry clearly had the military advantage, but Gregory still had sufficient support within the city to be able to maintain his base in Rome. Attempts at a negotiated settlement involving the calling of a synod ended in farce when, among other solutions, it was suggested that the pope would not actually perform the coronation of Henry, but pass him down the imperial crown on a stick from the battlements of Sant'Angelo.

• Odo's fall from Grace •

News of the events in Italy would have quickly found their way back to Normandy and England. There were strong familial ties with the Norman states in the Mediterranean, with a steady flow of individuals making their way in both directions. Robert Guiscard's origins were in the Cotentin, not that far from Bayeux, and, reputedly, he never forgot his upbringing there (Douglas 1969, 112). Guiscard's contacts with Norman bishops went back a long way; in the 1050s the young Geoffrey Mowbray, Bishop of Coutances had travelled to meet Robert in Italy and returned with treasures to help him rebuild his cathedral. Robert Guiscard's brother Count Roger, who was largely responsible for wresting control of Sicily from the Muslim emirate, is also recorded as retaining fond memories of his upbringing in the Cotentin as well as his early association with the Abbey of St Evroul.

Odo might have reasoned that Guiscard would welcome a wealthy fellow-Norman pope, who would surely be more accommodating than the stubbornly pious Gregory. Gregory was seen as 'fiery and passionate' but also as headstrong and a 'tactless individualist' (Hetherington 1994, 56). The Normans in the north had a poor opinion of the papacy and Odo would have been aware that elections to the Holy See had frequently been determined by money or violence. The theme of exploitation and corruption at Rome was common amongst eleventh-century satirists. Odo's protégé Serlo had written much on the failings of the papacy and claimed that wise men had pointlessly crossed the Alps to reach Rome, as no one listened to them (Bates 1975, 202). After 1077 the unity of the Anglo-Norman royal family began to break up and for the remaining decade of his life the king was at odds with his eldest son, Robert Curthose. Odo might have seen opportunities arising from the rift; but although it is likely that the bishop was in some way involved, he knew that there were limits to his secular power. It may have seemed to Odo that the chaotic state of papal politics offered him a unique chance to occupy the loftiest position in western Christendom and thus satisfy his undoubted ambition.

Odo was able to persuade a number of Anglo-Norman knights to support his cause, although only Earl Hugh of Chester is named. There is no suggestion that he made overtures to Guiscard to further his ambitions, but in the absence of firm evidence it is tempting to imagine the artful Odo employing his diplomatic skills in this direction in order to achieve his aims. Indeed, according to William of Malmesbury, he made advance arrangements in Rome by purchasing a palace in the city, furnishing it at great expense and fortifying it (Bates 1970, 247). Orderic Vitalis notes that, 'Odo bought a palace in Rome and bribed senators' and that he prepared to go there in the company of 'a goodly company of distinguished knights and Earl Hugh of Chester' (OV). The bishop is reported to have bribed some of the Roman gentry and even a number of cardinals to support his audacious bid. William of Malmesbury wrote that, 'He [Odo] had wonderful skill at accumulating treasure, possessed extreme craft in dissembling, so that absent, yet, stuffing the scrips [satchels] of the pilgrims with letters and money, he had nearly purchased the Roman papacy from the citizens' and he was intending to take vast amounts of gold and treasure out of the country, in quantities that 'surpassed anything that our age could imagine' (WM). He also claimed that after the bishop's arrest many sacks full of wrought gold were found in rivers, where they had been hidden.

Odo's wealth was legendary even during his own lifetime and he was obviously prepared to spend prodigious amounts of money in achieving his ambitions. Although revenues from the diocese of Bayeux were intended for the use of the Church, King William claimed that Odo failed to keep proper accounts, implying that he was guilty of embezzlement. Such a concept might have seemed foreign to Odo, who would have seen himself as inseparable from the Church he represented. His wealth and pomp would have reflected that of his Church and his grandeur was that of his cathedrals. It would have been the income from his various estates and activities in England that would have provided the bulk of his wealth. Some, if not most, of the resources required for rebuilding the cathedral after 1066 would have originated in England, and no doubt it was this source of income that formed the preponderance of the money he was going to spend in 1088.

If Odo was making these plans, there was nothing in his public *persona* to show it. He was in Normandy in the autumn of 1082 where, together with his two brothers, Robert and William, he witnessed a charter to the abbey at Grestain. This document agreed that gifts to Grestain should be held on the same terms as those given to the Conqueror's abbey of St Étienne in Caen. This event has been used to demonstrate William's special regard for the monastery where his mother was buried. Poignantly, this meeting of the three middle-aged brothers to protect the memory of their long-dead mother would have been the last time that William and Odo were together on friendly terms. A lifetime of co-operation between the two was about to come to an abrupt and acrimonious end.

Odo assembled his army on the Isle of Wight either in late 1082 or early 1083. When the king heard of the plot he hurried from Normandy and confronted the bishop as he was about to sail. William objected strongly to Odo raising a private army in England and taking it out of the country and in doing so depriving the king of knights required for the defence of the realm. Odo was brought before a council, probably at Winchester, but he objected that as a bishop he was subject only to the pope's jurisdiction. In reply, William of Malmesbury records that the king 'threw him into confinement, saying that he did not seize the bishop of Bayeux, but the earl of Kent' (WM i,

506–7). Reputedly, it was Lanfranc who was Odo's nemesis, by advising the king to give this artful response. Orderic Vitalis used the occasion to give William comprehensive and damning hindsight in condemning 'my brother, to whom I entrusted the care of my entire kingdom, has laid violent hands on her substance, has cruelly oppressed the poor, has seduced my knights on frivolous pretences, and has spread disorder through the whole of England by his unjust exactions' (OV). According to Wace, Odo was then taken to a nearby ship, which, as the wind was favourable, sailed directly to Rouen. Nothing was written about the fate of Odo's assembled troops or of the fleet that was to convey them to Rome. As so few details are provided, it suggests that the chroniclers were writing from anecdotal evidence rather than more reliable sources. The next stage of Odo's life is a complete blank. It is recorded that Odo was held in the Tower at Rouen Castle for four years, and was not allowed to leave it until the king had died (Wace, 9197–9222).

Some scholars simply do not accept the story of Odo's attempt on the papacy and believe that he was arrested for intriguing with Robert Curthose to usurp the king (Chibnall, 4, xxvii–xxx). Other sources are ambivalent. There was no strongly worded response from the pope about Odo's attempt to supplant him; in fact, Gregory seemed to support Odo's position on his trial and protested at the infringement of his clerical status. The pope complained bitterly to his papal legate Hugh of Lyons but adopted a more conciliatory tone when writing to King William. In 1087, not long before he was released, Urban II ordered that no harm should come to Bayeux Cathedral because of Odo's imprisonment, perhaps repeating a decree originally issued by Pope Gregory (Tabuteau 1988, 375). The absence of any reference to Odo's motives in the papal reaction does not necessarily mean that Gregory was unaware of them, for the pope had a great deal more on his mind in early 1083 'than the thwarted ambitions of an eccentric French bishop' (Bates 1975, 15). There also remains the unanswered question of why the king did not punish Hugh, Earl of Chester, who was said by Orderic to be Odo's chief supporter; his crime was, after all, identical to the bishop's. What is undisputed is that the bishop spent the next four years in prison.

• The Tower of Rouen •

We know nothing about Odo's time in prison, how he was treated or what degree of freedom he was allowed. He was presumably under the immediate detention of the constable of the ducal castle at Rouen, who would have been responsible to the *vicomte* of Rouen. The prison was in the keep or tower at Rouen, and the whole fortification came to be known as the 'Tower', like the Tower of London (Round 1892). Indeed, it has been suggested that the design of the White Tower in London was partly based on the Tower in Rouen (Le Maho 2000). There was a postern gate leading from the Seine to the Tower, which meant that Odo would have been shipped directly from the Isle of Wight straight into prison. The Tower had been built by Duke Richard I in the second half of the tenth century and would have probably been the first stone-built keep in Normandy. It was a large quadrilateral-shaped build, whose design seems to have been based on earlier castles at Chartres, Laon and Pithiviers. There is no surviving description of the castle, which was destroyed by the French king, Philippe Augustus, when he took over Normandy in 1204, but there are references to various parts of the Tower. There was a Tower chapel dedicated to St Romain, a kitchen, a reception room, ducal quarters and a gallery linking it to the great hall in the ducal palace. During its lifetime its size became legendary, leading to the twelfth-century expression, 'weighing as much as the Tower of Rouen' (Le Maho 2000, 73–5). Towards the beginning of the Bayeux Tapestry, at the point where Duke William is arranging the release of the captured Earl Harold, a prominent stone castle is depicted (colour plate 24). This grand building is generally believed to be Rouen Castle, but it has also been interpreted as representing Guy de Ponthieu's castle at Beaurain. On balance, its size and its close juxtaposition to William on the Tapestry favour a ducal rather than a comital fortification. In the middle of a crenallated wall there is a tower, or possibly the top of a motte with a tower sitting on it. In either case, this portrait has to be treated with caution, as many of the buildings depicted on the Tapestry are stereotypical rather than accurate representations of actual constructions (Musset 2005, 66–71). Nevertheless, it is ironic that the place where Odo spent what must have been a miserable and frustrating four years of his life is portrayed so proudly on the bishop's own greatest lasting creation.

William had a reputation for being cruel to his prisoners, but the records are silent on Odo's time in incarceration. It is unlikely that he was treated with the same consideration that Henry I is said to have extended to his brother Robert after he was imprisoned in 1106. According to Orderic Vitalis, the king described the conditions of his brother's captivity:

> I have not kept my brother in fetters like a captured enemy, but have placed him as a noble pilgrim … in a royal castle [Devizes, Bristol and Cardiff], and have kept him well supplied with abundance of food and other comforts and furnishing of all kinds.
> (OV, vi, 286–7)

Such imprisonment was known as 'free custody' or 'honourable captivity' and it seems unlikely that Odo did not buy himself preferred treatment whilst he was detained. We do know about one earlier event at the Tower which occurred c. 1000 – William of Hiémois, Duke Richard II's half-brother, escaped from here by climbing down a very long rope, hung from the highest window (van Houts 2000, 67).

There was no attempt to deprive Odo of his bishopric, although Bayeux Cathedral, the abbey of St Vigor and many of his diocesan parish churches were subject to attack and some were badly damaged. In Normandy, although some land was forcibly taken from the cathedral's estates, it seems to have been the bishop's own tenants, such as the *vicomte* of the Bessin, who were largely responsible for such actions. The bishop regained most of the land after his permanent return to Normandy in 1088. In England, however, William the Conqueror stripped Odo of his earldom and had started dismantling his massive English estates by the time Domesday Book was compiled in around 1086. It appears that the task of redistributing the bishop's enormous landholdings had only just begun as for the most part Domesday records Odo's estates as still intact and in his hands. It is possible that there remained doubts about the regularity of the procedure by which Odo was seized and tried; consequently, the royal court may have been reluctant to convict 'the bishop'. According to Domesday Book, Odo remained the largest single landholder in England after the king. Nevertheless, Odo's demesne lands in Kent had already been passed to royal administrators and were being farmed by Robert Latimer, while in Sussex and Gloucestershire his manors were listed along with those belonging to the king (Bates 1975, 17).

Some of Odo's principal vassals were also stripped of their English estates at the time of the bishop's imprisonment. For example, Wadard, who held land in several counties, was deprived of his holdings. However, his son Rainald was able to retain his Oxfordshire estates. William's anger towards Odo was extended even to those who had been helped by the bishop before his imprisonment. Abingdon Abbey felt the king's displeasure when he revoked a charter which had been signed by Odo, acting as regent while the king was in France, which confirmed the abbey's purchase of the manor of Nuneham Courtenay (Oxon). William deprived the abbey of the manor and gave it 'to an unknown person' (Cownie 1998, 41–2).

• Odo the Pontiff •

In Rome, the power struggle between the pope and the emperor continued, and in March 1084 the majority of Pope Gregory's supporters unwisely decided to surrender to the emperor, Henry. On Palm Sunday Gregory was formally deposed by Lombard bishops and the anti-pope Clement was consecrated as his successor. Although Henry did not have complete control of Rome, he was crowned Holy Roman Emperor on Easter Day 1084. On hearing the news from Rome, Robert Guiscard marched on the Holy City and on 24 May he set up camp outside the walls with a large army, which included a sizeable Muslim element. Henry did not stay to fight; he left the city with Clement three days before the Normans arrived, claiming urgent business in the north. Unwisely, the Romans did not surrender immediately and when Guiscard's troops did break into the city they resisted. As a result, the Norman army sacked Rome; there was a frenzy of murder, rape and pillage and much of the ancient city was destroyed by fire. Robert Guiscard had saved the papacy temporarily for Gregory, but it was impossible for the pope to remain in Rome, where the surviving citizens blamed him for the disaster that had fallen upon them (Brown 2003, 172).

The Normans left Rome at the beginning of July, taking Gregory with them. The pope moved to Salerno, within territory safely under Norman control, where he died in May 1085. His rather wistful epitaph was well chosen, 'I have loved justice and hated iniquity; therefore, I [now] die in exile.' His champion, Robert Guiscard, died just two months later of a fever on campaign on the island of Cephalonia. Gregory was succeeded reluctantly by Desiderius, abbot of Monte Cassino, who took the name Victor III. Victor's three-year reign as pope was neither a happy nor a successful one. He only spent short periods of time in Rome, alternating with the ever-present anti-pope Clement, and when he died in 1087 he was succeeded by the Cardinal Bishop of Ostia, Otho de Lagery (Champagne). The soothsayer's prophecy had proved correct: the new pope took the title of Urban II, and there was indeed a pope called Odo in Rome.

• The Death of the Conqueror •

William the Conqueror died on 9 September 1087. The custom was for the dying king to release prisoners who had offended against him. William followed the convention but specified that Odo should remain a prisoner, thus confirming his life sentence. Orderic Vitalis used his record of this occasion to air many of the negative opinions about Odo which have been repeated in order to portray the bishop as a thoroughly unsavoury character. Even though Orderic had a more balanced opinion of Odo than appears from this episode, in this instance the chronicler put words into William's mouth that were to blacken the bishop's name over the centuries. Orderic's account relates that when Odo's other brother, Robert, heard that the bishop was 'to suffer perpetual imprisonment by royal decree, he was sad at heart'. Robert then 'begged for mercy for his brother … and wearied the dying man with his entreaties'. After several others present joined with Robert in begging for Odo's release, the king replied:

> I am amazed that you do not appreciate what kind of man this is for whom you plead. Are you not interceding for a man who has long been an enemy of the church and a cunning instigator of treacherous rebellion? Have I not kept under restraint for four years this bishop who, when he should have been a most just viceroy in England, became the worst oppressor of the people and destroyer of monasteries?

The king went on to prophesy trouble if Odo were to be released, saying, 'I have imprisoned not a bishop but a tyrant. If he goes free, without doubt he will disturb the whole kingdom and bring thousands to destruction.' Interestingly, Orderic records no reference to Odo's attempt to gain the papacy or any other specific misdeeds, just the king's overwhelming sense of betrayal. Eventually, the exhausted king reluctantly relented, as all those around his bed had offered security for the bishop's future good conduct, but with one last expression of his deep misgivings, 'Unwillingly I grant that my brother may be released from prison, but I warn you that he will be the cause of death and grievous harm to many' (OV, vii, 99–101).

It was left to the poet Serlo to celebrate Odo's release from prison with a characteristically unctuous poem:

> While Odo had been in prison the flock had been without a shepherd, but with his release the sun had come out from behind the clouds. The cruelty and barbarity of the world no longer matter and the clergy need no longer fear its oppressions, for the storm has ended and the ship has its pilot again. The mother church is no longer a widow and the father's return has put all her enemies to flight. Nature is rejoicing, the clergy sing the praises of their great bishop and poets applaud their father in magnificent verses. Like Joseph Odo has returned from prison, the deliverer of this country and saviour of his church.
> (Bates 1975, 44–5)

• Odo and Duke Robert •

The death of Queen Matilda on 2 November 1083 had marked the beginning of a further deterioration in relations between the king and his eldest son, Robert. Matilda had acted as a buffer between the two and Robert may have felt unable to face his father by himself. Certainly, Odo in prison had been in no position to support the young prince, with whom he seemed to enjoy amicable relations.

> The peace between the king and his son which had taken so long to achieve was soon clouded. The stubborn young man contemptuously refused to follow or obey his father; the quick-tempered king continually poured abuse and reproach on him in public for his failings (OV, iv, 44).

Robert had left Normandy early in 1084 and never saw his father alive again. He spent almost four years in exile, only to return on his father's death to find that William had split his realm and that he was to inherit the lesser part – Normandy.

Odo was released in time to attend his brother's funeral at St Étienne in Caen. He would have been there both as the king's half-brother and as the bishop of the diocese in which this important event took place. It turned out to be an undignified occasion, interrupted by a man claiming that William had stolen his land to build the abbey church and culminating in William's corpse bursting and creating such a foul stench that the proceedings were rapidly brought to a conclusion. Odo made his peace with Duke Robert, who restored his Norman lands. The new duke appreciated that Odo's support in the Bessin would be important, as it had been to his father

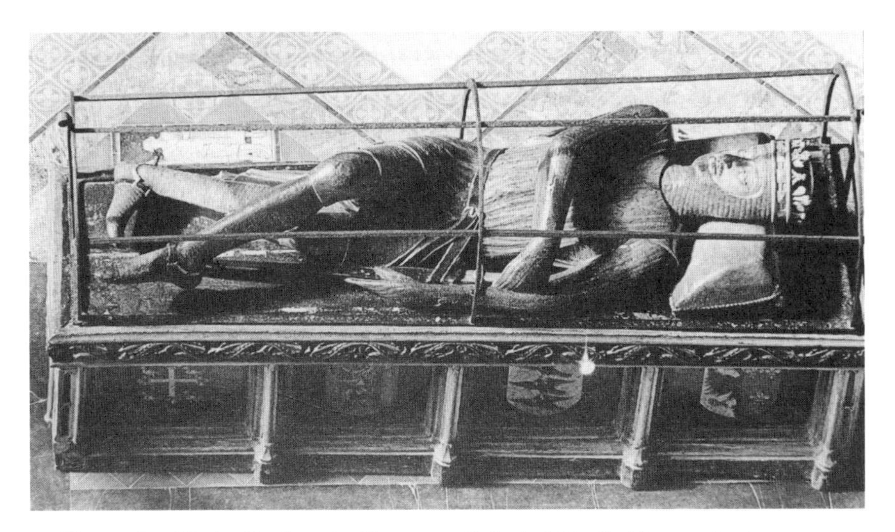

44 The tomb of Duke Curthose in Gloucester Cathedral. He died in 1134, having spent almost thirty years in prison in England.

before the Conquest. Orderic Vitalis used this occasion to praise the bishop, perhaps to balance the damning opinions he had given to the Conqueror to express, 'He was a man of eloquence and statesmanship, bountiful and most active in worldly business.'

Soon after William's funeral Odo returned to England, apparently without visiting Bayeux, such was his preoccupation with securing his vast estates on the other side of the Channel. It is not known if he was back in time to attend William II's coronation on 26 September 1087 as no record of that event survives, but he was in Canterbury in December. There, he ostensibly made peace with his old rival, Lanfranc, whom he assisted in the installation of a new abbot of St Augustine's. Abbot Scotland, who died in September 1087, had been an energetic leader who had encouraged Saxon artistic and literary traditions and probably provided Odo with the designer of the Bayeux Tapestry. St Augustine's had traditionally claimed a degree of independence from the metropolitan See and Lanfranc used the opportunity to bring them to heel by imposing Guy, a monk from Christ Church, as the new abbot. The monks of St Augustine's 'unanimously and with fervour' declared that they 'would neither obey him or receive him'. Despite these objections, Lanfranc still consecrated and enthroned Guy and ordered the arrest of 'those who were more vehement and had been ringleaders'. The archbishop deported some of the monks to other monasteries, imprisoned others and, reputedly, had one of their number who had threatened to kill Guy flogged at the abbey gates and driven from the city (Gem 1997, 54).

Odo seems to have been present in his capacity as Earl of Kent, representing the secular authority in the shire. Traditionally, the bishop had been a protector of St Augustine's, and was remembered as a friend and benefactor. The abbey had in the past called on Odo to advise on the translation of the relics of St Adrian and the bishop had seen the abbey as an ecclesiastical balance to Lanfranc's powers in Canterbury (Cownie 1998, 102). His presence alongside Lanfranc may have been an attempt to seek reconciliation with the archbishop and demonstrate his good intentions to the new king. Perhaps even at this stage he was not fully committed to rebellion and was keeping his options open. A few days later, Odo was present at the new king's Christmas court held at Westminster, along with most of the English bishops and many of the Anglo-Norman magnates. It was here that

45 The great seal of Henry I, from the foundation charter of Reading Abbey 1125.

he seems to have started sounding out those who were most likely to ally themselves with Duke Robert against the new king.

Initially, Robert may have been reasonably content with Normandy as his part of his father's bequest, but this was before he became aware that his father's prosperity had flowed from his English possessions. William Rufus had inherited the Treasury at Winchester, which, according to the *Anglo-Saxon Chronicle*, was overflowing with riches and 'it was impossible for any man to say how much was gathered there in gold, and in silver, and in vessels and in purple cloth and in gems and in many other precious things which are difficult to recount' (Aird, 110). In order to fulfil his father's deathbed wishes, Robert was obliged to dispense treasure to monasteries, churches and the poor, and he began to appreciate that a Norman duke without English financial support was not particularly wealthy. He also had to pay for the lavish celebrations marking his accession as duke and reward mercenary soldiers and his own backers; as a result, the Treasury at Rouen was soon exhausted. The duke was obliged to approach his younger brother Henry for money. Henry, who had been left no land but £5,000, struck a hard bargain – he would give £3,000 to Robert in return for a stake in Normandy, namely, the Cotentin.

Henry became Count of the Cotentin, a position that gave him possession of ducal lands and rights including castles; thus, the ducal administration of the Cotentin peninsula now functioned under his authority (Le Patourel 1976, 342). The sale of the most remote western part of the duchy might have seemed like a good deal to Robert at the time, as he could now concentrate his efforts on consolidating Upper Normandy and there was always the possibility that he would gain England – but he would come to regret allowing his brother a foothold within the duchy.

8

• 'The Bishop Abandoned the Dignity That He Had in This Land' •

The Conqueror's reluctance to release Odo was partly because he realised that the bishop would take advantage of his decision to divide the realm by fermenting division between the two brothers, William Rufus and Robert Curthose. His instincts were right; Odo, who appeared on the face of it like the Bourbons to 'have learnt nothing and forgotten nothing' (Talleyrand), wasted little time in resuming his career as a rebel leader. He would have calculated that once the initial enthusiasm had worn off, Robert would resent the crown of England passing to his younger brother, when according to natural justice it should have been his. The bishop also knew that he would not be able to regain his former positions as chief adviser and regent to the king – these positions were now occupied by Lanfranc and the Bishop of Durham, William de St Calais. Odo's best hope of re-establishing his former strength was by initiating a rebellion which would put Robert Curthose on the throne of England.

• Rebellion •

The Christmas court in 1087 had provided Odo with an opportunity to canvass support for a baronial uprising. Those barons who had land on both sides of the English Channel were worried by the prospect of having to serve two masters. 'How can we provide adequate service to two lords who are so different and live so far apart' (OV, 1968–80, VIII, 123). They argued that if they satisfied one it would probably be at the expense of upsetting the other; they would much prefer to have a ruler who was both King of England and Duke of Normandy. Orderic Vitalis articulated their thoughts:

> Then let us make Duke Robert ruler over England and Normandy to preserve the union of the two realms, for he is older by birth and of a more tractable character, and we have already sworn fealty to him during the lifetime of the father of both men. (OV, iv, 122–5)

It was the concerns of Bishop Odo and these powerful noblemen rather than Robert's ambition that fuelled the uprising. Indeed, it is not clear if Duke Robert was even aware of the plot being hatched on his behalf during the early part of 1088.

In addition to Odo, the list of conspirators included some of the most influential men in the Anglo-Norman world, such as his brother Count Robert of Mortain and Bishop Geoffrey of Coutances. Others, such as Roger de Montgomery, were ambivalent, although his son Robert de Bellême sided firmly with the rebels. Odo was said to have had a force of 500 men, but these did not include many of his Kentish vassals, who were loyal to their land and not to the bishop who, after all, had been in prison for four years. The plan was that the rebellion would break out simultaneously in different parts of the kingdom, but the heart of the rising would be in the south-east where Odo, Eustace III of Boulogne and Robert de Bellême were operating. The rebellion started at Easter 1088 and the absence of many of the conspirators from the king's Easter court would have indicated to William Rufus that he had a major problem on his hands. Odo is reported as having 'severely injured' his own earldom of Kent and 'utterly laid waste the king's land and the archbishop's, and he carried all the goods into his castle at Rochester' (Sharpe 2004, 139–57). Odo took advantage of the situation to settle some old grievances and is reported to have ravaged the lands of Lanfranc in particular. Over the next few weeks regional uprisings broke out at Bristol and Bath, at Berkeley in Gloucestershire, and in Worcestershire, Norfolk, Leicestershire and Northamptonshire. In response, at the end of April the king called an assembly to raise an army to suppress the rebellion; it was at this point that the Bishop of Durham, who up until then had been loyal to William Rufus, curiously chose to desert the king and flee to the north.

The king concentrated his response on Sussex and Kent, where the ringleader Odo was entrenched at Rochester with the small force, which Duke

Robert had sent from Normandy under Robert de Bellême and Eustace. The duke had promised to dispatch a larger army later. Rochester was well placed for raids on London and to receive reinforcements from Normandy up the River Medway. Although Odo and the other leaders would have been based in the castle, it appears that the rebels held the whole town, protected by the surviving Roman walls.

William's forces captured the rebel stronghold of Tonbridge, in doing so cutting off their line of communication to the north. Odo, anticipating reinforcements from the duke, had moved to the south-west to join his brother at Pevensey. The old Romano-British fort of *Anderitum* was once again at the centre of military action which would settle the future kingship of England. William Rufus, with Lanfranc in support, began a six-week siege of the rebels' stronghold, by land and by sea. Duke Robert did send a detachment of troops from Normandy, but the fleet carrying them to England was intercepted and destroyed by the king's ships. This setback delayed Robert's own departure from Normandy until it was too late and he never reached England. Eventually, lack of food forced Odo to seek a

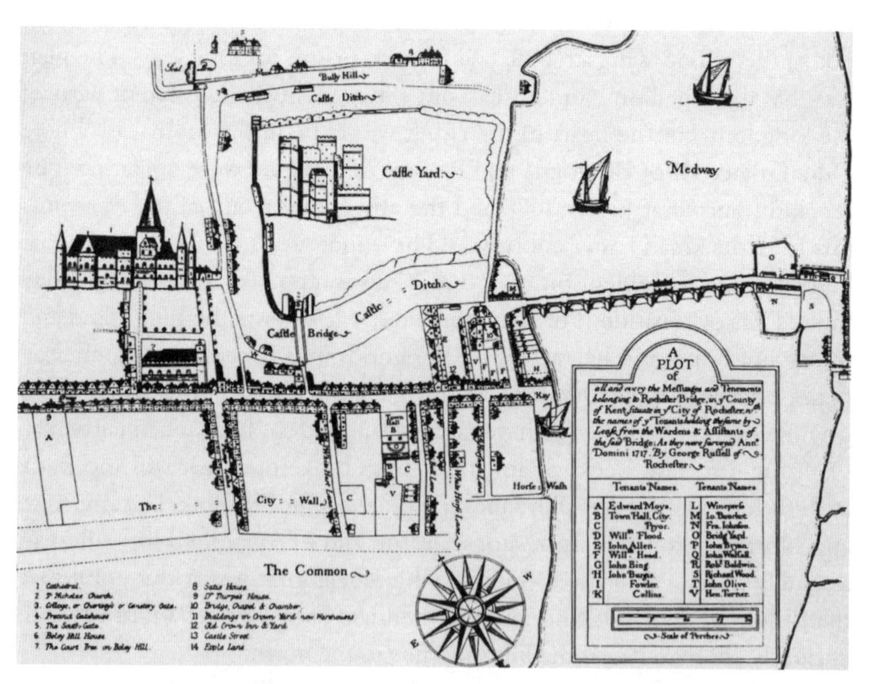

46 Bridge Warden's map of Rochester in 1717 showing the relationship of the castle to the bridge and the River Medway. *Allen Brown 1969, 15*

truce and he surrendered in the second week of June. Robert of Mortain seems to have been pardoned, but Odo was captured and offered his freedom on condition that 'he would go out of England and never more come into this country unless the king sent for him, and that he would render up the castle at Rochester' (*Anglo-Saxon Chronicle*). There is some confusion over what occurred next. Odo appears to have gone on ahead of the king to Rochester in order to negotiate the surrender. According to some sources, he reneged on his agreement with William by resuming his rebellion from within Rochester Castle, where the rebels were still hoping to be relieved by reinforcements from Normandy. Other accounts record that on his approach to the castle, Odo and his party were arrested and bundled inside. Irrespective of the details, William believed he had been betrayed and began a new siege, raising a large army of mainly native English soldiers. According to Orderic Vitalis, the king built two siege castles to block any exit from the beleaguered fortress at Rochester.

Conditions within the town and castle deteriorated rapidly. Orderic Vitalis writes graphically of the increasing distress of the garrison inside the walls, the death of men and horses from disease, and a dreadful plague of flies. The duke's long-awaited second relief fleet did not appear. Eventually, the rebels were forced to sue for peace and in early July were allowed a semi-honourable surrender. There were reports that Odo exited from Rochester to jeers and demands that he should be hanged. Several of

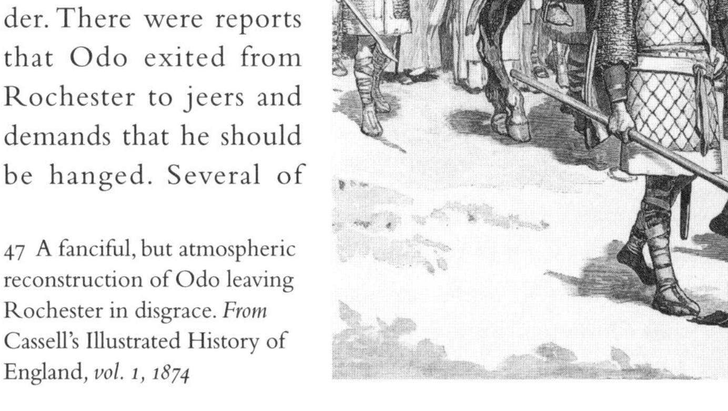

47 A fanciful, but atmospheric reconstruction of Odo leaving Rochester in disgrace. *From* Cassell's Illustrated History of England, *vol. 1, 1874*

the barons in the besieging force, such as Roger de Montgomery, had sons amongst the rebels and argued for clemency. The rebel leaders were spared their lives, but not their lands, and they were allowed out of Rochester with their horses and arms, but to the sound of royalist trumpets. It was far from the national uprising that was anticipated, given the number of eminent nobles who appeared to support Duke Robert's cause and elsewhere in England insurrections either collapsed or were controlled. Robert's own commitment to his own cause appears to have lacked conviction. In a charter to the abbey of Fécamp of 8 July 1088 Robert had added 'on the day when I should have crossed to England'. The date of the charter has been contested, but the sentiments are hardly those of a conqueror and it is hard to imagine his father, William, expressing them (Sharpe, 147).

In the aftermath the king acted with considerable lenience, given the treacherous nature of the rebels' intentions. Odo was allowed to return to Normandy, but the bishop lost his Kentish earldom for the second and final time. It was a defining moment in Odo's life. The *Anglo-Saxon Chronicle* reported that the king regarded Odo's treason as particularly serious as it was compounded by his defiance of Rufus at Rochester after submitting to him at Pevensey. The other ringleaders, Eustace of Boulogne and Robert de Bellême, also lost their English lands. Odo's brother Robert of Mortain and Geoffrey of Coutances returned to Normandy but kept their estates in England. Orderic observed that Rufus 'shrewdly spared the older barons ... out of love for his father whom they had served long and faithfully ... In any case he knew that disease and speedy death would soon put an end to their activities' (Aird 2008, 117). Ironically, William de St Calais, Bishop of Durham, who only a few months earlier Odo had viewed as an impediment to his gaining the confidence of William Rufus, was tried and banished as well. However, this particular prelate's role in the 1088 rebellion was soon forgiven and he was allowed back into England and restored to his bishopric.

• Banishment •

The *Anglo-Saxon Chronicle* often concisely summed up events in a pithy sentence, whereas writers such as William of Poitiers and Orderic Vitalis would spread the same incident over many paragraphs. In 1088 the *Chronicle* laconically describes Odo's banishment from England as follows: Odo 'went over sea, and the bishop thus abandoned the dignity that he had in this land'.

Odo may have left England in disgrace, but he appears to have wasted little time in attempting to establish himself as Duke Robert's principal adviser. Although the chroniclers continue to portray Odo in a familiar light during the last decade of his life, as ambitious and power hungry, there is another, even more basic motive underpinning his activities – self-preservation and the protection of his legacy. Odo had gambled everything on the replacement of William Rufus by Robert Curthose as King of England. Now, having been banished from England, with the loss of all his English lands and revenues, he had become vulnerable to the attentions of King William and his younger brother, Henry, now in occupation of the Cotentin. He was back where he had been before the invasion, but in a far weaker position.

Although Orderic Vitalis claimed that the 'vanquished' and 'very angry' bishop now prowled the duchy 'like a fire eating dragon', Odo appreciated that he had little time to lose if he was going to re-establish his power base in Bayeux. When Duke Robert sold the Cotentin to his younger brother, Henry had taken the title of Count of the Cotentin. A later grant to Henry included land to the east and south of the Cotentin and embraced the overlordship of the Avranchin, including Mont-Saint-Michel and the Bessin, but excluding the cities of Bayeux and Caen. This presented a real threat in Odo's own backyard; his room for manoeuvre would be strictly limited if he was unable to dislodge Henry quickly. Not only did Henry have control of the Bessin but he would have been the overlord of the diocesan estates across western Normandy. The political landscape of Normandy had changed dramatically from the one Odo had known before his imprisonment. Odo's own wealth had also been severely diminished with the loss of his English estates. One of the bishop's first acts when back in Normandy was to advise the arrest of Count Henry. The 1088 rebellion had shattered the trust between William the Conqueror's three sons and over the next few years they wrestled with one another intermittently within the Duchy of Normandy.

• The Imprisonment of Count Henry •

Henry was the only one of the Conqueror's sons to have been with him when he died and it is generally believed that he was disappointed not to have been given any land, but he used the money left him by the king to great effect. Henry's role in the 1088 rebellion was ambivalent, but he took no active role in the insurrection and remained in Normandy until it was clear that it had failed. Nevertheless, it was Henry's money, paid to the duke for the Cotentin, which Robert had used to raise a fleet and an army against William Rufus. Henry sailed to England in late July 1088 with the intention of claiming his mother's lands, which he believed had been left to him. He was cordially received by the new king and undertook some business with him, but was unable to secure his mother's estates, which William had already given away to secure support during the rebellion.

Henry returned to Normandy in the autumn of 1088 in the company of Robert de Bellême, one of the rebels at Rochester who had been forgiven by the king. Robert had lost relatively little from the abortive uprising, but he was already a considerable force in Normandy. The extensive Bellême lands stretched across the south of the duchy towards Maine, and Robert was also due to inherit the adjacent Hiémois and Seois estates on the death of his father, Roger de Montgomery. Robert, who already had a reputation for cruelty and violence, was destined to be a major player in later Anglo-Norman politics.

Odo viewed both these passengers on the incoming ship as a danger to himself and to the new duke and had little difficulty in persuading Duke Robert, who is said to have 'stood in great fear of Odo' (OV, iv, 148), that Henry and Robert de Bellême had formed a conspiracy with William Rufus against him. It seems unlikely that this was strictly true, but Odo's assessment of the danger the two posed was eventually to prove correct. Part

48 Nineteenth-century drawing of Odo's castle at Neuilly l'Évêque, showing Romanesque arches dating from Bishop Odo's castle, which have since been destroyed. *Casset*

of William the Conqueror's policy to maintain peace in Normandy had been to place his own garrisons in the castles of his barons, including those of Robert, but on his death in 1087 Robert had immediately driven out the king's men and replaced them with his own soldiers.

Henry and Robert were seized as they were disembarking and were consigned to the bishop's custody. Henry was imprisoned in Bayeux, while Robert de Bellême was incarcerated in the episcopal prison at Neuilly l'Évêque, about 30km to the west of Bayeux. The duke took advantage of Henry's imprisonment and reclaimed the Cotentin. Odo also urged the duke to re-establish control of Maine in order to broaden and secure his base as well as reclaiming control of the Bellême castles. William the Conqueror had annexed Maine to Normandy, but the Norman hold on the county was insecure. The Conqueror himself had been obliged to mount repeated campaigns in the region and Robert Curthose had inherited his father's problems there. Orderic Vitalis recounts a story that in 1089 Robert appealed for help to quell a revolt in Maine. Count Fulk le Rechin of Anjou, the duke's overlord in the county, agreed to help if Robert would procure for him a noted beauty, Bertrada de Montfort, who was a ward under the protection of her uncle, William of Évreux. Despite disingenuous protestations from her uncle, Bertrada was handed over to Fulk as his third wife in return for his own uncle's estates. Odo's name was mistakenly associated with a later episode in Bertrada's life. In 1092 King Philip of France developed a passion for Bertrada, for whom he deserted his wife, while Bertrada left Count Fulk, fearing that he was going to repudiate her as he had his previous two wives. 'So the absconding concubine left the adulterous count and lived with the adulterous king,' thundered Orderic, before going on to accuse Bishop Odo of performing an illicit marriage ceremony for the pair; on this occasion he was not guilty (OV, VIII, 20), although there remained suspicions that the bishop was in some way complicit in the affair.

Odo was so concerned about subduing Maine that he took command of part of the ducal army himself. In the event, Robert captured one of the Bellême castles near Alençon and Maine was easily pacified on this occasion. At this point, the duke was approached by Roger de Montgomery seeking a truce and the release of his son Robert de Bellême. The duke believed that he had completed his expedition successfully and Bellême was freed from Odo's custody. In retrospect, even the duke would have admitted that this was foolhardy, as once out of prison Bellême 'took vengeance daily in every way he could' (OV, iv, 150–8). According to Orderic, Prince Henry was released in the spring of 1089, following representations from the duke's magnates. Although Henry did not formally have his comital title restored, he proceeded to act as if it had been. As Odo saw his plans unravelling he must have been in despair. By way of compensation Robert issued a charter, witnessed by the duke's supporters, confirming lands granted to the cathedral church of Bayeux. In order to enforce this charter, it concluded with the threat that anyone interfering with episcopal estates would be anathemised (cursed) personally by the Archbishop of Rouen (Hollister 2001, 66–8). The summer of 1089 seems to have been a turning point in Odo's relationship with the duke. In April the bishop was with Robert at the castle of Vernon as the duke was preparing for an expedition to enlist the French king's help. It may have been the fear that Robert would not return or that he would be heavily defeated which made Odo insist that Robert confirmed the possessions of Bayeux Cathedral. On 20 July the bishop was present at the siege of Eu, which was in the hands of William Rufus's allies; at this time Odo obtained a confirmation from the duke of his establishment of St Vigor (Allen, 152). Coincidentally, it was here that Odo made the acquaintance of Abbot Gerento of St Bénigne in Dijon, who was present on business concerning his abbey and St Étienne in Caen. Gerento was known as a deeply pious man and the contrast with Odo has been pointed out by several historians, perplexed by their friendship. It is possible that the two men discussed the future of St Vigor at this time, but what is certain is that six years later Odo was to trust his abbey into the care of Gerento. The bishop was present at an impressive court gathering sometime before 9 September where episcopal business was carried out. Thereafter, up until his preparations for the crusade in 1096, Odo did not play an important role in ducal affairs. He seems to have largely remained within his own diocese and concerned himself with Church matters.

• Duke Robert II and King William II •

Many historians of the time and later have dismissed Duke Robert II as being weak and vacillating; and there certainly was considerable inconsistency in his policies in Normandy after 1088. Opinions differ over whether Odo was responsible for these vagaries or his advice was not heeded enough or, more probably, that he became increasingly politically impotent. It is not surprising that there was a lack of resolution after the 1088 rebellion, as both men faced a new and unusual situation in the Anglo-Norman world. Under the Conqueror, England and Normandy had been ruled as one, with a single powerful leader who had immense wealth and considerable military capacity. After 1087 England under William Rufus had become a powerful neighbour, looking towards Normandy as part of the realm that had become detached. From 1089 Normandy was divided, with a competent, hungry and militarily active Count Henry in charge of the Cotentin, while parts of Upper Normandy were effectively in the pay of William Rufus. The rest of Normandy, under Duke Robert, was a shadow of William the Conqueror's pre-1066 duchy, particularly its security and wealth, and it is scarcely surprising that Robert tried several ways of raising funds and increasing the number of his supporters – he was operating in difficult and unknown political territory.

Duke Robert had little experience of ruling in his own right and should perhaps have been grateful for the advice of the seasoned political campaigner Bishop Odo. On the other hand, he would have been aware of Odo's reputation for duplicity and, consequently, may not have taken Odo's counsel all that seriously. He would also have been aware of the antipathy existing between his brothers and the bishop as they became increasingly active in the duchy. Robert may have thought it sensible to leave Odo outside his circle of close advisers, except on Church affairs and matters relating to the defence of the Bessin. Nevertheless, according to Orderic, probably soon after his banishment Odo instructed Robert how best to perform his duties at the ducal palace in Rouen. He explained that the protection of the Church and the weak in society was his primary duty as duke. Odo provided Robert with a list of role models to emulate, including King David, Alexander the Great, Caesar and Robert's own father, William the Conqueror. These men, Odo explained, were able to alternate kindliness with severity as the occasion demanded. Odo concluded to general applause from the court:

> Reflect carefully on all that I have said; and stand up worthily as a good prince should for the peace of holy Mother Church and for the defence of the poor and helpless; put down all opponents with resolution.
> (OV, iv, 152–3)

Most observers tended to agree with William of Malmesbury's assessment of Robert's character, that is, it did not meet Odo's requirements. The chronicler claimed that the duke preferred the straightforward problems of the battlefield to those of the subtleties of the court. He was 'a man with no memory for the wrong done to him, and forgave offences beyond what was right; to all who came to him he gave the answer they desired rather than send them away disappointed …'. Malmesbury went on to say that this generosity should have won the duke the affection of his subjects, but instead they held him in contempt. Robert's kindliness was not always in evidence; after capturing the Bellême castle of St Ceneri, for instance, he is said to have blinded the castellan and mutilated its garrison. Such cruelty might have been in response to similar actions by Robert de Bellême, but it was not politically adept as he was about to release Bellême from captivity (Hollister 2001, 66).

In England, William Rufus had not forgotten about the 1088 rising and, according to Orderic Vitalis, developed a bitter grudge against his uncle Odo for his prominent role in the rebellion. He also continued to take a keen interest in Norman affairs, with a view to turning the tables on his brother and re-uniting the duchy with England under his rule. He summoned his barons to Winchester in 1090 and explained why he needed to intervene in Normandy. Firstly, it was to avenge himself on his brother the duke and the treacherous Bishop Odo and secondly, to save the Norman Church from the anarchy that prevailed in the duchy. It was a neat reversal of his father's justification to invade England to save the English Church in 1066. With these ends in mind, the king bought the support of several powerful barons in Upper Normandy, some of whom had land on either side of the Channel. These lords prepared for civil war by garrisoning their castles with mercenaries paid for by the king. In the west, Henry was also placing his castles on a war footing, with the intention of making the Cotentin independent of Normandy.

Duke Robert seemed to be facing extinction when King William instigated a riot in Rouen in October 1090. The merchants of the city were suffering as a result of the general anarchy and also because of the loss of their direct link with London markets and traders. The leader was the wealthiest Rouen merchant, Conan, son of Gilbert Pilatus, supported by a contingent of royalist mercenaries. However, on this occasion Count Henry and Robert of Bellême joined forces with the duke. William had miscalculated; Henry and Robert preferred a weak duke as an overlord, rather than a strong king, and were prepared to help Duke Robert in return for the normal spoils of war. Their intervention was critical; the uprising was suppressed and savage reprisals were inflicted on the townspeople by the ducal soldiers. Henry himself is said to have thrown Conan to his death from the top of the Tower where Odo had been imprisoned (Barlow 1983, 274–5).

This setback did not deter the king, who early in 1091 launched an invasion of Normandy with a view to annexing the duchy. In the event there was very little fighting, possibly because William was worried that the duke would ally himself with the French king, Philip I, and thus he would be presented with a much more serious adversary. Robert and his brother signed a formal treaty at Rouen in February 1091, where the duke agreed to hand over the county of Eu, which the king already effectively occupied, and the abbeys of Fécamp, Mont-Saint-Michel and Cherbourg. These were significant concessions, but in return the king gave Robert substantial but unspecified gifts, probably treasures and money as well as estates in England. The most significant part of the treaty was that the king and the duke made each other heir to each other's lands, thus removing from Henry any hope of inheriting either of their titles while one of his brothers lived (Aird, 140). Ironically, the peace negotiations to settle relations between the duke and the king seem to have been orchestrated by Odo's former rival, the banished William of St Calais, Bishop of Durham, whose skilful diplomacy seems to have earned him reconciliation with William Rufus.

There followed a short period of co-operation between William and Robert. They joined forces to subdue Maine once again, but their brother Henry was now causing trouble in the west, probably in response to the unpalatable contents of the Rouen treaty. Therefore, the king and duke marched westwards and besieged Henry, who had taken refuge at Mont-Saint-Michel. Eventually, Henry was allowed to leave and a short-lived truce was established between Henry and Robert. The combined army did not move back to Maine as there were now problems in England and the king accompanied the duke and returned to fight against the Welsh and the Scots. At the end of an inconclusive Welsh campaign and a more successful one against Malcolm III of Scotland, Duke Robert quarrelled with the king and returned to Normandy (Aird, 142–5). Both Robert's brothers continued to make trouble for him in the duchy between 1093 and 1095, and on at least one other occasion he was obliged to call on the French king for assistance again. There is no indication that Odo played a significant role in the various military campaigns that occupied Duke Robert in this period, although he may have accompanied the duke on an expedition to Maine early in 1094 (Allen 2009, 87–112).

• The Diocese of Bayeux 1090–95 •

Bishop Odo was conspicuously absent during these significant events, at least as far as the contemporary historians were concerned. He does not appear either as a counsellor or as a warrior. Some scholars have suggested that Odo grew tired of Robert's shifting policies, others that the duke had grown to distrust his uncle so much that he no longer asked for his advice. A third explanation is more probable, that Odo was now intent on guarding his own backyard. The bishop must have given up all hope of regaining his title and lands in England; indeed, this had been deliberately left out of the Rouen agreement. Odo may have felt obliged to concentrate on protecting the Bessin during such troubled times. His nephew Henry seems to have ravaged the region in early 1091 and would have been a constant threat to the bishop and his estates.

Odo would have appreciated by this stage that his only real tangible legacy would be the Church he had enriched so much. He turned his attention to securing the resources of the cathedral and to trying to nurture a monastery in Bayeux worthy of his memory. The diocese had been subject to the pillaging of abbeys and churches by Odo's own men during his imprisonment and preoccupation with ducal politics. With these issues in mind, Odo drew up a legal framework that governed his relations with the most senior secular lord in his diocese, Ranulph, *Vicomte* of the Bessin. This agreement not only regulated their relations with each other, but also made explicit their loyalty to the duke. The agreement with Ranulph was only concluded by the bishop making considerable concessions, including the giving of hostages. On another occasion he demanded a written declaration of obedience from Arnulf, the new abbot of Troarn; there is also a record that they met at one of the bishop's houses in Caen to discuss a dispute relating to the church at Dives-sur-Mer. Such micro diplomacy must have seemed trivial to the bishop, compared to the elevated heights of Anglo-Norman politics where he was used to operating, but it was desperately important for him as he found his powers increasingly restricted. These agreements, together with the 1091 charter confirming the Bayeux diocesan estates, suggest that Odo was concerned that his diminishing power base was going to disappear altogether. There may also have been an element of self-preservation in Odo's failure to appear alongside Duke Robert during many of his military engagements in the 1090s. Robert's main adversaries were his brothers William and Henry, both of whom held grudges against the bishop. Odo might have avoided direct military action against them because of the fear that they would seek him out or that he would be betrayed by one of Robert's knights for the huge price that he would have commanded. If captured, the best he could have hoped for would be to spend the rest of his days in prison and this time he knew that there would be no hope of a reprieve.

• The Abbey of St Vigor •

The records of Odo's activities between 1090 and 1095 are primarily concerned with Church affairs in the Bessin, although he does appear in the ducal entourage on a number of occasions, for instance, at Bonneville-sur-Touques in December 1093, but he rarely strayed far outside Lower Normandy. Earlier, in the summer of 1091, he attended a council to elect a new bishop of Sées; he also witnessed an act for the abbey of Jumièges issued at Lisieux by the duke in December 1093. In 1094 he witnessed charters for the abbey of La Trinité de Vendôme on the River Loir. In the early 1090s Odo raised funds to restore a monastic order at his abbey of St Vigor. During his imprisonment the abbey had been closed and partly destroyed. The abbot, Robert de Tombelaine, a notable musicologist appointed by Odo, had left for Rome in 1082 to serve Pope Gregory VII. Before his imprisonment Odo had reinstated a series of annual processions between St Vigor and Bayeux Cathedral, including one held on Ash Wednesday for penitent clergy. At the start of this ceremony the bishop, in full regalia, blessed the relics and then absolved all the penitents in front of the high altar. After the service the procession moved out to St Vigor for prayer and then returned to the cathedral. Further processions took place on Wednesdays and Fridays during Lent, visiting the parish churches in the vicinity of the city. At Whitsuntide every parish priest was required to lead his flock to the cathedral, where each householder had to bring one pennyworth of wax for lighting the church. It appears that processions were made from places such as Isigny, and even St Stephen's in Caen was not exempt from this obligation (Bates 1970, 158). The processions were carefully orchestrated, possibly by Abbot Tombelaine, and included complex arrangements of liturgical chant.

Odo also decreed that he and all subsequent bishops and canons of Bayeux should be buried at St Vigor; in the event, only Bishop Richard III (d. 1142) was interred there. Although St Vigor had been abandoned by

1087, not all the monks had dispersed. Richard de Cremelle had managed to keep some of them together in a house in the town, and he was presumably created prior of the re-created monastery after Odo's release.

• Endgame •

The early 1090s must have been a melancholy time for the aging bishop. Several men, with whom he had worked closely in building a powerful Duchy of Normandy and conquering and colonising England, died. On 3 February 1093 Odo attended the funeral of his old associate and fellow prelate Geoffrey of Mowbray, Bishop of Coutances. It is not known if the two bishops were close – probably not – but they did share memories of momentous occasions. He and Geoffrey had been together during the Conquest of England, more than a quarter of a century earlier, and in the abortive coup of 1088, just five years before. In many respects, Geoffrey's career ran parallel to that of Odo. He had been an energetic reforming bishop in Normandy before the Conquest, and he had contributed ships to the invasion fleet and participated at Hastings. After the coronation he was richly rewarded with lands, particularly in south-western England. He appears as a military commander suppressing English rebellions and as a judge, notably, at Odo's suit on Penenden Heath. He even joined insurrections against the monarchy, as in 1088 against William II, but he never quite reached the heights of achievement or the depths of ignominy which characterised Odo's life. Orderic Vitalis observed that Geoffrey was more skilled in teaching knights in hauberks to fight than clerks in vestments to sing psalms, but, like Odo, he was never accused of neglecting his duties as a bishop (Le Patourel 1944, 129–61). Geoffrey's final years were to prove traumatic; although he had been forgiven for his involvement in the 1088 rebellion, he found himself at odds with Count Henry and his barons. Coutances lay within Henry's territory and, as a consequence, the bishop had to endure the pillaging of his goods, the burning of his houses and the destruction of his parks; furthermore, in 1091 his new cathedral had been partly destroyed by an earth tremor (Allen 2010, 93). In response to such attacks, Geoffrey issued an anathema which 'blessed the defenders and consolers of the church of Coutances [and] smote its invaders and devastators with an anathema of eternal malediction' (Tabuteau 1988, 207).

In July 1094, another of Odo's contemporaries and close neighbour Roger de Montgomery, died in the abbey which he had founded at Shrewsbury. Roger had been a trusted friend of the Conqueror and had remained in Normandy in 1066 as an advisor to Matilda. He was given the *castlery* of Arundel and made Earl of Shrewsbury, becoming the most successful of the Marcher barons. He was ambivalent about Odo's rebellion in 1088 and managed to remain on good terms with William Rufus. At the time of his death he had taken over from Odo as the wealthiest tenant-in-chief in England (Mason, J., 2004–2011).

In early December 1095 Odo's brother Robert of Mortain died and was buried at the abbey of Grestain, alongside his father and first wife. Robert had been extremely wealthy and had made generous endowments to Grestain and other Norman foundations. He seems to have remained in Normandy after the 1088 rising, although he, unlike Odo, was pardoned. He was succeeded as count by his son, William, who, on Odo's death in 1097, attempted unsuccessfully to claim the earldom of Kent. In 1104 William rebelled against Henry I and, as a consequence, lost the Mortain lands in England. At the Battle of Tinchebrai (1106) he fought alongside Duke Robert and lost his Norman lands as well. Reputedly, he died as a Cluniac monk at Bermondsey in 1140 (Allen 2010).

These two deaths must have brought home to the bishop that he too was reaching the end of his life and that

49 Stone marking the burial of Odo's mother, father and brother at the Abbey of Grestain, set up in the early twentieth century.

there was little time left for further achievement; his appreciation that time was short would have influenced his decision to join the duke's contingent on crusade the following year. During this period Odo's movements were largely restricted to western Normandy, where the duke hardly ever appeared. It is probable that Robert felt confident about the bishop's ability to maintain ducal order in the Bessin, and it was obvious that he was never as interested in this area of Lower Normandy as in his heartland around Rouen or his southern and eastern borders. Or it could have been that Odo was carefully avoiding contact with King William and Count Henry in the years leading up to his departure on crusade, and that he felt safer on his own territory, where he could rely on his own guards not to betray him.

9

• 'God Wills It' – Odo's Last Expedition •

Odo's final expedition took him to the island of Sicily in the Mediterranean, where he died ostensibly on his way to the First Crusade. Sicily had only recently come under the control of the Normans who, led by one of the Hauteville brothers, Count Roger I, were establishing a new Mediterranean dominion, characterised by its cultural and ethnic diversity. Southern Italy had come to be seen as a potential source of wealth as well as refuge. It was the land of opportunity for the Normans, who came here to acquire land, fortunes or spiritual salvation. It was also the destination of many who had fallen out of favour with the duke or the king, who were exiled or fled here to resume their lives amongst their kinfolk. Sicily was to become the heart of the Norman Empire in the south during the following century.

• *Deus le Volt* – God Wills It •

In November 1095 Bishop Odo, acting as Duke Robert's emissary, attended the Council of Clermont in the Auvergne. He was accompanied by his fellow Norman Bishops Gilbert of Évreux, nicknamed 'the Crane' because of his great height, and Serlo of Sées. He also took his dean and an archdeacon from Bayeux. Odo seems to have obtained a private meeting with the pope, possibly to seek further protection for his abbey of St Vigor, but this was not held until after the main council. Pope Urban II presided over an assembly of 300, largely French, clerics which spent the first nine days discussing issues such as lay investiture, clerical marriage and the Truce of God. Then, on 27 November, the pope made a statement that was to make an impact on the Christian and Islamic worlds alike for centuries to come. He appealed to western Christians to help their brethren in the East against the Saracens. The Byzantine emperor had asked for assistance against the Seljuk Turks, who had taken over parts of Anatolia and were pressing him hard in Constantinople. No mention was made of Jerusalem at this stage, but his appeal was soon interpreted as an invitation 'to liberate the Church of God which had been trampled underfoot by savage peoples for a long time' (Lack 2007, 75). Pope Urban II was an accomplished orator, who spoke with fervour, and the response to his call to arms was immediate and emphatic: cries of '*Deus le Volt*' – 'God Wills It' interrupted his speech. The pope had ignited an emotional and spiritual fire that was to spread throughout Christian Europe; soon, tens of thousands were taking the cross with the intention of fighting for Christ and freeing Jerusalem from the heathen Muslims. At this point, Odo may have seen a chance to escape from Normandy, which was becoming increasingly claustrophobic and dangerous for the bishop. Odo would also have recognised that the crusade, like the Conquest of England, was an opportunity to blend spiritual salvation with the possibility of worldly enrichment.

The pope argued that it was better for Western armies to fight a 'righteous war' against the infidel than to slay each other in the myriad of local disputes which characterised eleventh-century western Christendom, in which Odo had often played his own part. In addition to political conflict leading to hostilities between neighbouring principalities, other forms of aggressive behaviour were commonplace. A contemporary chronicler from the abbey of St-Benoît-sur-Loire described violence, particularly among the young, as endemic and wrote that epicene youths 'full of themselves in their youthful vigour and enterprise rode the countryside with musicians at the head of their march, charmingly terrorising the neighbourhood in search of money for their pastimes' (Crouch, 110). Conflict with one or more neighbours was regarded as standard practice in the principalities of France; this was coupled with internal disputes which often resulted in violence. For those that died on crusade there would be absolution and remission of sins, and for those that survived considerable earthly rewards were promised. One of the immediate results in Normandy of the call to arms against the Muslims were anti-Semitic riots in Rouen, one of many such episodes in the cities of Western Europe resulting from the misunderstanding of the fiery preaching of enthusiasts of a Holy War.

• The Normans Prepare for Holy War Again •

Following Odo's return from Clermont, Archbishop William 'Bona Anima' of Rouen convened a provincial synod in the ducal capital for February 1096. William had himself been on a pilgrimage to Jerusalem accompanied by the abbot of St Evroul in 1058. Although there was no direct reference to the proposed expedition during the proceedings, the decrees of Clermont were promulgated. Subsequently, edicts issued at Rouen were concerned with establishing peace in Normandy, which was seen as a prerequisite of a Norman contingent joining the crusade. Odo was one of those 'men of religion' who, according to Orderic Vitalis, persuaded Duke Robert to take the cross, and in February or March 1096 Robert resolved 'to go on pilgrimage to Jerusalem to make amends to God for his sins' (OV, v, 26–7). Conditions at home were difficult for Robert; he had failed to gain England, his barons were restless and, in the view of some scholars, Normandy was rapidly falling into anarchy, and so perhaps the answer lay in the Holy Land (Bates 1970, 276). Some scholars have questioned the assumption that Robert was looking for an escape from his troubles at home, pointing to the duke's piety as another strong motive for his joining the crusade, as 'it was recognised, even by his critics, that his devotions went beyond the merely formulaic' (Aird, 2008, 159). The duke's great-grandfather Richard II had sponsored a pilgrimage

50 Twelfth-century illustration of a crusader taking the cross from a bishop.

to the Holy Land in 1026 and donated a large sum of money to rebuild the damaged church of the Holy Sepulchre. He may have felt that it was his duty to follow in the footsteps of his grandfather (Duke Robert the Magnificent), whose name he shared, to the Holy Land, this time with the specific purpose of freeing Jerusalem from the infidel. Robert was very conscious of his ancestors' involvement in the Holy Land and was said to gain courage on the battlefield by recalling 'his noble lineage'. It seems clear that he was not looking for permanent territorial gains for himself in the East and that it was always his intention to return to Normandy (Aird, 161). We cannot imagine what he thought his brothers William and Henry would be doing to the duchy in his absence; perhaps he believed that as a crusader he was immune from the malignant designs of those who had not taken the cross. Certainly, the Church took responsibility for the protection of pilgrims' lands and families. In addition to the Cotentin, William Rufus confirmed his brother Henry's overlordship of the Bessin, excluding Bayeux and Caen, Avranches and Mont-Saint-Michel, while the king maintained direct control of the remainder of the duchy. Robert's other great problem at home was his lack of money, and stories of the wealth that might be gained by a successful crusading leader may have been an important factor in persuading him to take the cross. Perhaps the duke imagined himself returning to Europe swathed both in silver and in sanctity – a far more powerful ruler than when he had set out.

In April 1096 Abbot Gerento of St Bénigne in Dijon, acting as papal legate, undertook a mission to England to negotiate terms for Robert's surrender of Normandy to his brother for the duration of the expedition. The duke was to receive 10,000 silver marks from William Rufus for 'mortgaging' the duchy, which was used to equip and sustain his large military entourage. By all accounts, the king did not find it easy to raise this sum and was obliged to levy a tax of 4*s* on the hide in England. Many abbeys, which had suffered in the decade after the Conquest, had difficulty in finding the sums demanded by William Rufus and were ordered to melt down their treasures to meet the king's demands. The *Worcester Chronicle* observed that, 'Bishops, abbots, abbesses broke up their silver ornaments, earls, barons, sheriffs despoiled their knights and villeins and gave the king a large sum of gold and silver.' It took until September for the king to collect the money, when William went in person to deliver sixty-seven barrels of bullion coin to Rouen and formally take possession of Normandy (Aird, 162).

• The Bishop Counts the Cost •

It would have been inconceivable for Odo to have remained in Normandy without the protection of Duke Robert. Normandy was to be under the direct rule of William Rufus, against whom he had rebelled in 1088 and who had developed a particular antipathy towards his uncle. Orderic Vitalis reported that the enmity between the bishop and the king was such that mediators were unable to bring about reconciliation (OV, v, 208–9). Added to this, just to the west of Bayeux and the Bessin was Count Henry of the Cotentin, whom he had imprisoned in Rouen; the potential treatment of the old bishop at Henry's hands would have been as bad if not worse than at his brother's. He knew that under the new regime it would just be a matter of time before he would be imprisoned or even executed. It is possible that Odo always intended to leave Robert's contingent in Italy and not continue on to Jerusalem, possibly with the hope of taking up a position in Norman Sicily. Alternatively, the bishop might already have been ailing and known that he would not return from the journey. Perhaps, he reasoned, it would be better to die a free man on a holy mission than a prisoner in the Tower of Rouen once more. If anyone was using the crusade as an opportunity to escape his troubles in Normandy, it was not Duke Robert, but Bishop Odo.

The cost of mounting a campaign to travel to the Levant was formidable, even for a minor baron; the duke could not have managed it without the English king's money. Odo was still wealthy, but his loss of revenues from England would have diminished his resources considerably and he would probably have had to invest most of his surviving wealth in the expedition. Costs included the maintenance of a large number of horses, not only mounts, but also warhorses, pack animals and draught teams, all of whom had to be equipped and fed. Only a limited amount of fodder could be carried, so the crusaders needed money to buy supplies along their route. Each knight would have taken up to three grooms and a squire and the duke's contingent would have included cooks, huntsmen and falconers. There were also foot soldiers, ordinary pilgrims using the army as a shield, wives, children and many other non-combatants. There would be expensive ordnance – armoury, tools and spare horse equipment. It has been estimated that the leading crusaders spent four times their annual income equipping their contingents.

There were other considerable expenses on the way to Jerusalem. The Bishop of Passau, Wolfger, when travelling along the pilgrimage route to

Rome a century later, paid 30*s* for a cook, 23*s* for bread and 20*s* for wine during an overnight stop for his contingent at Viterbo. He also paid 35*s* for grass and fodder for his horses (Birch 1998, 66). Odo, like Wolfger, was an important and wealthy prelate and would have obtained comfortable and expensive lodgings whenever they were available. Odo would have taken a much larger contingent with him on crusade than Wolfger, so his expenses would have been correspondingly that much greater. It is, therefore, probable that Odo took as much of his treasure as could be carried; if he had left it in Normandy it is unlikely that it would have remained untouched by his nephews for very long.

In the months before the Norman contingent left, Odo set about tidying up some loose ends, aware that he was unlikely to return. During his time in prison his abbey of St Vigor in Bayeux had been disbanded, mainly because the abbot had left to serve Pope Gregory in Rome, and several of the monks had returned to Mont-Saint-Michel, from where they had originally come. Odo had restored the order in the early 1090s, but he knew that the abbey remained vulnerable as he was so closely associated with it. Therefore, in order to guarantee St Vigor's future, he bestowed it as a priory to the abbey of St Bénigne in Dijon, an establishment that had been closely linked to the revival of the Norman Church early in the eleventh century. William of Volpiano had been the abbot from Dijon who had been brought to Fécamp with a number of monks by Duke Richard II in order to reform the monastic life of the duchy. St Bénigne had been granted property by earlier dukes and had a considerable number of well-managed priories. Odo hoped that St Vigor would eventually become a daughter abbey of Dijon, as provision was made for the election of an abbot. It is not known if Odo made any special arrangements for the protection of his cathedral, apart from invoking the papal sanction against anyone damaging property belonging to crusaders. The bishop had created a healthy chapter which, despite some problems, had managed to cope with Odo's long absences in the past.

In the event, the consequences of Odo's crusade and consequent death were to prove disastrous for his diocese. His successor as Bishop of Bayeux was Turold d'Envermeu (c. 1099–1107), who appears to have been unsuitable in almost every way and, consequently, 'his episcopate is remarkable only for the series of disasters that afflicted the diocese of Bayeux during his reign' (Allen 2009, 161). Turold's power base was in Upper Normandy around Dieppe, remote from the Bessin, and he obviously lacked the skills to hold together the diocesan structure he inherited from Odo. Diocesan lands were subject to plunder, mainly by Robert fitz Hamon, lord of Creully and Torigni, who was captured by the citizens of Bayeux in 1105, which provoked Henry I into besieging and burning the city.

Odo's own crusader party included Arnulf of Hesdin, William son of Ranulf, *Vicomte* of the Bessin and William Columbiers. The only other noble from the Bessin recorded as joining the crusade was William of Bayeux, the great-nephew of Hugh of Avranches, Earl of Chester (Riley-Smith 1997, map 2). Indeed, the number of Norman noblemen joining the crusade was surprisingly small, particularly when compared with the large number of nobles who came from territories adjacent to Normandy. Among Robert's entourage were old friends, whose number included Ivo and Aubrey de Grandmesnil, as well as men who had opposed the duke, such as Gerard de Gournay and Walter de St Valery. There were many from outside the duchy in the Norman contingent, including men from Brittany, Maine, Artois and Perche. There were also those from within the duchy who, like Odo, were fearful of their future under William Rufus, and those that stayed behind were perhaps equally fearful of leaving their lands unguarded.

Odo would have travelled in style, as befitted a king's brother, bishop, and former earl and regent, but perhaps not as grandly as Thomas Becket did on a mission from London to Paris in 1158. Becket was travelling as an envoy for King Henry II with a retinue that was designed to impress. It consisted of 200 horsemen:

> Knights, clerks, stewards, squires and the sons of nobles. There were eight great wagons, each drawn by five great horses; two of the wagons carried top-quality beer. The chapel, chamber, store and kitchen each had their own wagon, while the remainder carried food, drink, tapestries and bedding. Twelve packhorses bore the chancellor's gold and silver plate, his money, clothes and the sacred vessels and books for the chapel. Tied to each wagon was a hunting dog and sitting on the back of each packhorse was a monkey. As the retinue entered the villages and fortresses of Northern France, the two hundred and fifty footmen in the van sang English songs. The hounds, hunt servants and wagons followed, then the packhorses, squires and their masters' shields, horses and falcons, then the household officials, followed by knights and clerks, riding two by two, and finally Becket and his close friends.
> (William fitz Stephen's description in Barlow 1990, 56–58)

• The Journey to Rome •

Having raised the necessary funds for Duke Robert, Abbot Gerento and Hugh de Flavigny returned to Normandy. They met with Odo and Robert in Bayeux before travelling to Rouen together in the summer of 1096. It had been agreed that the crusading armies should be ready to depart on the Feast of the Assumption (15 August), but the Norman contingent left later than the others because of the delay in the arrival of the money from England. As soon as it did arrive in mid-September 1096, Robert started off promptly, anxious to avoid the fate of Aelfsige, Archbishop of Canterbury, who was frozen to death in the Alps whilst on his way to Rome to collect his pallium in AD 959 (Birch 1998, 56). For the first section of the journey the Normans were accompanied by the papal legate and chronicler Hugh

51 Odo's final journey to Palermo.

de Flavigny. It is estimated that Robert's contingent consisted of as many as 1,000 knights and 6,000 foot soldiers, together with an indeterminate number of followers, thus forming one of the largest of the crusader armies (France 2001, 91–2). At Pontarlier in the Jura the Normans joined company with the contingents of the counts of Flanders, Blois-Chartres and Vermandois. Stephen of Blois was married to Robert's sister Adela, who had remained behind to administer his lands. Stephen was accompanied by the priest Fulcher of Chartres, who later wrote a chronicle of the expedition. The cavalcade, probably now numbering well over 10,000, then headed into the Alps along the *Via Francigena*. This was a well-established pilgrim road, which crossed the Alps by way of the Great St Bernard Pass, with many shrines, monasteries and hospices along the route providing accommodation and help, particularly for those that could pay for it. A century later, Wolfger, Bishop of Passau reported that the pilgrim hospices were able to provide more than meals, a bed for the night and stables. At many, medicines could be obtained, and some seem to have been able to offer a bath and a laundry service (Birch 1998, 61). Leaving the Alps by way of the old Roman town of Aosta, the road passed through Pavia and Piacenza; at Parma the road turned southwards to cross the Apennines. A convoy of this size would do well to travel 25km in a day, particularly across the Alps and Apennines. The Norman crusaders had, therefore, made good progress to arrive at the ancient Tuscan city of Lucca by mid-November, a distance of about 1,000km from Rouen.

Lucca was an important pilgrimage centre in its own right, where the cathedral housed the famous *Volto Santo*, a crucifix 'in the image of God Himself', which was set on a huge wooden cross and, reputedly, spoke (Birch 1998, 54). The duke's entourage had a meeting with Pope Urban II who was also on his way to Rome. The papacy was still divided, despite the crusades, and parts of Rome were in the possession of the obstinate anti-pope Clement III. Before they left, the pope gave his personal blessing to the leaders of the crusade. From Lucca it was a relatively easy journey for the northern warriors, on a straight road down to Rome. The crusaders arrived at the gates of Rome in the second week of December, where they found that St Peter's on Vatican Hill, outside Rome's city walls at that time, was in the hands of the supporters of the anti-pope. Fulcher was shocked by their greeting:

> And when we had entered the church of St Peter, we found before the altar men of Wibert [Clement III] the false pope, who with swords in their hands

> wrongly snatched the offerings placed on the altar. Others ran up and down on the timbers of the church itself and threw down stones at us as we were prostrate praying. For whenever they saw someone faithful to Urban, they immediately longed to massacre them. In one part of the vault of the church were Lord Urban's men, who carefully guarded it loyally for him, and resisted their adversaries as best they could. We were sorely troubled when we saw such a great disgrace …
> (Lack, 85)

At this stage, a number of Robert's contingent, perhaps disillusioned by their sour welcome in Rome, decided to return to Normandy. The remainder of the contingent reassembled and moved south-eastwards to the great abbey at Monte Cassino, before crossing the Apennines once again. They were the guests of their fellow Normans in this part of Italy, now under the rule of Roger Borsa, Duke of Apulia and son of Robert Guiscard. Roger 'welcomed the duke of Normandy with his companions as his natural lord and provided liberally for all his needs' (Aird, 169). They probably met with him in the new capital of Salerno, where a grand new cathedral was being erected. They then turned east towards the Adriatic coast, but their progress to the Holy Land was delayed when they reached Bari, the main embarkation port for the crusaders. Robert's late departure from Normandy meant that he was too late to commission ships to cross the Adriatic, a sea that was notoriously dangerous in winter. Shipping throughout much of the Mediterranean came to a halt between November and March because of potentially treacherous storms. Contingents sailing from Bari earlier in the year had been involved in heavy losses of transport ships, and local sailors were unwilling to participate in another winter crossing, particularly with such a large consignment. Despite the dangers, Robert of Flanders decided to leave the Normans and risk the crossing with a smaller detachment. Count Roger helped Robert secure ships, in which he was able to sail to Durazzo (*Dyrrachium*) in modern Albania without incident. Duke Robert and Stephen of Blois elected to spend the winter in Calabria as the guests of Count Roger. Despite their warm reception, it was reported that the Normans 'spent the harsh winter weather' in Calabria (Lack, 88). Here, Duke Robert met Sibyl, daughter of Count Geoffrey of Conversano and granddaughter of Robert Guiscard, whom he was to marry on his return from the crusade in 1099/1100. Orderic Vitalis reported that Robert 'fell in love' with Sibyl and that 'she was truly good in character' (Aird, 191), but, although it may well have been an unusual contemporary example of a love match, Robert succeeded in raising sufficient funds as a result of the marriage to redeem Normandy from William Rufus. In effect, he had achieved part of his crusading objective before even leaving Italy.

• Odo's Final Journey •

Sometime towards the end of 1096 Odo left the Crusaders and probably crossed the Tyrrhenian Sea by boat to Sicily, to attend Count Roger I's splendid cosmopolitan court in Palermo. In order to fit the known dates he would have had to leave the rest of the Norman group at Rome or Capua. Possibly, he took a boat directly from Rome's medieval port at Portus on the Tiber estuary. Alternatively, if he travelled by land, he would have followed the Appian Way to Capua and then the *Via Popilia* to Reggio, the short sea crossing to Messina and finally along the north coast of Sicily to Palermo. It is unlikely that his real motives for going to Sicily will ever be

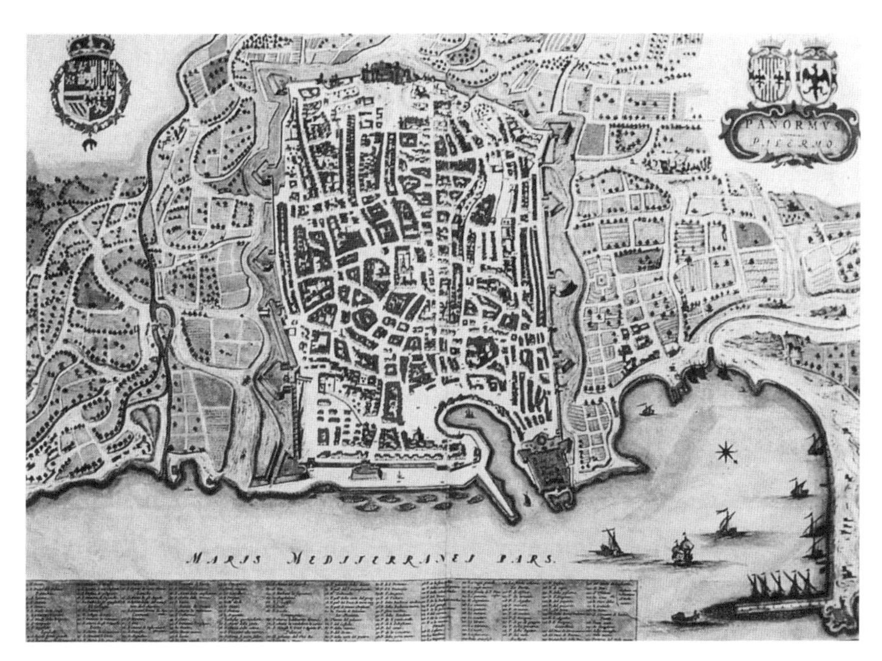

52 Plan of Palermo in the mid-seventeenth century. The city was still contained within its medieval walls. The Norman palace lies at the top of the walled area; the cathedral is in the centre. The Moslem area lay to the left of the harbour. *Bleau, J., Amsterdam, 1663 in Chirco, 1992*

known. Palermo had not long been taken from the Muslims and he may out of curiosity have wanted to see a city that had recently been freed from the control of the infidel, particularly if he felt that there was little chance of his seeing Jerusalem. If, indeed, he was already sick he could have believed that the Arabic and Greek doctors of Palermo, whose reputation would have reached Normandy, might have been able to cure him.

When Palermo fell to the Normans in 1072 it was a busy cosmopolitan city with an estimated population of 350,000; there were 300 mosques, numerous markets, exchanges, streets of craftsmen and a thriving port. Amatus noted that the Normans shared out 'the palaces … and gave to the nobles the pleasure gardens full of fruit and watercourses; while even the knights were royally provided for in what was veritably an earthly paradise'. In the late twelfth century, Ibn Jubayr, who was the Andalusian Muslim secretary to the Almohad governor of Granada, wrote a description of Palermo on his return from pilgrimage to Mecca. He describes the cultured elegance of the city where Odo died, in between cursing the Christians who had supplanted its Muslim creators:

> Palermo is the capital of the island, the union of the benefits of both opulence and grace. It possesses all the beauty, both internal and external, that you could desire and all the necessities of life, both ripe and verdant. The city is ancient and elegant, wondrous and gracious and seductive to gaze upon. It presents its courtyards with gardens, broad roads, and thoroughfares, it pleases the eyes with the beauty of its outstanding appearance. It is a marvellous place, built in the style of Cordoba, all of it constructed of a stone known as kaddān [a soft limestone]. A river divides the city and four springs flow into it perennially from its remote areas.
>
> The king roams through the gardens and courts for pleasure … The Christian women of this city follow the fashion of Muslim women, are fluent of speech, wrap their cloaks about them, and are veiled.

Ibn Jubayr also noted that the king 'has doctors and astrologers for whom he has great concern and tremendous enthusiasm' (Jansen et al. 2010, 236).

Odo might also have wanted to visit some of his many relatives who had taken up residence on the island after the defeat of the Muslims. For instance, Count Roger of Sicily's second wife was the daughter of one of Odo's cousins and several of her brothers had acquired Sicilian estates. There were also a number of Norman clerics in Sicily, including one of

53 Painting of St John of the Hermitage, Palermo by Wolton, 1840. The coloured domes are characteristic Sicilian Arabic tradition used in a Christian church. *Chirco, 1992*

the new bishops, who came from Rouen. Whatever his motives, it was here that Odo fell seriously ill and died early in 1097. The cause of Odo's death is not known, but he was by now an old man well into his 60s and even if he was not already sick the arduous journey from the north would have taken its toll on his health. Neither is it certain exactly when he died; his death was commemorated on 6 January at Bayeux, on the 4th at St Augustine's, Canterbury and on the 2nd at Jumièges, while Orderic Vitalis records it as being in February. On his deathbed he was attended by Bishop Gilbert of Évreux, who ten years earlier had preached the obsequies at the funeral of Odo's half-brother the Conqueror. Gilbert appears to have returned home to Normandy soon after Odo's burial and was certainly present at the consecration of the abbey church at St Evroul in 1099. Odo's final act was to leave his movable wealth to his close friend Arnulf of Chocques, chaplain to the Norman crusader army. Arnulf had been tutor to Odo's niece, William the Conqueror's daughter Cecile. He was later to become a controversial

Latin Patriarch of Jerusalem, briefly in 1099 and again from 1112 to 1118. Although it had been Odo's wish to be buried at St Vigor in Bayeux, it is recorded that a fine tomb was erected for him by Count Roger in Palermo Cathedral. Before the Muslims occupied Sicily the cathedral had been dedicated to St Gregory, but in the late ninth century it had been converted to a mosque and it would have been in this building that Odo was interred. This monument appears to have been dismantled in the late twelfth century, when the church was rebuilt by an English archbishop, Walter of the Mill. Nothing of his tomb has survived, although it is possible that Odo's bones were removed and deposited along with those of other Norman nobles in the side chapel dedicated to Mary Magdalene.

The final episode in Odo's eventful life might be seen as an anticlimax. Just like the Bayeux Tapestry, it ended before reaching a gratifying conclusion. The Tapestry should have ended with William the Conqueror's triumphal entry into London and his coronation in Westminster Abbey. Perhaps Odo's story was meant to finish with the bishop participating in the siege of Jerusalem and his triumphal entry into the Holy City, and perhaps even being appointed Patriarch. Although the fall of Jerusalem did not actually occur until over two years later, in July 1099, there is, nonetheless,

54 Engraving of Palermo Cathedral in 1761 by A. Bova. This church was built by King Roger in the twelfth century and replaced the church in which Odo was buried in 1097. *Chirco, 1992, 33*

55 Portrait of Odo from the Baron Gerard Museum in Bayeux, it originally hung in the Bishop of Bayeux's castle at Neuilly l'Évêque.

a form of symmetry here. Palermo was a long way from Conteville, but both were integral parts of Odo's story and of the Norman achievement at the end of the eleventh century. What is more, Odo was one of a select group of Normans who participated (albeit briefly) in the First Crusade and who had also been at Hastings over thirty years earlier. His life spanned the most important years of Norman achievement in northern and southern Europe and his activities touched upon all the most significant events of that turbulent era. No Norman king or duke had seen as much as Odo; he was the true embodiment of that Norman story, in all its accomplishments and all its flaws. Odo suffered from a 'bad press' after his death, particularly from Orderic Vitalis who described the bishop variously as 'frivolous and ambitious', 'the greatest oppressor of the people' and 'the destroyer of monasteries'. These were themes taken up and elaborated by later chroniclers and in time they became self-perpetuating. Yet, by the standards of his time, he had not been a particularly wicked or a cruel man; he achieved much in many spheres, but perhaps his 'sin' was that he was never content and always wanted still more, 'wishing only to have authority as pope over the Latins and all the people of the earth' (OV, 1968–80, VIII, 41).

None of the three surviving versions of Odo's epitaph are likely to be authentic, but this seventeenth-century version is preferable to Serlo's obsequious offerings and is more wistful and pious than might have been expected from the man himself:

> To what good have I been bishop of Bayeux? Glory, praise and honour are they not manifestation of sin? Already I am tearing myself from the storms of the abyss, having ruled a bishopric for forty-eight years, and coming to Palermo on my road to Jerusalem I lie dead, a pauper in the Lord. Therefore, O priest, remember me whom I have always loved. Utter for me some prayers of pleasant odour, and groans, and some tears, remembering the sinful woman who obtained grace by tears. Meanwhile by regarding my own death look to your own destinies and see that there is no happy life. This and the joys of life are found in God alone, whence, hastening, my brethren, return.
> (Bates 1970, 281–2)

• Bibliography •

Aird, W.M., *St Cuthbert and the Normans: The Church of Durham, 1071–1153* (Woodbridge: Boydell Press, 1998).
Aird, W.M., *Robert 'Curthose', Duke of Normandy (c. 1050–1134)* (Woodbridge: Boydell Press, 2008).
Allen, R., 'The Norman Episcopate, 989–1110', PhD thesis, 2 vols. (University of Glasgow, 2009).
Allen, R., 'Robert Curthose and the Norman Episcopate', *Haskins Society Journal*, 21 (2009).
Allen Brown, R., *Dover Castle* (4th ed. English Heritage, HMSO, 1985).
Armstrong, K., *A History of Jerusalem: One City, Three Faiths* (London: Harper Collins, 1996).
Barlow, F., *William Rufus* (London: Methuen, 1983).
Barlow, F., *Thomas Becket* (Berkeley: University of California Press, 1990).
Barlow, F. (ed. and tr.), *The Carmen de Hastingae Proelio of Guy Bishop of Amiens* (2nd ed. Oxford: Clarendon Press, 1999).
Barlow, F., *The Godwins: The Rise and Fall of a Noble Dynasty* (Harlow: Longmans, 2003).
Bartlett, R., *Trial by Fire and Water: Medieval Judicial Ordeal* (Oxford: Oxford University Press, 1986).
Bates, D., 'Odo of Bayeux 1049–1097', PhD thesis (University of Exeter).
Bates, D., 'The Character and Career of Odo, Bishop of Bayeux (1049/50–1097)', *Speculum* 1 (Jan 1975).
Bates, D., *William the Conqueror* (Stroud: Tempus, 1988).
Bates, D., 'The Conqueror's Adolescence', *Anglo-Norman Studies*, 25 (2003).
Bates, D., 'Odo, earl of Kent (d. 1097), bishop of Bayeux and magnate', *Oxford Dictionary of National Biography* (Oxford: Oxford University Press, 2004–11).
Bates, D. and Gazeau, V., 'L'abbaye de Grestain et la famille d'Herluin de Conteville', *Annales de Normandie*, 40 (Caen: CRAHAM, 1990).
Bates, D., 'The land pleas of William I's reign: Penenden Heath revisited', *Bulletin of the Institute of Historical Research*, li (1978).
Bayle, M., 'Les Évêques et l'architecture normande au XIe siècle', in Bouet, P., et Neveux, F. (eds), *Les Évêques normands du XIe siècle* (Caen: Presses Universitaires de Caen, 1995).
Beech, G.T., 'The Breton Campaign and the Possibility that the Bayeux Tapestry was Produced in the Loire Valley (St Florent of Saumur)' in Lewis, M.J., Owen-Crocker, G.R. and Terkla, D. (eds), *The Bayeux Tapestry: New Approaches* (Oxford: Oxbow Books, 2011).

Berkhofer III, R.F., Cooper, A., and Kosto, A.J. (eds), *The Experience of Power in Medieval Europe, 950–1350* (Aldershot: Ashgate, 2005).
Birch, D.J., *Pilgrimage to Rome in the Middle Ages: Continuity and Change* (Woodbridge: Boydell Press, 1998).
Bond, G.A., *The Loving Subject: Desire, Eloquence and Power in Romanesque France* (Philadelphia: University of Pennsylvania Press, 1995).
Bosanquet, G. (tr.), *Eadmer's Historia Novorum in Anglia* (London: The Cresset Press, 1964).
Boswell, J., *Christianity, Social Tolerance, and Homosexuality* (Chicago and London: Chicago University Press, 1981).
Bouet, P., '1000–1100: La Conquête' in Bouet, P. and Neveux, F. (eds), *Les Normands en Mediterranée* (Caen: Presses Universitaires de Caen, 1994).
Bouet, P., and Neveux, F, *les Évêques normands du xi siècle* (Caen: Presses Universitaires de Caen, 1995).
Bouet, P., Levy, B., and Neveux, F. (eds), *The Bayeux Tapestry: Embroidering the Facts of History* (Caen: Presses Universitaires de Caen, 2004).
Bridgeford, A., *1066: The Hidden History of the Bayeux Tapestry* (London: Fourth Estate, 2004).
Brown, G.S., *The Norman Conquest of Southern Italy and Sicily* (Jefferson, NC and London: McFarland & Co., 2003).
Brown, S.A., 'Auctoritas, Consilium et Auxilium: Images of Authority in the Bayeux Tapestry' in Foys, M.K., Overbey, K.E., and Terkla, D. (eds), *The Bayeux Tapestry: New Interpretations* (Woodbridge: Boydell Press, 2009).
Burgess, G.S. (tr.), *The History of the Norman People: Wace's Roman de Rou* (Woodbridge: Boydell Press, 2004).
Caple, C., *Objects: Reluctant Witnesses to the Past* (Abingdon: Routledge, 2006).
Casset, M., *Les évêques aux champs* (Mont Saint Aignan: Publications des Universités de Rouen and du Havre, 2007).
Chibnall, M. (ed. and tr.), *The Ecclesiastical History of Orderic Vitalis* (6 vols, Oxford: Clarendon Press, 1968–1980). Appears as OV.
Christiansen, E. (tr.), *Dudo of St Quentin: History of the Normans* (Woodbridge: Boydell Press, 1998).
Clout, H.D. (ed.), *Themes in the Historical Geography of France* (London: Academic Press, 1977).
Colvin, H.M. (ed.), *The History of the King's Works*, II (London: HMSO, 1963).
Combes, P., and Lyne, M., 'Hastings, Haestingaceaster and Haestingaport: a question of identity', *Sussex Archaeological Collection*, vol. 133 (1995).
Cooper, A., 'Extraordinary privilege: the trial of Penenden Heath and the Domesday inquest', *English Historical Review*, vol. 116, issue 469 (Nov 2001).
Cooper, A., 'Protestations of Ignorance in Domesday Book' in Berkhofer, R.F. III, Cooper, A., and Kosto, A.J. (eds), *The Experience of Power in Medieval Europe: 950–1350* (Aldershot: Ashgate, 2005).
Cowdrey, H.E.J., 'Towards an Interpretation of the Bayeux Tapestry', *Anglo-Norman Studies*, 10 (1988).
Cowdrey, H.E.J., *Lanfranc* (Oxford: Oxford University Press, 2003).
Cownie, E., Religious Patronage in Anglo-Norman England: 1066–1135 (Woodbridge: Boydell Press, 1998).
Cownie, E., 'Conquest, lordship and religious patronage in the Sussex rapes, 1066–1135', *Sussex Archaeological Collections*, vol. 136 (1998).
Crouch, D., *The Normans: The History of a Dynasty* (London and New York: Hambledon, 2002).
Darby, H.C., and Campbell, E.M.J., *The Domesday Geography of South-East England* (Cambridge: Cambridge University Press, 1971).
Darlington, R.R., McGurk, P., and Bray, J. (eds. and tr.), *The Chronicle of John of Worcester*, vols 2 and 3 (Oxford: Clarendon Press, 1995 and 1998).
Davis, R.C.H., and Chibnall, M. (eds and tr.), *The Gesta Guillelmi of William of Poitiers* (Oxford: Clarendon Press, 1998).

Delacampagne, F., 'Une maison urbaine Bayeux (IXe–XVIIIe siècle)', in Bouet, P., et Neveux, F. (eds), *Les villes normandes au Moyen Âge* (Caen: Presses Universitaires de Caen, 2006).
Delauney, H.F., Origine de la Tapisserie de Bayeux prouvée par elle-même (Caen: Mancel, 1824).
de Nogent, Guibert, 'A Treatise on Relics', in Coulton, C.G. (ed. and tr.), *Life in the Middle Ages*, vol.1 (New York: Macmillan, 1910).
Dodwell, C.R., 'The Bayeux Tapestry and the French Secular Epic', *The Burlington Magazine*, 108, no. 764 (Nov 1966).
Dodwell, C.R., *Anglo-Saxon Art* (Manchester: Manchester University Press, 1982).
Douglas, D.C., *William the Conqueror: The Norman Impact upon England* (London: Eyre Methuen, 1964).
Douglas, D.C., *The Norman Achievement, 1050–1100* (Berkeley and Los Angeles: University of California Press, 1969).
Dunbabin, J., *France in the Making 843–1180* (Oxford: Oxford University Press, 1985).
Farmer, D.H., *The Oxford Dictionary of Saints* (2nd ed. Oxford: Oxford University Press, 1987).
Flatrès P., 'Historical Geography of Western France', in Clout, H.D. (ed.), *Themes in the Historical Geography of France* (London: Academic Press, 1977).
Foys, M.K., Overbey, K.E., and Terkla, D. (eds), *The Bayeux Tapestry: New Interpretations* (Woodbridge: Boydell Press, 2009).
France, J., 'The Normans and Crusading' in Abels, R.P., and Bachrach, B.S. (eds), *The Normans and their Adversaries at War* (Woodbridge: Boydell Press, 2001).
Freeman, E.A., *The History of the Norman Conquest of England* (6 vols, Oxford: Clarendon Press, 1867–76).
Fulford, M., and Rippon, S., *Pevensey Castle, Sussex: Excavations in the Roman Fort and Medieval Keep, 1993–95*, Wessex Archaeology Report, No. 26 (Salisbury: Wessex Archaeology and University of Reading, 2011).
Galbraith, V.H., 'Notes on the Career of Samson, Bishop of Worcester (1096–1112)', *English Historical Review*, 83 (1967).
Gardiner, M., 'Shipping and Trade between England and the Continent in the Eleventh Century', *Anglo-Norman Studies*, 29 (Woodbridge: Boydell Press, 2000).
Gazeau, V., Normannia Monastica: Princes normands et abbés bénédictins: Xe–XIIe siècle (Caen: CRAHAM, 2007).
Gem, R. (ed.), *English Heritage book of St Augustine's Abbey Canterbury* (London: Batsford and English Heritage, 1997).
Gibson, M., *Lanfranc of Bec* (Oxford: Clarendon Press, 1978).
Gleason, S.E., *An Ecclesiastical Barony of the Middle Ages* (Cambridge, Mass.: Harvard University Press, 1936).
Golding, B., 'Robert of Mortain', *Anglo-Norman Studies*, 13 (Woodbridge: Boydell Press, 1990 (1991)).
Green, J., 'The Sheriffs of William the Conqueror', *Anglo-Norman Studies*, 5 (1982).
Greenway, D. (ed. and tr.), *Henry, Archdeacon of Huntingdon: Historia Anglorum* (Oxford: Clarendon Press, 1996).
Hagger, M., *William: King and Conqueror* (London: I.B. Tauris, 2012).
Henige, C., 'Putting the Bayeux Tapestry in its Place' in Owen-Crocker, G.R. (ed.), *King Harold II and the Bayeux Tapestry* (Woodbridge: Boydell Press, 2005).
Herrick, S.K., *Imagining the Sacred Past* (Cambridge, Mass.: Harvard University Press, 2007).
Hetherington, P., Medieval Rome: A Portrait of the City and its Life (London: Rubicon Press, 1994).
Hicks, C., *The Bayeux Tapestry: The Life Story of a Masterpiece* (London: Chatto and Windus, 2006).
Higham, N.J., *The Death of Anglo-Saxon England* (Stroud: Sutton Publishing, 1997).

Hill, D., and McSween, J., 'The Storage Chest and the Repairs and Changes in the Bayeux Tapestry' in Lewis, M.J., Owen-Crocker, G.R., and Terkla, D. (eds), *The Bayeux Tapestry: New Approaches* (Oxford: Oxbow Books, 2011).
Hollister, C.W., *Henry I* (New Haven: Yale University Press, 2001).
Ivens, R.J., 'Deddington Castle, Oxfordshire, and the English honour of Odo of Bayeux', *Oxoniensia*, 49 (1984).
Jaeger, C.S., The Envy of Angels: Cathedral Schools and Social Ideals in Medieval Europe, 950–1200 (Philadelphia: University of Pennsylvania Press, 1994).
Jansen, K.L., Drell, J., and Andrews, F., *Medieval Italy: Texts in Translation* (Philadelphia: University of Pennsylvania Press, 2010).
Jope, E.M., and Threlfall, R.I., 'Recent Medieval Finds in the Oxford District', *Oxoniensia*, xi/xii (1946/7).
Kapelle, W.E., *The Norman Conquest of the North: The Region and its Transformation, 1000–1135* (London: Croom Helm, 1979).
Keats-Rohan, K.S.B., 'Through the Eye of the Needle: Stigand, the Bayeux Tapestry and the Beginnings of the *Historia Anglorum*', Roffe, D. (ed) *The English and their Legacy 900–1200* (Woodbridge: Boydell Press, 2012).
Kent County Council, *Kent Historic Towns Survey* (Kent County Council and English Heritage, 2003).
Lack, K., *Conqueror's Son: Duke Robert Curthose, Thwarted King* (Stroud: Sutton Publishing, 2007).
Mason, J., 'Montgomery, Roger de' (*DNB*, 2004–11).
Lawson, M.K., *Cnut: England's Viking King* (Stroud: Tempus, 1993).
Legge, M.D., 'Bishop Odo in the Bayeux Tapestry', *Medium Aevum*, 56 (1987).
Le Maho, J., 'La Tour-de-Rouen, palais du duc Richard 1*er* (d. 996)' in de Beaurepaire, F., et Chaline, J.-P. (coordination), *La Normandie vers l'an mil* (Rouen: Societé de l'Histoire de Normandie, 2000).
Le Patourel, J., 'Geoffrey of Montbray, Bishop of Coutances, 1049–1093', *English Historical Review*, vol. 59, no. 234 (1944).
Le Patourel, J.H., 'The Reports of the Trial on Penenden Heath' in Hunt, R.W., Pantin, W.A., and Southern, R.W. (eds), *Studies in Medieval History Presented to F.M. Powicke* (Oxford: Clarendon Press, 1948).
Le Patourel, J., *The Norman Empire* (Oxford: Oxford University Press, 1976).
Lewis, M.J., 'Identity and Status in the Bayeux Tapestry', *Anglo-Norman Studies*, 29 (Woodbridge: Boydell Press, 2007).
Lewis, M.J., Owen-Crocker, G.R., and Terkla, D. (eds), *The Bayeux Tapestry: New Approaches* (Oxford: Oxbow Books, 2011).
Loyn, H.R., *The Making of the English Nation: From the Anglo-Saxons to Edward I* (London: Thames and Hudson, 1991).
Lyne, M., *Excavations at Pevensey Castle, 1936–1964*, British Archaeological Report, British Series, 503 (Oxford: Archaeopress, 2009).
Musset, L., *The Bayeux Tapestry* (Woodbridge: The Boydell Press, 2002).
Mynors, R.A.B., Thomson, R.M., and Winterbottom, M. (eds. and tr.), *William of Malmesbury: Gesta regum Anglorum*, 1 (Oxford: Oxford University Press, 1998).
Neveux F., 'Les diocèses ecclésiastiques de Rouen du Xe au XIIe siècle' in Bouet, P. and Neveux, F. (eds), Les Évêques normands du XIe siècle (Caen: Université de Caen, 1995).
Neveux, F., Bayeux et Lisieux: villes épiscopales de Normandie à la fin du Moyen Age (Caen: Éditions du Lys, 1996).
Orme, N., *Medieval Schools* (New Haven and London: Yale University Press, 2006).
Overbey, K.E., 'Taking Place: Reliquaries and Territorial Authority in the Bayeux Embroidery' in Foys, M.K., Overbey, K.E., and Terkla, D. (eds), *The Bayeux Tapestry: New Interpretations* (Woodbridge: Boydell Press, 2009).
Owen, D.D.R. (tr.), *The Song of Roland* (Woodbridge: Boydell and Brewer, 1990).

Owen-Crocker, G.R., 'Brothers, Rivals and the Geometry of the Tapestry' in Owen-Crocker, G.R. (ed.), *King Harold II and the Bayeux Tapestry* (Woodbridge: Boydell Press, 2005).
Palliser, D.M., 'Domesday Book and the "Harrying of the North"', *Northern History*, 29 (1993).
Pastan, E.C., and White, S.D., 'Problematising Patronage: Odo of Bayeux and the Bayeux Tapestry' in Foys, M.K., Overbey, K.E., and Terkla, D. (eds), *The Bayeux Tapestry: New Interpretations* (Woodbridge: Boydell Press, 2009).
Paul Drury Partnership, *Rochester Castle Conservation Plan, Part 1* (Teddington: 2009).
Potts, C., 'When the Saints Go Marching: Religious Connections and the Political Culture of Early Normandy' in Hollister, C.W. (ed.), *Anglo-Norman Political Culture and the Twelfth-Century Renaissance* (Woodbridge: Boydell Press, 1997).
Power, D., 'Angevin Normandy' in Harper-Bill, C., and van Houts, E.M.C. (eds), *A Companion to the Anglo-Norman World* (Woodbridge: Boydell Press, 2003).
Renn, D.F., *Norman Castles in Britain* (London: John Baker, 1968).
Renoux, A., 'Palais épiscopaux des diocèses de Normandie du Mans et d'Angers (XIe–XIIIe siècle): état de la question' in Bouet, P., et Neveux, F. (eds), *Les Évêques normands du XIe siècle* (Caen: Presses Universitaires de Caen, 1995).
Riley-Smith, J., *The First Crusaders, 1095–1131* (Cambridge: Cambridge University Press, 1997).
Round, J. H., *Geoffrey de Mandeville* (London: Longmans, 1892).
Rowley, T., 'William the Conqueror' in Kightly, C., and Cyprien, M., *A Traveller's Guide to Royal Roads* (London: Routledge and Kegan Paul, 1985).
Sharpe, R., '1088 – William II and the Rebels', *Anglo-Norman Studies*, 26 (2004).
Stenton, F.M. (ed.), *The Bayeux Tapestry: A Comprehensive Survey* (London: Phaidon Press, 1957).
Stephenson, P., 'Where a Cleric and Aelfgyva …' in Lewis, M.J., Owen-Crocker, G.R., and Terkla, D. (eds), *The Bayeux Tapestry: New Approaches* (Oxford: Oxbow Books, 2011).
Sumption, J., *Pilgrimage* (London: Faber and Faber, 1975).
Tabuteau, E.Z., *Transfers of Property in Eleventh Century Norman Law* (Chapel Hill and London: University of North Carolina Press, 1988).
Tsurushima, H., '*Hic Est Miles*: some images of three knights: Turold, Wadard and Vital' in Lewis, M.J., Owen-Crocker, G.R., and Terkla, D. (eds), *The Bayeux Tapestry: New Approaches* (Oxford: Oxbow Books, 2011).
van Houts, E.M.C. (ed.), The Gesta Normannorum Ducum of William of Jumièges, Orderic Vitalis and Robert of Torigni (Oxford: Clarendon Press, 1995).
van Houts, E.M.C. (ed. and tr.), *The Normans in Europe* (Manchester: Manchester University Press, 2000).
van Houts, E.M.C., 'Serlo of Bayeux', *Oxford Dictionary of National Biography* (Oxford: Oxford University Press, 2004–11).
Whitelock, D. (ed.), Douglas, D.C., and Tucker, S.I., *The Anglo-Saxon Chronicle: A Revised Translation* (London: Eyre and Spottiswoode, 1961).
Williams, A., *The English and the Norman Conquest* (Woodbridge: Boydell Press, 1995).
Williams, A., 'The Anglo-Norman Abbey' in Gem, R. (ed.), *English Heritage book of St Augustine's Abbey Canterbury* (London: Batsford and English Heritage, 1997).
Winterbottom, M., and Thomson, R.M., *William of Malmesbury: Gesta regum Anglorum*, 2 (Oxford: Oxford University Press, 2002).
www.catholic.org/saints consulted 27/11/2011

• Index •

Abingdon Abbey 81, 143–4
Adam fitz Hubert 119
Adela, Countess of Blois, Daughter of William the Conqueror 175
Aelfgifu, on Bayeux Tapestry 89–91
Aelfsige, Archbishop of Canterbury 174
Aethelric II, Bishop of Selsey 120
Adrian, St, relics of 148
Agatha, daughter of William the conqueror 54, 66
Alençon, Orne 12, 26, 157
Alexander II, Pope 19, 31, 70, 85
Alfred, brother of Edward the Confessor 25–6, 65
Al-Hakim, Caliph, 32–3
Amatus of Montecassino 33–4, 136, 178
Anglo-Saxon Chronicle 22, 44,64, 69, 65, 76, 80, 82, 101, 109, 128 134, 149, 154
Ansgot, Bishop of Rochester 118
Arnost, Bishop of Rochester 120
Araegenus (Vieux-la-Romaine) 15
Arnulf of Choques 179–80
Arnulf of Hesdin 173
Arnulf, Bishop of Troarn 162
Athelney Abbey 133
Aure, River 16, 46

Baiocasses, territory of 15
Baldwin, Count of Flanders 69
Bari 35, 36, 176
Baron Gerard Musée 87
Baron's Revolt 122, 127
Bates, David 7, 23, 25–6, 27, 42, 111, 135
Battle, Sussex 75–8
Baudri de Bourgueil 94, 103
Bayeux Tapestry 7, 10, 15, 17, 21, 22, 30, 53, 59, 64–70, 74, 76, 77, 78, 83–106, 116, 123, 142, 143, 180
Bayeux 46–9, 63, 70, 104, 138, 146, 170, 173, 174, 180
  Augustodurum 15
Bishop's Palace 44, 53
  Bourgs 44, 47–8
  Castle 15, 92, 157
  Canons of 19, 48, 53, 60, 61, 123, 172
  Cathedral 9, 41–3, 50–62, 66–7, 76, 85, 96–7, 100, 103, 114, 122–4, 140, 141, 162–3, 163, 179
  Chapter 10, 22, 46, 48, 60, 61, 123, 172
  Diocese 14–17, 24, 41–3
  Doyen Hotel du 88
  Musée de la Tapisserie 88, 101
  Noviomagus Badiocassium 15
  St Vigor see Vigor-le-Grand
  Survey of bishops lands (1133) 42
Beaurain Castle, Ponthieu 89, 142
Bec, Abbey of 122
Becket, Thomas 100, 173
Berenger, Count of Bayeux 15
Bellême 11, 13, 41, 156, 160
Berkhamsted 30, 82, 132, 133
Bessin 13, 14, 15, 40, 42, 43, 46, 49, 50, 54, 56, 57, 143, 146, 155, 159, 162, 163, 166, 170, 171, 173

Vicomte of 143
Ranulph, *vicomte* of 162, 173
Beaumont, Roger de 70
Bermondsey Abbey 165
Bertrada de Montford 157
Bishopstone 133
Bonneville-sur-Touques, castle 66, 70, 100, 163
Bosham, Sussex 89, 90, 104
Bramley, Surrey 130
Braose, William de 75
Brittany 12, 17, 41, 67, 91, 115, 173

Caen 12, 15, 36, 44, 48–9, 50, 70, 73, 99, 155, 162, 170
La Trinité (Abbaye aux Dames) 70, 71,122
St Stephens Abbey (St Etienne) 49, 52, 122, 140, 146, 163,
stone 12–13, 49
Cambremer, Calvados 16, 44
Canterbury 79, 97, 98, 100, 135
Castle 108
Christ Church 121, 124, 133, 147–8
St Augustine's 95, 98, 104, 124, 179
Castle Rising 124, 130–1, 132
Cerisy Forest 46
Cerisy Abbey 50, 56
Charlemagne 93, 105
Charles the Bald 10
Charles the Simple, King 10
Cherbourg, Abbey, King 161
Clermont 167–8, 169
Cluny 32
Cnut, King 26
Columbiers, William 173
Conan of Bayeux 48, 63
Conan, son of Gilbert Pilatus 160–1
Conan II, Count of Brittany 91
Constantinople 36, 37, 168
Conteville 99, 181
Cotentin 12, 13, 15, 30, 138, 139, 149, 155, 156, 157, 159, 160, 170, 171
Cousenon, River 91
Coutances Cathedral 51,56, 60, 164
Crusade, First 10, 32, 106, 167–82
Crusaders, Norman contingent 173, 174–6

Deer Parks 44
Deddington Castle 111, 119, 124, 129–30, 132
Dinan 91, 92
Dives, River 16, 73
Dives-sur-Mer 162
Dol 91, 92, 103
Domesday Book 23, 30, 61, 73, 74, 76, 108, 111, 112, 113, 116, 119, 121, 124, 127, 128, 133, 143
waste 79–80
Domfront, Orne 27, 91,
Douglas, David, C 27, 35
Dover 21, 66, 70, 79–80, 99
Castle 99, 103, 104, 108, 109, 111, 112–13, 124
Dudo of St Quentin 21
Dunston St 84
Durham Cathedral 116

Eadmer 23, 65, 89
Ealdred, Archbishop of York 68, 82, 107
Edgar Aetheling 68, 81, 82, 108
Edward the Confessor, King 25, 26, 65, 67–9, 88–91, 93
Edith, Queen 68, 79, 101,
Edwin Earl of Mercia 67, 72, 82, 108
Emma, Queen 25, 65
Ethelred II, the Unready 25, 65
Eustace II, Count of Boulogne 70, 101, 102–03, 112–13
Eustace III, Count of Boulogne 151, 154
Evreux Cathedral 122
Expurius, Saint 58

Fécamp, Abbey 29, 34, 35, 49, 54, 56, 60, 70, 133, 154, 161, 172
Forests 45–6
Freeman E.A. 9
Fulbert, Herleva's father 25
Fulcher of Chartres 175–6
Fulk III, Count of Anjou 34, 36
Fulk IV (le Rechin), Count of Anjou 157

Gate Fulford, Battle of 72
Geoffrey, Bishop of Coutances 40, 44, 63, 76, 100, 107, 113, 133, 136, 138–9, 151, 154, 164
Gerento, Abbot 158, 170, 174
Gilbert, Bishop of Evreux 167, 179
Gilbert Maminot, Bishop of Lisieux (1077–1101) 43
Glaber, Ralph 25, 32
Glastonbury Abbey 133
Gloucester 111
Godwin, Earl of Wessex 65, 121
Goscelin of St Bertin's 99
Gregory VII, Pope 116, 136–9, 144, 172
Grestain, Notre Dame de 30–2, 133, 140, 165
Guilbert, anti-pope Clement III 138–9, 144, 175

Guilbert de Nogent 58, 134
Guy, Abbot of St Augustines 147
Guy, Count of Ponthieu 89, 92, 142
Gyrth 96

Hakon, Earl Harold's nephew 65
Halley's Comet 69, 88, 93
Harald Hardrada 71–2
Harefoot, Harold, Regent 65
'Harrying of the North' 113–14, 116
Harthacanut, King 65
Hauteville, Tancred de 35
Harold, Earl and King 59, 64–70, 75–8, 83–93, 95–7, 99, 100, 104
Harold, Viking lord 15
Hastings, Battle of 7, 9, 17, 21, 22, 42, 64, 70, 72, 73–8, 80, 82, 96, 99, 100, 102, 104–5, 107, 132, 164, 181
  Castle 74, 92
Henry I, French King 35
Henry I, King of England (1100–35) 63, 149, 155–63, 164, 166
Henry IV, Emperor (1031–60) 136–9, 144
Herbert fitz Ivo 119
Herleva, Odo's mother 24, 25, 27,30
Herluin, Odo's father 27, 30
Hiémois 13, 24, 143, 156
Himmler 87–8
Hoo, Kent 130
Hugh, Bishop of Bayeux (1015–49) 14, 39, 43, 50
Hugh, Earl of Chester 139, 141
Hugh of Flavigny 25, 174–5
Hugh of Lyons 141
Hugh de Port 119
Hugh de Montford 108, 113
Huntingdon, Henry of 23, 132

Ibn Jubayr 178
Ilbert de Lacy 119
Investiture Conflict 137
Isigny 163
Isle of Wight 70, 140, 142

Jerusalem 27, 32–7, 106, 107, 168, 169, 170, 171, 178, 180, 182
  Holy Sepulchre 170
John, Odo's son 18
John of Ravenna 29
John of Worcester 23, 68, 115
Jumièges Abbey 12, 51, 54, 163, 179
Jumièges, William of 21, 25, 26, 36, 41, 68
Jumièges, Robert, Archbishop 65, 121

Lanfranc, Archbishop of Canterbury 120–2, 135, 141, 147–8, 150, 151, 152
Launceston, Cornwall 133
Leo IX, Pope (1049–54) 34
Leofwine 96, 107
Liege Cathedral School 61
Lieuvin 13, 27
Lincoln Cathedral 53
Lisieux, Calvados 16, 18, 27, 31, 44, 163
  Bishop of 29, 31, 40, 43
  Council 18
Loir, River 10, 101
London 31, 71, 72, 75, 76, 80–1, 82, 96, 98, 108, 118, 132, 152, 160, 173, 180
  Tower of 128, 142
Longsword, William, Duke of Normandy (1127–42) 11, 15
Lucca 175
Lugdunensis Secunda 13

Mabel de Bellême, wife of Roger de Montgomery 41
Maine 10, 114, 156, 157, 161
Maldon, battle of 85
Malcolm III, King of Scotland 161
Marbod of Rennes 43–4, 62,
Matilda de Montgomery, first wife of Robert of Mortain 30, 41
Matilda, Queen 50, 54, 70, 79, 85, 86–7, 111, 114, 122, 146, 165
Montacute, Somerset 30, 133
Monte Cassino 176
Mont-Saint-Michel 54, 91, 97, 155, 161, 170, 172
Morcar, Earl of Northumbria 67, 72, 82, 108
Mortain 30, 41, 60
Muriel, Odo's sister 30

Napoléon 86
Nicaea 36, 37
Neuilly l'Évêque castle 44–6, 156, 157, 181
Northmanni 10–11
Nuneham Courtenay, Oxfordshire 144

Orderic Vitalis 17–19, 21–2, 41, 51, 61, 69, 100, 109, 111, 112, 114, 120, 121, 134, 139, 141, 142–3, 145, 146, 150–1, 153, 155, 157, 159, 160, 164, 169, 171, 179
Orne, River 14, 16, 49

Palermo 9, 10, 174, 177–82
Penenden Heath, Trial of 23, 99, 119–22, 164

Pevensey Bay 73–4,
Pevensey Castle (*Anderitum*), Sussex 73–4, 80, 124–8, 132, 133, 152
Phillipe I, King of France 115, 157
Picot, Sheriff of Cambridgeshire 112
Plessis-Grimoult 114
Poitiers, William of 19–20, 27, 39, 50, 64, 65, 68, 77, 79–80, 100, 102, 107, 108, 109, 154
Poppa, daughter of Berenger, Count of Bayeux 15

Ralph, Earl of Norfolk 115
Ralph de Courbépine 119
Ralph fitz Turold 118
Ramsey Abbey 120
Rennes 92, 120
Richard, Bishop of Bayeux (1108–33) 61
Richard, Bishop of Bayeux (1135–42) 61
Richard III, Bishop of Bayeux (d. 1142) 163
Richard de Cremelle 164
Richard I, Duke of Normandy (942–96) 15, 40
Richard II, Duke of Normandy (996–1026) 24–5, 92, 143, 169–70, 172
Richard III, Duke of Normandy (1026–7) 25, 26, 34, 35
Richard fitz Gilbert 124, 127
Richard du Hommet 18
Robert de Bellême 151, 152, 154, 156–7, 160
Robert Curthose, Duke of Normandy (1087–1106) 10, 22, 115–16, 139, 141, 146–63, 158–60, 162–3, 165, 166, 167, 169, 170–1, 173, 174–7, 181
Robert, Count of Eu 75, 113
Robert of Flanders 175, 176
Robert of Jumièges 65, 121
Robert Guiscard 136, 138, 139, 144, 176
Robert fitz Hamon 173
Robert Latimer 143
Robert the Magnificent, Duke of Normandy (1027–35) 24–38
Robert de Mortain 27, 29–30, 41, 54, 64, 70, 74, 95, 102, 113, 117, 127, 132–3, 140, 145, 151, 153, 165
Robert de Tombelaine, Abbot of St Vigor 163
Rochester 80, 99, 124, 156
  Castle 99, 108, 111, 124, 128, 129, 132, 151–4
  Cathedral 124, 128
  Gundulf, bishop of 112, 128
Roger Bigot 119
Roger Borsa 176
Roger, Count of Sicily 139, 167, 177–80
Roger, Earl of Hereford 115
Roger de Montgomery 30, 31, 41, 70, 74, 111, 132, 151, 154, 156, 157, 165
Rollo, Duke of Normandy (911–27) 10–11, 15, 21, 22
Roman de Rou 21
Rome 35, 42, 103, 134–5, 137, 138–41, 144, 163, 172, 174–6, 177
  Castel Sant' Angelo 138
Roncevalles, Battle of 105–6
Rouen 10, 11, 12, 13, 15, 16, 26, 39, 41, 43, 44, 48, 49, 52, 56, 57, 60, 66, 67, 70, 85, 89, 100, 116, 134, 141, 142, 159, 160–1, 162, 166, 168, 169, 170, 171, 174, 175, 179
  Cathedral 56
  Church councils at 41
  Mauger, Archbishop of 40
Robert, Archbishop of 18, 35, 40
Rotomagus 13
  Tower 89, 92, 141–3, 171
  Treaty of 161, 162
  Treasury at 149
  vicomte of 142
  William I Bonne-Ame, Archbishop of 159

Salerno 34, 136, 144, 176
Samson, Bishop of Worcester (1096–1112) 61
St Aquilinus 15
St Albans Abbey 124, 133
St Austell 17
St Bernard Pass 35, 175
St Benigne Abbey, Dijon 158, 170, 172
St-Benoit-sur-Loire 168
St Evremond 15
St Evroul 15
St-Evroul-en-Ouche, Abbey of 21, 41, 139, 169, 179
St Florent de Saumur, abbey 101, 103,
St Germans, Cornwall 133
St Marcouf 15
St Méon 17
St Mere-Église 16–17
St Ouen, Abbey 12, 54, 56, 60
St Rasyphus and St Ravennus 58–9, 60
St Regnobert 60
St Riquier Abbey 56
St Pierre-sur-Dives 16
St Samson 7
St Stephen relics 36
St-Valery-sur-Somme 73
St Wandrille, Abbey 12, 54, 60

Samson, Bishop of Worcester (1096–1112) 61
Scotland, Abbot of St Augustine's 91, 99, 104, 147
Serlo, poet 19, 30, 48, 53, 62–3, 122, 139, 145–6, 182
Serlo, Bishop of Sees 167
Ship List 79
Sibyl of Conversano (m. Robert Curthose 1100) 176–7
Sicily 36, 60, 136, 139, 167, 171, 177, 178, 180
Snettisham 111, 124, 130
Song of the Battle of Hastings (Carmen de Hastingae Proelio) 21, 100
Song of Roland 78, 105–6
Southwark 81
Stamford Bridge, Battle of 72, 76
Stenton, F.M. 83, 97
Stephen of Blois 175, 176
Stigand, Archbishop of Canterbury 68–9, 81, 93, 108, 130
Sussex Rapes 74–5, 107–8

Talleyrand 150
Textus Roffensis 128
Thomas Archbishop of York (1070–1100) 61, 124
Tinchbrai, Battle of (1106) 22, 165
Tonbridge Castle 108, 124–7, 154
Totaire, Rodulf 53
Tosny, Roger de 26
Tostig, Earl of Northumbria 67, 69, 71, 72
Truce of God 168
Tovi 133
Turold, Odo's vassal 89, 98–100, 118
Turold d'Envermeu (1099–1107) 172–3
Turpin, Archbishop 78, 105–6,

Urban II, Pope (Otho de Lagery) 144, 167–8, 175

Val-es-Dunes, battle of (1047) 39, 114
Victor III, Pope 144
Viducasses 15
Vigor, Saint 56, 57
Vigor-le-Grand, Saint, abbey 16, 47, 50, 56–7, 143, 158, 167, 172, 180
Vikings 10–12, 14, 15, 50, 54, 88, 98, 103
Vire, River 14, 15, 16, 46
Vire Valley, Bishops rights 46
Vital 42, 95, 98–100
Vital of Savigny 29

Wace, Robert 22, 36, 78, 134
Wadard 42, 94, 98–100, 118, 119, 143
  Rainald son of 143
Walcher, Bishop of Durham 116
Wallingford 81
Walter of the Mill, Archbishop of Palermo 180
Waltheof, Bishop 115
Wandrille, Saint, Abbey 60
Warenne, William de 74, 117
Westminster Abbey 69, 80, 82, 93, 180
  Palace 99, 111, 148
William the Conqueror, 9, 21, 24, 26, 27, 30, 34, 38, 39, 40, 43, 54, 62, 64–82, 83–104, 106–11, 112, 115, 139, 140–3, 145–9, 150, 154, 155, 157, 159, 165, 179, 180
William de Mortain 165
William of Malmesbury 23, 24, 29, 34, 36, 89, 114, 139–40, 159–60
William of Evreux 157
William of Heimois
William fitz Osbern 70, 108–14
William Rufus, King of England (1087–1100) 17, 116, 147–56, 158–60, 164, 165, 166, 170–1
William de St Calais, Bishop of Durham 150, 151, 154, 161
Wilton nunnery 101, 133
Winchester 69, 74, 79, 109, 111, 128, 132, 149, 160
  Treasury at 149
Windsor 81, 111
Wolvesey Palace 132
Wolfger, Bishop of Pasau 171–2, 175
Wootton Hundred, Oxfordshire 119
Worcester Chronicle 170
Wulfnoth, Earl Harold's brother 65
Wulfstun, Bishop of York 43

York Cathedral 124